Advance Praise for *Real Leader*

Anyone interested in running a company—high-tech or otherwise—will treasure Steve Tobak's book. It provides new insights that clearly spell out what it takes to be successful in a competitive world. This book will be immensely useful to both first-time and seasoned entrepreneurs!

—PHILIPPE KAHN, CEO OF FULLPOWER TECHNOLOGIES, FOUNDING CEO OF BORLAND, CREATOR OF THE CAMERA PHONE

The media-hyped tsunami of entrepreneurship is creating a drought of true innovation and leadership. Is this business book heresy? Nope. Just real insight and clear thinking from Steve Tobak—a highly successful business executive, entrepreneur and damn good writer who knows of what he speaks. Steve gets it right and tells it straight. *Real Leaders Don't Follow* is an extraordinary read that no aspiring entrepreneur or business leader should do without.

—JIM McCANN, FOUNDER AND CEO, 1-800-FLOWERS.COM, INC.

This book is spot-on for today's business climate. Steve's incisive analysis of today's "wantrepreneur" craze is a refreshingly honest, well-informed read. If you're looking for a solid guide to inform business decisions—not only for tomorrow's entrepreneurs, but for anyone who wants to apply useful lessons—pick it up.

—RICK MYERS, FOUNDER AND CEO, TALENT ZOO

Steve covers a wide range of topics on entrepreneurism, business building and leadership in *Real Leaders Don't Follow*—and you'll appreciate the way he consistently takes a strong position that will have you reflecting on and challenging your own core beliefs. Every emerging or veteran leader can take away powerful lessons from this book to apply on their own journey.

—Doug Mack, CEO of Fanatics,
former CEO of One Kings Lane

REAL LEADERS
DON'T FOLLOW

BEING EXTRAORDINARY
IN THE AGE OF THE ENTREPRENEUR

STEVE TOBAK

Ep
Entrepreneur
PRESS®

Entrepreneur Press, Publisher
Cover Design: Andrew Welyczko
Production and Composition: Eliot House Productions

This publication is designed to provide accurate and authoritative information
in regard to the subject matter covered. It is sold with the understanding that
the publisher is not engaged in rendering legal, accounting or other professional
services. If legal advice or other expert assistance is required, the services of a
competent professional person should be sought.

Library of Congress Cataloging-in-Publication Data
    Tobak, Steve.
      Real leaders don't follow: being extraordinary in the age of the
entrepreneur / by Steve Tobak.
      pages cm.
      ISBN-13: 978-1-59918-575-0 (paperback)
      ISBN-10: 1-59918-575-X (paperback)
      1. Entrepreneurship. 2. Leadership. 3. New business enterprises—
Management. I. Title.
      HB615.T627 2015
      658.4'092—dc23   2015022191

Printed in the United States of America

19 18 17 16 15   10 9 8 7 6 5 4 3 2 1

For tomorrow's business leaders.

CONTENTS

ACKNOWLEDGMENTS. xiii

PREFACE

REAL ENTREPRENEURS DON'T FOLLOW xv

PART I

THE ENTREPRENEURIAL MOVEMENT

CHAPTER 1

A CULTURAL REVOLUTION IS BORN 3

    One Device to Rule Them All 6

    A Blogger Is Born 8

CHAPTER 2

THE GREAT MILLENNIAL MYTH 11

    Millennial in a Boomer Body 12

The Entrepreneurial Generation 15

The Golden Age of Fads 16

CHAPTER 3

THE IDIOCRACY EFFECT 21

The Spiral of Silence 26

CHAPTER 4

CHOOSING THE MORE EVOLVED PATH 29

You Are Not a Zombie. 29

The Blue Pill or the Red Pill 32

PART II

THE REAL ENTREPRENEUR

CHAPTER 5

RULING YOUR OWN DESTINY. 41

Trust Your Gut. 42

Trial By Fire 47

CHAPTER 6

YOU ARE NOT A PRODUCT 51

The Good News Is, You're Fired 52

Your Product Is Your Brand 54

Bad-Tasting Medicine 59

CHAPTER 7

ALL THAT GLITTERS IS NOT GOLD. 67

Think Happy Thoughts 72

CHAPTER 8

MAKING YOUR OWN LUCK. 77

Opportunity Meets Desperation 80

CHAPTER 9

THE REAL SECRET TO PERSONAL PRODUCTIVITY. 83

Do Only What Matters 84

Priorities, Focus, and Discipline 88

CHAPTER 10

COMPETENCIES FOR A CHANGING WORLD 93

Critical Thinking 94

Focus and Discipline. 96

Being Human 97

Getting Things Done. 99

Competitive Spirit. 101

CHAPTER 11

FINDING POINT B 105

Looking for a Career in All the Wrong Places 106

Entrepreneurial Mythology 111

Know Yourself, Face Your Fear, Follow Your Heart 116

PART III

THE REAL BUSINESS

CHAPTER 12

STARTUP = ENTREPRENEUR + VENTURE CAPITAL 121

First, Lose the Label. 122

There Are Entrepreneurs and There Are *Entrepreneurs* 126

CHAPTER 13

STARTUP 101: THINK LIKE A VC 133

Never Tell Me the Odds 134

What Problem Are You Solving?. 137

How Will You Beat the Competition? 138

Do You Have the Right Team? 141

Do You Have a Credible Business Plan? 142

CHAPTER 14

BUSINESS IS ALL ABOUT RELATIONSHIPS 147

People People 149

Why I Like Going to the Dentist 151

Engage With Purpose. 152

Relationships, Texas Style 156

You're Not as Introverted as You Think 159

CHAPTER 15

DESTIGMATIZING SALES 161
You're Not Selling Used Cars 162
Selling Is a Marathon, Not a Sprint 163
Go Big or Go Home 164
Never Turn Down a Paying Customer 166
You're Always Selling 167
Cold Calling Does Not Mean Wasting People's Time 168
Be Your Genuine Self 170

CHAPTER 16

UNRAVELING THE MYSTERIES OF MARKETING 173
Principle 1: In Competitive Markets, It's Winner Takes All 177
Principle 2: Innovators Turn Ideas
Into Products People Can Use 178
Principle 3: Marketing Is Like Sex:
   Everyone Thinks They're Good at It 179
Principle 4: Differentiate or Die 180
Principle 5: You Can Never Afford to Lose a Customer 182
Principle 6: Your Product Is Your Brand 184
Principle 7: Competitive Barriers Work Both Ways 185

CHAPTER 17

WHICH WAY IS UP? 189
Strategic Planning 101 193
If You're Not Growing, You're Dying 196
The Myth of the One-Trick Pony 197
I See Products in Your Future 200

CHAPTER 18

FAILURE HAPPENS 203
Pitfall 1: Running Out of Cash 204
Pitfall 2: A Little Success Can Be a Dangerous Thing 205
Pitfall 3: Solutions in Search of Problems 206
Pitfall 4: Lousy Vision 207

Pitfall 5: Lack of Focus...208

Pitfall 6: The Dinosaur Effect 210

Pitfall 7: Fear of Flying...211

Pitfall 8: The Dysfunctional Founder Problem...................212

PART IV

THE REAL LEADER

CHAPTER 19

THE NO BS LEADER...217

The Bill Gates School of Leadership...........................218

The Warren Buffett School of Leadership 221

The Andy Grove School of Leadership..........................222

The Knights of the Round Table School of Leadership 224

The *You* School of Leadership..................................226

CHAPTER 20

THE MYTH OF THE ROCK STAR LEADER 227

The Myth of the Extroverted Leader 227

The Myth of the Visionary Leader 230

When It Comes to Communication, Less Is More..................232

The Problem With "Fake It 'Til You Make It" 237

CHAPTER 21

UNDERSTANDING COMPANY CULTURE..............................239

Empowerment, Not Engagement 240

Cult-Like Cultures 242

David vs. Goliath 243

Think (and Act) Different 245

Hire the Best, Organize the Least 247

Only the Adaptable Survive 248

CHAPTER 22

THE POLITICALLY INCORRECT LEADER 251

Diversity and Discrimination 252

The Merits of Meritocracy.....................................256

CHAPTER 23

THE TAO OF LEADERSHIP 259

    Embrace the Chaos 263

    Think Less, Feel More 265

    A Question of Balance 268

CHAPTER 24

THE EVOLVED LEADER 273

    Losing the HP Way 274

    Will You Lead or Follow? 282

EPILOGUE

HUMANITY VS. INDIVIDUALITY 285

ABOUT THE AUTHOR 289

INDEX 291

ACKNOWLEDGMENTS

CAROLE JELEN, MY AGENT AT WATERSIDE, was instrumental in helping me flesh out the book's concept. Without her guidance, encouragement, and efforts, this book would not have been possible. I'm also grateful to Jillian McTigue of Entrepreneur Press for her faith in a first-time author and for being such a great publisher to work with.

Many thanks to my editor, Jennifer Dorsey, whose feedback and contributions to the development, readability, and flow of the manuscript were invaluable. And thanks to Karen Billipp and her team at Eliot House Productions for the editing, fact checking, and magic that turns a bunch of words into a quality book.

I'm indebted to Jeff Misenti, chief digital officer at Fox News and Fox Business, and Ray Hennessey, editorial director at Entrepreneur Media, for providing me with a platform with which to engage a broad audience. Not to mention the prophetic Michael Kanellos, who gave me the initial idea and opportunity to blog about management and careers way back in 2007.

Nobody tells you how insane it is to write a book on a deadline without taking time off from your day job. I didn't think I could do it and I couldn't have without Kim's support, guidance, and patience. Her capacity to listen while her neurotic husband explores every notion in his head, and keep him sane without going nuts herself, is the stuff of legend. And throughout the process, one creature never left my side: my always loyal and entertaining best friend, Daphnie.

REAL
ENTREPRENEURS
DON'T FOLLOW

THIS IS A STORY ABOUT A KID WHO GREW UP in a tiny rent-controlled apartment in the Big Apple. His folks were working-class people who didn't have much, but they worked hard every day at their lousy jobs for one reason: to ensure their children had a chance at a better life.

With a powerful work ethic and a strong sense of self-reliance, this kid, the youngest of two boys, left the streets of Brooklyn behind, graduated from college, found his way to the high-tech industry, and beat the odds to become a successful senior executive.

Life was good, but after a decade of corporate leadership, our hero surprised everyone by walking away from that lucrative gig to become an entrepreneur. Then the merchant gods smiled down on him, blessed his righteous quest, and bestowed all good things upon his management consulting business. And he lived happily ever after. The end.

Pretty inspiring stuff, huh? Except that's not exactly how it happened. At least, that's not how it happened to me. You see, I'm that kid.

The first part—about my parents, my early life, and my high-tech career—is entirely true. But I didn't actually give up the life of a high-powered executive to *become* anything. I did it because, after 23 years of climbing the corporate ladder like some crazed workaholic monkey, I simply couldn't do it anymore. My candle, which had burned so very brightly for so long (yes, at both ends), had burned out.

As I told an executive recruiter who contacted me about a CEO position soon thereafter, "I don't need this crap," I said. "I'm done."

"Are you just *sort of* done," he asked, "or are you 'stick a fork in me I'm done' done?"

"Get a fork," I replied. "I'm *done* done."

That was 11 years ago—12 if you count the time it took to write this book. I'm not sure that last year spent writing wasn't the toughest of all, but that's a story for another time. Suffice to say there were no gods, no blessings, and no bestowings involved. This new life is no less stressful or more gratifying than the previous one.

But I had no illusions it would be otherwise. It's not as if I set out to change the world. I'd already spent a couple of decades helping to bring digital technology like advanced computer chips, low-cost personal computers, and mobile devices to the masses. That was all the world changing I intended to do.

No, I quit the corporate life and struck out on my own because it was time to change *my* world. All I really wanted to do at that point was stop moving and sit still for a while. I was tired of all the meetings, all the conflict, and all the politics. I was tired of living on airplanes and waking up in hotel beds with no idea what city or country I was in. I needed a break.

Besides, that was early 2003. Everyone was still reeling from the dotcom bomb. There was no Web 2.0—no blogosphere, no social media, no user-generated content—and no smartphone revolution. There was certainly no entrepreneurship craze. All that would come later.

Don't get me wrong. When the internet bubble burst it put a damper on things, but there were still plenty of startups, founders, and VCs around—the same ones I'd been working with for decades.

Real entrepreneurs with real businesses. Real CEOs who ran real companies. Real investors with real venture funds.

We still have those same *professional entrepreneurs*, for lack of a better term, but now we've added something new: a much larger group of entrepreneurial amateurs and enthusiasts. It seems that everyone wants to be an entrepreneur these days.

You know what I'm talking about. Everyone's a *wantrepreneur*: a CEO of a one-person company, a crowdfunder, a self-proclaimed leader, a personal brand, a social media guru, a content marketer, a cause junkie, or a solopreneur with a few irons in the fire.

I'm talking about millions of people binging on massive amounts of content in the hopes of boarding this global flight to entrepreneurship. They're digesting countless books and articles, following hordes of bloggers and influencers, and watching millions of videos and webinars.

Ever wonder where all that online content comes from? This may come as a real shocker, but they don't call it *user-generated content* for nothing. It mostly comes from the same people that are consuming it. Like content cannibals, they're all blogging, posting, and tweeting their hearts out in an endless quest for clicks and followers to boost their personal brands and social media presence. The vast majority of it is nothing but eyeball candy.

Meanwhile, big media companies further propagate and magnify all that popular nonsense while making enormous profits off the advertising, as do popular online media platforms such as Google, Facebook, and LinkedIn.

Make no mistake. User-generated content and the entrepreneurial craze it spawned are the new opiates of the masses, which is why you may have a hard time digesting what I'm about to tell you: There really is no entrepreneurial movement. It's a myth, a fad, a fairy tale, a complete fabrication.

Wait, what? "Blasphemy!" you say.

Given all the hype, we should be seeing the mother of all business creation movements, but we're not. What we are seeing is a massive long-term decline in new startups and small businesses across all demographics and geographies. We'll get into this in more detail later, but for now, suffice to say that new business creation has dropped a whopping 28 percent from 1977 to 2011, according to U.S. Census Bureau data. The greatest irony of all is that the steepest declines are coming from those aged 20 to 34, who created just 22 percent of all new companies in 2013, down from 34 percent in 1996. That's right. The *entrepreneurial generation* is nothing of the kind. It's just a media fabrication. (Not to mention that unemployment and underemployment rates among Millennials are almost twice that of the general population.)

With new business creation and workforce participation rates at multidecade lows across the board—especially among young people—the truth is inescapable: Instead of enabling and empowering a new generation of successful innovators and business leaders, this mythical movement and all the virtual content it generates is leading countless would-be entrepreneurs down a utopian path toward a dream that simply doesn't exist.

Why all the gloom and doom? For starters, you can't fix a problem until you identify it. And the only way any of you are going to become the innovators and business leaders of a new generation is if someone has the guts to tell you the truth, get you off the Kool-Aid you've been drinking, and set you on the right path.

Do you have any idea how easy it would have been to write a book that fed right into all the hype? To pen an inspiring piece of feel-good fluff and add my voice to the relentless entrepreneurial drumbeat that's indoctrinating the masses? I didn't do that because my parents taught me right and I'm an honest guy who believes in karma. Besides, I didn't get to where I am by taking the easy way out. I didn't beat the odds by following the path of least resistance. And I certainly didn't achieve all I've achieved by following the masses.

If there's one lesson I learned the hard way, it's that you never get ahead by following anyone down a gilded path. I learned that fighting for my identity on the streets of a crowded inner city. I learned it competing head-to-head with tech giants like Microsoft and Intel. I learned it in the boardrooms of Silicon Valley and beyond. That singular lesson enabled a kid who started with nothing to lead an extraordinary life on his own terms, a life he never dreamed possible. That same lesson is so ingrained in the blood and bones of every successful entrepreneur, executive, and business leader that it's become part of our DNA.

Nobody ever changed the world by doing what everyone else is doing. That's not just common sense—it's biology. Species evolve when beneficial genetic mutations arise out of competitive ecosystems and take over. Likewise, civilization advances when unique individuals who think and act differently shatter the status quo and forever change how we do things.

Leaders lead. Followers follow. You can't be both. Real leaders don't follow, and neither do real entrepreneurs. That's a choice each of us has to make somewhere along the line. I made mine early on, as many of my contemporaries did. The problem is that far too many of you have made the wrong choice without realizing it.

I wasn't on any kind of mission when I started this journey 11 or 12 years ago, but I'm certainly on one now. In many ways, entrepreneurialism is broken, and I'm going to fix it. Since that's a pretty big job, this book has a pretty broad scope.

It provides a unique inside perspective on a technological revolution that is transforming our culture on a global scale . . . and how it affects all of us. It exposes popular myths that masquerade as common wisdom to help you find a truer career path. It explains how real entrepreneurs start, build, and run successful companies in highly competitive global markets. And it builds a foundation for a new generation of executives and business leaders.

The book's lessons and stories come from decades of experience working with thousands of founders, executives, and VCs in the cradle of entrepreneurial America—Silicon Valley—and with our customers around the world.

While the focus is on high-tech, we've all learned by now that, as the technology industry goes, so goes the world. Whatever business you're in, the anecdotes and advice will resonate and relate in meaningful ways. Professional courtesy and confidentiality agreements sometimes kept me from naming names, but rest assured the stories are reasonably accurate given that human perception is always subjective. God knows, I'm definitely human.

My overarching goal for this book was to provide unique insights from an insider perspective to help you make better-informed career, business, and leadership decisions. You might not always agree with my conclusions—nor should you—but if the book serves to challenge popular doctrine and your own beliefs, I'll consider its mission accomplished.

Our journey begins as the clock strikes midnight, ushering a new millennium into the Santa Cruz Mountains bordering Silicon Valley.

PART I

THE
ENTREPRENEURIAL
MOVEMENT

CHAPTER 1

A CULTURAL
REVOLUTION
IS BORN

STREAMS OF SILLY STRING FLEW THROUGH THE AIR as someone popped yet another bottle of overpriced champagne, as if anyone could tell the difference between Dom Perignon and Diet Sprite at that point. Feeling a little woozy, I plopped down in an overstuffed chair and closed my eyes just for a second.

When I woke up the sun was shining, my head was pounding, and I had absolutely no idea how or when I'd gotten into bed. The new millennium began just like any other New Year's Day—and far too many *normal* Saturday mornings, I'm afraid.

But there was good news. Contrary to months of Y2K fear mongering, the world's servers didn't suddenly lose their programming at the stroke of midnight. Elevators didn't stall in mid-descent and 747s didn't fall out of the sky. That was a relief.

Monday was just like every other Monday in Silicon Valley. Rush-hour traffic was hell. Work was work. And my job was senior vice president of marketing and sales at Tessera, a late-stage San Jose-based high-tech startup. We'd just finished raising $35 million in a mezzanine round of funding and were starting to think about taking the company public.

The next couple of months were also uneventful—if you can call the $165 billion AOL Time Warner merger, the Nasdaq climbing another 1,000 points, and 142 initial public offerings (IPOs), half of which doubled or tripled on their first day of trading, uneventful. After all, it's not as if we didn't know we were in a bubble. We just chose not to think about it popping.

The IPO market couldn't be hotter, so we chose our underwriters, completed the always entertaining due diligence process and S-1 prospectus, and got our roadshow pitch done in record time. That's when the unthinkable happened—the biggest bubble in stock market history burst. After peaking at 5,132 on March 10, the Nasdaq plummeted 2,000 points over the next ten weeks. When the dust settled, hundreds of internet startups had gone belly-up, commercial realtors in Silicon Valley were practically giving away office space, and investors had lost trillions.

And of course, we had no choice but to hit the pause button on our public offering. It would be a very, very long pause.

That's all ancient history, but here's what isn't. The big takeaway to come out of the historic dotcom bust is not how blind everyone was to irrational exuberance. Don't get me wrong: It *was* crazy to assume demand for telecom infrastructure would continue to accelerate unabated until the end of time. It *was* nuts to value any company with dotcom in its name at more than $1 billion no matter how ludicrous its concept and nonexistent its business model.

And it's still hard to fathom how an industry full of brainiacs with enormous IQs had their sights set so far off in the distance that they couldn't focus on what was happening right in front of their noses. Now, we know you just can't see change coming when you're in the thick of it, but I guess we had to learn that lesson the hard way.

What really came out of the long and desolate nuclear winter that followed the internet bust had nothing to do with any of that. It was the mother of all creative destruction. What happened over the coming years became the foundation for the most powerful cultural transformation since the '60s hippie movement and the summer of love.

The change we couldn't see coming was the rise of the social web, aka Web 2.0.

When you consider that some of the most valuable, powerful, and successful products and companies in the history of technology—products that would come to shape our everyday lives in unimaginable ways—were formed during the years following the dotcom bust, it's hard to believe it wasn't part of a grand design dreamed up by some mad genius. Or maybe it was; I'm not saying one way or the other. But if it was, the inspiration must have come from Stanford University. After all, nearly everyone who had anything significant to do with the coming revolution was schooled in Palo Alto, home to the Stanford Cardinal and half the geeks in the valley.

Speaking of geeks, against the advice of pretty much everyone they knew, a couple of Stanford grads named Larry Page and Sergey Brin decided the world wouldn't be right without another search engine. It's only fitting that, after striking out with the venture capital community and all the big internet firms, it was a Stanford alum—Sun cofounder Andy Bechtolsheim—who wrote the guys a $100,000 check. That angel investment would come to be worth more than $2 billion.

More important than the search algorithms themselves was the notion that small businesses might be willing to pay to boost their search results. Prior to launching AdWords in October 2000, the search market was actually highly fragmented and still up for grabs. Google's share was only about 8 percent. It was AdWords that would turn Google into one of the most powerful brands on Earth and create one of the most commonly used verbs in the English language.

Also following the demise of the first internet boom, developers began to envision a transformation of the World Wide Web from a collection of published static pages to an interactive medium using open-source tools for user collaboration, social networking, and sharing of user-generated content.

The main catalyst for what came to be known as Web 2.0 was WordPress, a free and soon to be ubiquitous content management system developed by Matt Mullenweg and Mike Little. Launched in May 2003, WordPress would power most of the blogosphere and come to be used by more than 60 million websites, give or take.

Meanwhile, online payment innovator PayPal went public and was soon acquired by eBay. That created an exodus of key employees, known as the *PayPal Mafia*, who went on to found and fund some very important startups. Among this elite group of entrepreneurs was another Stanford grad named Reid Hoffman, who launched the first business social networking site, LinkedIn. He and PayPal cofounder Peter Thiel also provided early funding for Mark Zuckerberg's Facebook venture.

Three more PayPal employees would go on to found YouTube, the digital world's video hub that would ultimately boast more than one billion users.

Interestingly enough, PayPal, Google, LinkedIn, and YouTube all received early-stage funding from the same venture capital firm, Sequoia Capital.

Finally, Evan Williams—who actually coined the term "blogger"—joined forces with Biz Stone, Jack Dorsey, and Noah Glass to develop Twitter. The microblogging site went viral at Austin's 2007 South by Southwest Interactive confab and went on to become one of the world's most popular online social platforms.

The key point is that it was the vision, capital, and hard work of a surprisingly few extraordinary entrepreneurs and VCs that enabled a global cultural movement, the social web, to come to life. But for Web 2.0 to reach its full potential, users would have to be set free from their PCs. A revolution in mobile computing was yet to come.

ONE DEVICE TO RULE THEM ALL

While Page and Brin were off registering the Google.com domain in 1997, Apple chief executive Gil Amelio was acquiring NeXT Computer, a pivotal event that brought Steve Jobs back to the company he cofounded. Never mind that Jobs thought the guy was a pompous ass, which he probably was. Jobs seemed to revel in making fun of some of the things Amelio would say, including this classic analogy: "Apple is like a ship with a hole in the bottom, leaking water," he would say, "and my job is to get the ship pointed in the right direction." Think about it. What's the point in steering a sinking ship?

So it came as no surprise to anyone that, in a matter of months, Amelio was gone and Jobs was acting CEO of the nearly bankrupt company.

At the same time, National Semiconductor, which Amelio had run before jumping ship to Apple, acquired microprocessor maker Cyrix for $550 million. Why is that important? Cyrix had been the catalyst behind a revolution in low-cost computing that made it easier for everyday consumers to get online. It was developing a breakthrough mobile device that would fuel the tablet movement, the WebPAD. And the merger brought its marketing veep to National. That would be me.

One day an executive who was working with me on a special project, John Mallard, popped into my office to say he was leaving National to cofound a startup and make what he described as a sort of handheld solid-state jukebox that could store and play hundreds of songs.

That company, PortalPlayer, was chosen by Apple to develop the platform for its first portable music player, the iPod. The device, which launched with iTunes in 2001, became Apple's initial foray beyond computers and a pivotal product for the Cupertino company—not because it changed how people bought and listened to music but because of what it led to next.

It was the breakout success of the iPod that got Jobs thinking about a phone. Whether that was a defensive move to protect Apple's hot new product, a strategy to beat competitors to the next level of handheld integration, or just Jobs being Jobs and somehow managing to divine the next big thing, nobody knows. But soon enough that would all be academic. In 2003, Apple began a secret project to develop a product that would define a generation: the iPhone.

Meanwhile, I'd gotten sick of the big-company politics at National and moved on to help run Tessera and, several years later, another Silicon Valley company, Rambus. That's when I finally decided to call it quits, cofounded a management consulting firm, and spent the next few years advising CEOs on a variety of strategic matters, from new business development and public offerings to corporate positioning and restructuring.

While that was fun and paid the bills, I craved something more. Having played a significant role in the technological and management landscape for so long, a growing part of me wanted to share my observations, experience, and insights with a far broader audience. That opportunity would soon come my way.

A BLOGGER IS BORN

It's funny how many life-changing events begin with a phone call. In this case, the caller was Michael Kanellos, editor-at-large at CNET and an old media friend from back in the day. It was a cold, rainy day in January, my consulting business was in a lull, and the distraction was welcome. Besides, I loved Kanellos. He was a great guy who always made me laugh.

After the usual catching up, Kanellos explained that he and CNET editor-in-chief Jai Singh were putting together a contributor blog network, and he was calling to see if I wanted to be part of it.

"So, are you interested?" Kanellos asked.

"In what?" I said.

"In writing a blog for us?"

"What's a blog?"

"It's just like a column except online, so readers get to comment and you get to comment back," he said. "There's also social media interaction."

I really had no idea what he was talking about, but it sounded like it could be good promo for the consulting business, which I sorely needed. It also sounded like fun. After decades in the high-tech industry, I certainly had a lot to write about. And my philosophy has always been, if it sounds even remotely like an opportunity, just say "yes." So I did.

"Sure," I said. "Why not? Just one question. What do I *blog* about?"

Kanellos reminded me how many of our conversations over the years—especially the late-night ones involving alcohol—had deteriorated into bitch-fests about the industry and all the dysfunctional executives we've known and occasionally worked for. Then he said something that proved so prophetic it still gives me chills.

"Focusing on career and management might pay off. People spend their whole lives bitching about work, and yet we never read about it," he said. "Climbing the ladder sucks and everyone is obsessed with it, yet few speak out on it. You know the topic, could put out a lot of stuff on it, and can be funny about it. You could even rip on insane bosses you have known."

So *that* was his angle. Dishing the dirt on the tech industry's notorious dysfunctional executives. Well, there certainly was a lot of material to work with. And he was right about work, bosses, and climbing the corporate ladder. They were all we talked about over beers and margaritas after work, but the mainstream media ignored it. It seemed like a great idea, but at the time there was no career, management, or leadership commentary to speak of. Still, CNET wanted everything to have a tech angle, so five days after Apple launched the first generation iPhone, CNET ran my very first blog post, "Why the iPhone scares the crap out of me." The article was eerily predictive of what was to come:

> "It's ironic. I make fun of people who drive around with [phones] glued to their ears. I imagine they can't stand a minute alone with themselves and their thoughts. Hungry for distraction, desperate for human contact, they talk, talk, talk.

> "I have a neighbor who I think had her cell phone surgically attached to her head. It has to be; it's always there. I heard that one of her kids was actually born that way. I'm thinking it's a new genetic mutation that will eventually propagate through the entire human race."

Then, after describing a near-death experience with a freeway embankment while texting, I wrote:

> "The only saving grace is that cell phones are primarily just that—phones.
> . . . Although we all screw up from time to time, there's really no excuse

for not keeping our eyes on where we're going when we're on the phone. Until now.

"The iPhone may not be the first, but it will without a doubt be the most popular phone with a decent visual interface and some really cool features for Web browsing and whatever else you choose to strain your eyeballs on.

"I don't know about you, but that scares the crap out of me. . . . On the other hand, if Jobs made it, [Walt] Mossberg liked it, and all of you are waiting in line to shell out $599 to buy it, who am I to say, 'Look out for the embankment!'"

The iPhone would, of course, become the most successful and lucrative single product in tech history. Its annual revenues alone would be bigger than those of nearly every company in the S&P 500, including Procter & Gamble, Boeing, Microsoft, Johnson & Johnson, Pfizer, Intel, Cisco, Coca-Cola, and Goldman Sachs.

More important, the iPhone's iconic design, innovative multitouch display interface, virtual keyboard, and unprecedented web browsing capability would launch a smartphone revolution. Along with the iPad and Google's rival Android platform, Apple would bring social media, video, user-generated content, messaging, and millions of applications to the everyday lives of more than a billion people.

Together, smartphones and Web 2.0 spawned a cultural revolution. And once CBS bought CNET in 2008, I found myself in the thick of it with a popular leadership blog called The Corner Office. The blog afforded me a powerful media platform from which to explore a broad range of topics, and I became drawn to the increasingly convoluted intersection of business, technology, and culture. At the focal point was the generation that had come of age during this cultural upheaval, Millennials.

CHAPTER 2

THE GREAT
MILLENNIAL
MYTH

AS THE FIRST GENERATION TO GROW UP WITH PCs and the internet, Millennials took to coding as if it were second nature. They didn't just embrace Web 2.0; they reveled in it. With wunderkinds like Zuckerberg and Mullenweg achieving rock-star status as developers of some of the web's hottest sites and platforms, the media started calling Millennials the *entrepreneurial generation*.

At the same time, the press was also blasting the newest generation to hit America's workforce as entitled and self-centered. The challenges of managing Millennials became a popular and trending topic throughout the mainstream media and the blogosphere.

How much of the hype surrounding Millennials in the workforce is perception and how much is reality? Are they more entrepreneurial and entitled than others, or are those just popular myths? With Millennials expected to overtake baby boomers as the nation's largest demographic this year, according to U.S. Census Bureau data, it's time we separate fact from fiction about those we're counting on to be our next generation of executives and business leaders.

Let's start with the general concept of *generational profiling*. Whether any of the labels the media has attached to Millennials are true is irrelevant. In the business world everyone should be viewed as an individual and personnel decisions should be based entirely on meritocracy. That's how effective leaders manage their teams and smart executives run their companies. It's also common sense.

Behavioral characterizations about any group of people are largely artificial media constructs. Our culture loves to label groups. Sure, there's usually a thread of truth in there somewhere, but the media is adept at weaving those threads into entire tapestries that are little more than fabrications. They do it because it's dramatic, and people love drama. Drama draws eyeballs and page views. Drama sells, especially in a post-Web 2.0 world.

Inevitably lost among the overhyped surveys and studies is the fact that people are not static. We mature as we age, and competitive markets are always changing. For example, research from Ernst & Young, as reported in *USA Today* in 2013, says that "Generation Y managers are widely perceived as entitled." But that's not unusual for young up-and-comers in any era. In time, they'll learn to adapt, change the rules, or fall by the wayside. That's the way the business world works. That's how it's always been.

From a practical business and management standpoint, generational labels are essentially nonsense. People are individuals, and individuals are defined by their behavior.

MILLENNIAL IN A BOOMER BODY

I'd like to tell you a true story that I think will go a long way toward explaining the problem with generational profiling. Let me know if it sounds at all familiar.

It's about a guy who got a bachelor's degree from a state college but couldn't get a job in his field. It was during a recession; there were no jobs. So he worked part time as a vault attendant at the local bank for minimum wage. It was depressing, to say the least.

Even worse, he was saddled with all sorts of debt from student loans. And although he eventually went to grad school, too much time had elapsed, so the interest and penalties piled up until he ended up owing twice the original amount he borrowed. When he finally got a *real* job after grad school, it took years to pay it all back.

Speaking of that first job, the hours were 8 to 5. This guy was *not* a morning person. He couldn't stand getting up that early and was always lobbying his bosses for flexible hours. After all, why should he have to be there when everyone else was? It drove him crazy to sit in meetings when he could have been doing something productive . . . like sleeping.

And he had absolutely no respect for management, for *the man*. His boss had a sign in his office that said, "I may not be smart, but I sure am experienced." The young man thought it would be funny if he made a sign that said, "I may not be experienced, but I sure am smart" and hung it in his claustrophobic little cubicle—which, by the way, he also despised. His boss didn't think that was very funny. But you know, the guy really didn't mean it as a joke. He actually believed it. That's how overblown his ego was.

And he didn't like the way they wanted him to dress, either. He wore tight-fitting, trendy clothes, torn jeans, funky sneakers, and T-shirts. He didn't buy into the whole *dress for success* thing. He wanted to be unique. Stand out. Have his own image. Above all, he never wanted to become a corporate drone.

One thing about work was cool, though. This guy was an engineer, and the industry had a new technology called computing. You could design semiconductor chips a lot faster and more accurately with software tools that ran on big mainframes. The old guys at work had trouble adapting, but not the young engineer. And before long, he ended up managing people twice his age.

Since he had to move to where the jobs were, the young engineer didn't know a soul there. All his friends were from work. They'd go out after work, grab some food and beers, and complain about management: how they didn't understand them or how to motivate them. How inflexible they were. Then they'd all go back and work way into the night. Work-life balance? No such thing, but they didn't care.

Ultimately, this guy decided he couldn't stand the whole corporate machine: the layers of management, the bureaucracy, the politics, the whole "ranking and rating" review system some called "ranting and raving." So he moved to California and worked with some entrepreneurs in startup companies. That suited him much better, and his career flourished.

Sound familiar? I'm sure you recognize all the Generation Y workplace themes we hear over and over again these days: recession, no jobs, student loan debt, inflexible workplace, no work-life balance, new technology, even personal branding.

The only difference is that this story happened more than 30 years ago, and it happened to me. Not only is every word true, but most of my friends felt exactly the same way I did.

But then a funny thing happened. I grew up. I didn't lose what made me different. I didn't go to sleep one day and wake up a zombie pod person. I just learned from experience. And in time, I became a top executive.

One of the things I learned along the way is that, in business as in culture, things change. Some things change because they should. Some things change even though they shouldn't. And the more things change, the more they stay the same. Somehow, that's always true.

You know what else I learned? Change isn't generational. Change isn't revolutionary; it's evolutionary. When I was a young worker, I wanted to change management. That didn't happen. First I had to prove myself; then I became management. And that's when I got to change things—from the inside. That's how it works: one person at a time.

Don't just take my word for it. Download and listen to the words of "Won't Get Fooled Again" by The Who. The best line is the last one: "Meet the new boss, same as the old boss." It was written 45 years ago, and it's still true today.

THE ENTREPRENEURIAL GENERATION

Perhaps the stickiest label attached to Millennials is that they're the "entrepreneurial generation." In 2006, *USA Today* ran an article, "Gen Y makes a mark and their imprint is entrepreneurship," which boldly proclaimed a new American movement. Here's an excerpt:

> "They've got the smarts and the confidence to get a job, but increasing numbers of the millennial generation—those in their mid-20s and younger—are deciding corporate America just doesn't fit their needs.
>
> "So armed with a hefty dose of optimism, moxie and self-esteem, they are becoming entrepreneurs."

That piece and others like it sparked a cultural wave that indelibly branded Gen Y as the entrepreneurial generation.

Influential organizations like the Young Entrepreneur Council, dozens of popular Millennial blogs, and books such as Scott Gerber's *Never Get a "Real" Job* and Donna Fenn's *Upstarts! How GenY Entrepreneurs Are Rocking the World of Business* ensured that Millennials would forever be linked with entrepreneurship in our minds and theirs.

But that link turned out to be far more myth than reality.

Despite how strongly those in Generation Y identify with entrepreneurs, that connection never materialized. Contrary to popular belief, not only has entrepreneurship in America been on a long, steep decline, that troubling trend is far worse among young adults.

The number of startups created in America on an annual basis has fallen nearly 28 percent from 1977 to 2011, according to a 2014 *Los Angeles Times* analysis of U.S. Census Bureau data. And the percentage of startups relative to all businesses and the size of the working population have both fallen by more than 50 percent over the same time frame. *The Atlantic* provides a similarly bleak analysis of the data in a 2012 article: "For roughly 30 years, new businesses have made up a steadily shrinking portion of companies in the United States while generating a declining fraction of new jobs."

The downward trend is not absolutely linear. There was, interestingly, a five-year uptick beginning around the start of 2001 and corresponding to the time frame directly following the dotcom bust. But unfortunately it did not last, as business creation fell off a cliff around 2006.

In any case, the multidecade trend is across the board in every region and every industry. It's most pronounced among those aged 20 to 34, who created just 22 percent of all new companies in 2013, down from 34 percent in 1996. That trend is reversed for baby boomers, who surpassed Gen Y in starting 23 percent of new businesses last year, up from 14 percent in 1996.

Meanwhile, unemployment and underemployment rates among Millennials are staggering, almost twice that of the general population. And that's led to the lowest workforce participation rate in 40 years. On top of that, Gen Y is by far the most indebted generation in history. By mid-2013, U.S. federal student loan debt topped $1.2 trillion. And that's up 20 percent in less than two years.

THE GOLDEN AGE OF FADS

If you're wondering how such an enormous disconnect could be possible and starting to doubt your sanity or mine, consider this:

We live in a post-Web 2.0 world dominated by social media and user-generated content. One survey of a thousand young people who would rather rule their own destiny than slave away in corporate America is all it takes. Once it's gone viral on Twitter, Facebook, and LinkedIn, that sentiment becomes doctrine in people's minds. Throw in some books, blogs, and seminars by the hordes of hungry consultants who smell money, and you've got a bona fide movement built mostly on hot air.

In terms of its ability to magnify stories and trends—whether or not they're true—social media under Web 2.0 is like traditional media on steroids.

Yes, there have always been fads. The more they're promoted, the more people want them to be true, and the more hype they create, the more tenacious they tend to be. In the old days, communications were limited and word-of-mouth was inefficient, so crazes came and went without much consequence. Today, it's a much different story.

Take Tony Robbins, for example. Thirty years ago, you'd see him on late-night infomercials having sessions with small groups in Hawaii. After decades of seminars and a couple of bestselling self-help books, Robbins amassed a large following and, by all accounts, a significant fortune.

Never mind that his platform is built on people believing he has some formula for success when, at least to me, that formula appears to be getting people to pay to hear his formula for success. Does that sound like circular reasoning? Welcome to the wonderful world of self-improvement.

Anyway, fast-forward to today. There are hundreds of Tony Robbins types floating around. You can't visit a media website without bumping into three or four of them. That's because you don't have to be a Stephen Covey or Brian Tracy to develop a huge following anymore. All you need is a blog and a Twitter account. As a result, the self-improvement industry has exploded from about $2.5 billion in 2000 to more than $12 billion today.

The truth is that we are living in the golden age of fads. While we tend to think of them as relatively short-lived and mostly harmless, their time frames are getting longer and longer all the time. And while some are inconsequential, others can be quite destructive.

In an era of unparalleled scientific and technological sophistication, the pervasiveness of mystical remedies and magical cures such as homeopathic medicine, acupuncture, nutritional supplements, colon cleansing, and detoxing—most of which do little to no good whatsoever—is striking.

For years, we were told that saturated fat is bad for us. Then, in 2014, we learned from the *Wall Street Journal* that the "link between saturated fat and heart disease" was essentially based on botched studies and "dubious science." Meanwhile, if you live in Hollywood and you're not vegan, vegetarian, gluten free, or at least paleo, you're an outcast.

How about all the weight-loss systems, diet systems, workout systems, nutrition bars, vitamin waters, club memberships, and fitness bands? It's ironic that the more obsessed we are about health and fitness, the more obese and unhealthy we actually become. It's a global crisis.

And who can keep track of all the things that are supposed to cause cancer or fry our brains? Wifi radio signals. Microwave ovens. Plastic bottles. Aspartame. Mercury in fillings. Toxins. What toxins? Nobody knows, but you still have to flush them out. Meanwhile, the anti-vaccine fad based on a completely unsubstantiated rumor that vaccines cause autism has brought back diseases once thought to be eradicated like whooping cough and measles.

It's a dizzying roller coaster of dubious claims, somehow made plausible by the nature of the social media marketing beast. Now apply that to the entrepreneurship craze. What probably started as a revolt against corporate downsizing and outsourcing has gotten completely out of hand.

Granted, if there ever was such a thing as corporate loyalty to employees, it has all but disappeared. But that's not necessarily a bad thing. I, for one, have always preferred the notion of grooming myself for the future instead of relying on a corporation to do it for me. I had no qualms about bouncing from one company to the next for a better opportunity, unpopular as that was at the time.

While the concept of managing your own career has thankfully become the norm, far too many people have bought into the belief that entrepreneurship is the only way to go.

I don't know if the problem is parents telling their children to never trust the man or the blogosphere going overboard with the ludicrous notion that ruling your own destiny somehow means never working for someone else and that getting a real job means you're doomed to a life of poverty and misery. Perhaps it's a little of both. But the mainstream media has run with the hype (the entrepreneurial generation does make for great drama), and not surprisingly, the social media crowd is all too happy to go along for the page views.

Look around. Today, everybody's an entrepreneur. Everybody's a CEO. Everybody has a blog and Twitter, Facebook, and LinkedIn accounts so they can make their voice heard. Everybody's an influencer.

Everybody's special. Never mind that they rarely have any employees, customers, revenues, or profits.

Bizarre as it may sound, a joint oDesk and Millennial Branding study from 2013, "Millennials and the Future of Work," says Millennials view entrepreneurship as a state of mind that has nothing to do with actually starting a business. They see themselves as risk takers, self-starters, and visionary leaders, even without the real-world experience to back it up.

I'm not sure how legitimate it is to hang that on a whole generation, but it definitely goes hand in hand with the decidedly circular relationship that amateur entrepreneurs or "wantrepreneurs" have with social media. They are both masters and slaves of the social media universe, both enormous generators and consumers of online content. That means they spend a great deal of time online breathing their own fumes.

Meanwhile, when asked about their skills, Millennials reportedly cite blogging, social media, and content marketing above all others. But Web 2.0 is essentially free and open-source by design, so the market is flooded with online content and services and nobody's making any money. In other words, the business case for making a living within the confines of Web 2.0 is virtually nonexistent.

It certainly doesn't help that our increasingly intimate relationship with our gadgets is making us all more distracted, disengaged, and disassociated. Our attention spans are becoming more and more limited to sound bites, and we rarely have the time or inclination to question or verify anything anymore. If we did, we wouldn't be as quick to accept fads as facts.

One thing's for sure: Today's massively overhyped entrepreneurial craze is not helping Millennials—or anyone else—become real entrepreneurs. On the contrary, it appears to be having the opposite effect.

CHAPTER 3

THE
IDIOCRACY
EFFECT

SINCE AMERICANS NOW SPEND MORE TIME IN the digital domain than watching TV—more than five hours a day, according to eMarketer—it's tempting to see our growing obsession with online social connectivity and the entrepreneurial movement it spawned as a technological phenomenon. While that's at least partly true, it's actually more about biology.

Around the time of Apple's 2007 iPhone launch, I rented a movie—something we used to do back in the dark ages—called *Idiocracy* by Mike Judge (of *Beavis and Butt-head* and *Silicon Valley* fame).

The movie is about an average Joe—that was actually his name, Joe—who goes into hibernation and wakes up 500 years later. During that time, human evolution hits a serious snag. Hundreds of years of natural selection reward sex-addicted idiots with tons of kids while smart people presumably had better things to do with their time than procreate.

As a result, intelligence becomes an endangered human trait.

As mankind becomes dumber and dumber, the best scientific minds are all working on nonsense like computer games, erectile dysfunction, and monster trucks. By the time Joe awakens, intelligence has been bred out of the human race, making *average Joe* the smartest person alive.

Vulgar advertising and commercialism run rampant in this Orwellian dystopia full of media-addicted morons, fast-food junkies, and shows that make *Jackass* and *Jersey Shore* look like Oscar material.

When Joe is brought to the White House, he meets a Cabinet member who declares, "I'm Secretary of State, brought to you by Carl's Jr." Even cheesier is the U.S. president, a porn star and five-time wrestling champion named Dwayne Elizondo Mountain Dew Herbert Camacho, who takes one look at Joe and says, "So you smart, huh? I thought your head would be bigger. It looks like a peanut."

This bizarre version of the federal government charges Joe with solving the consumerism-crazed culture's biggest problem: Their crops are all dying, the world is turning into a planet-sized dust bowl, and everyone is starving. It turns out they water their crops with a sports drink resembling Gatorade.

Since nobody's smart enough to maintain their cities, the only structure left standing on the ruins of civilization is a Costco so enormous it disappears into the horizon. It even has a commercial jet crashed into its roof that nobody seems to notice. A public defender named Frito actually got his law degree there.

The weird thing about *Idiocracy* is how what was clearly intended to be a sci-fi satire hits so close to home. It struck a nerve with me in so many ways it was jarring, right down to its over-the-top mega-conglomerate version of AT&T (a phone call yields the automated message, "Welcome to AOL Time Warner Taco Bell U.S. Government long distance").

And I'm definitely not alone. Today, the movie that almost nobody saw in theaters has an enormous cult following, not just because it was so remarkably prophetic but, since the movie is set in the 26th century, we seem to be getting there way ahead of schedule. The *Idiocracy* entry on the Urban Dictionary site reads, "A movie that was originally a comedy, but became a documentary."

It's chilling, when you think about it.

We are, in a very real sense, devolving—maybe not genetically, as portrayed in the movie (at least not yet), but behaviorally. That's why *Idiocracy* resonates with us. We see its signs everywhere we look. It's undeniable that our attention spans and engagement in what really matters are rapidly shrinking as we replace long-term goals and meaningful relationships with a constant need for instant gratification and thousands of distractions.

We are addicted to an ever-growing list of obsessions, from Facebook and Twitter to YouTube and LinkedIn, from video games and reality TV to eating and buying everything in sight, whether we can afford to or not. We have so much stuff we have nowhere to put it all, but all we think about is how much more stuff we want. It's never enough. In addition to watching an average of five hours of TV a day, Americans now spend an additional five hours with their eyes glued to a computer display of some sort, according to eMarketer. Young Millennials say their mobile phone is the most important thing in their daily lives—more important than personal hygiene. And a 2014 Bank of America study reports that nearly half of all adults say they couldn't last more than a day without their phone.

The effect that's having on our behavior is alarming and far-reaching. We are becoming more entitled and less empathetic, more disassociated and less organized, more anarchistic and less civilized, more impulsive and less thoughtful, more distracted and less focused. And we are losing our ability to discern fact from fiction, truth from lies, and real insights from complete bullshit.

While the dramatic shift in our behavior and its visible effect on our culture is not a direct result of breeding, it is, strangely enough, very much related to human evolution and natural selection.

For instance, did you know there's a caveman's brain living inside your head? No, I'm not kidding. It's called the *limbic system.* Here's the back story on it:

Millions of years ago—long before we evolved frontal lobes and the ability to think rationally—we were creatures of instinct and emotion. We were all about survival. And that meant eating when food was available, seeking out shelter and safety in numbers, and, of course, pursuing members of the opposite sex, although we weren't smart enough to understand why. Since we were unable to reason logically, our brains produced powerful neurotransmitters like dopamine and serotonin that induced a narcotic-like euphoria to reinforce those behaviors critical to survival. In other words, meeting one of the survival imperatives was rewarded with biochemical reactions that made us feel good.

That behavioral reinforcement mechanism helped us to evolve as herd animals and as social creatures. In the meantime, our brains continued to evolve, eventually adding a neocortex for higher-level thinking. We became more social but also more organized. Our communities became larger, more complex, and more civilized, generally speaking.

But beneath the folds of gray matter, buried deep in our subconscious minds, still lies the brain of a caveman. The limbic system, the feeling and reacting portion of the brain, regulates involuntary and hormonal functions, including the adrenaline fight-or-flight response to emotional stimuli.

After all this time, the limbic system is still responsible for our survival. It still reinforces the same behavior through the same powerful mechanism. To the limbic system, not much has changed over the millennia.

In particular, the limbic system strongly reinforces the sort of social behavior that enabled our survival long ago by making us feel good when we eat, have sex, are sheltered, and socialize with others. While we're usually not aware of the effect, it's always there. And it deeply influences our behavior in profound ways.

Millions of years ago when the limbic system evolved, people weren't so easy to find. Landing a mate was pretty damn competitive. It took a lot of work and time to hunt for and harvest food. Likewise for finding and building shelter. So those *feel good* impulses occurred infrequently, as they should.

To say that's *not* the case today is a wild understatement. The overabundance of all the survival imperatives in modern society makes us all like kids in a candy store—except, in this case, the "candy" triggers powerful, euphoria-inducing chemicals to be released in our brains. Prepared food is everywhere and instantly available. So is pornography. And we can virtually meet or communicate with people at the push of a button. The same is true for buying stuff that makes us feel sheltered and part of the community. And, as of just a few years ago, broadband and wireless *everything* plans have made all that relatively cheap and convenient.

Our current situation is just like the behavioral conditioning experiments conducted by B. F. Skinner at Harvard back in the 1930s. Skinner trained lab rats to press a lever to get food pellets whenever a light came on. The rats learned fast, because they have the same reinforcement mechanism we do: limbic system, neurotransmitters, and all.

Your limbic system works the same way as Skinner's lever: It rewards you with chemicals that reinforce good behavior, including eating, having sex, and connecting with others. The system worked quite well until we became a socially connected world. Now we're all feeling that powerful tug to text and tweet, to ego search and take selfies, to desperately seek attention and followers, to post details of our lives that nobody cares about, to check our email and answer calls 24/7 when we really don't have to. We do these things because biochemical reactions in our brains give us pleasure when we do. It's the same process as any addiction. And like it or not, it's the same process that made those lab rats keep pressing a lever to get food.

Today, for the first time in history, we can satisfy our most basic needs at the click of a button or the tap of a display. So that's what we do. Over and over again, just like drug addicts or lab rats in a Skinner box.

In short, the nearly irresistible tug of the socially connected world is causing us to revert back to ancient instincts. Behaviorally and organizationally, we are indeed devolving. It's dramatically affecting our culture, including the way we live and work. I call it the *Idiocracy* Effect. The only problem is, unlike the movie, it's not fiction. It's absolutely real. It's affecting each and every one of us in ways we're not consciously aware of. And it has far-reaching implications.

THE SPIRAL OF SILENCE

Another key factor that enhances and accelerates the *Idiocracy* Effect is the way our survival instincts help drive cultural conformity. If you've ever wondered how societal norms occur, then perhaps you've heard of an evolutionary theory called the *spiral of silence*: Those who openly support the majority viewpoint on an issue are lauded, so that behavior is reinforced. Dissenters, on the other hand, are denounced, so they clam up for fear of being isolated or ostracized.

Animals that are isolated from the herd usually don't live very long. That's the reason behind the core survival instinct of safety in numbers that's reinforced by the limbic system. This applies to all pack animals, including humans. That's why when you socialize you're rewarded by those powerful neurotransmitters that make you feel good, make you feel safe.

This tendency to self-censor also explains why it is so difficult to change the status quo. People are generally afraid to voice public support for an opinion they perceive to be unpopular, so it takes quite a bit of individual courage and effort to build support and overturn the majority view.

In a sense, the spiral of silence has served to maintain cultural or organizational stability. It provides balance between a quiet majority sustaining the status quo and a vocal minority agitating for change.

That said, the modern online world has thrown that equilibrium into chaos. A 2014 Pew Research and Rutgers University study shows that the spiral of silence effect is far more pronounced on social media than on other public forums. For example, social media users are about half as likely to discuss controversial issues online as they are in person, especially if they think their friends and followers might disagree with them.

So Web 2.0, user-generated content, and social networks actually stifle diversity of thought. The more we live online, the more we think alike and behave as a social collective. The pressure to conform is enormous.

In other words, online personas and personal brands only give the illusion of uniqueness. In reality, the opposite is true. You may think your smartphone and Twitter account give you a bold, unique voice when, in reality, you're mostly just talking to an echo chamber. The truth is, the global shift from physical to virtual interaction actually suppresses diversity, creativity, innovation, and differentiation.

These are some of the biological, technological, and cultural factors that have led to a wildly overhyped entrepreneurial movement and, perhaps more concerning, threaten to turn a billion people and counting into a growing pack of self-perpetuating group thinkers. The pack thinks and acts alike while deluding itself into believing the opposite is true.

To summarize, three factors have led to an overhyped global entrepreneurial movement:

1. *The biology.* The four ancient survival imperatives—food, sex, shelter, and safety in numbers—are all reinforced by the limbic system and satisfied by social interaction. That's why humans evolved as social creatures and what gave rise to culture and civilization.
2. *The technology.* Web 2.0, user-generated content, social networks, and mobile technology opened the floodgates for social connectivity. For the first time in history, technology has made

all our survival imperatives readily available at the touch of a button or the tap of a display.

3. *The culture*. Influenced by the *Idiocracy* Effect and the spiral of silence, the social collective goes viral. Everyone is connected 24/7. Cultural acceptance is off the charts with Millennials as the focal point. The pressure to conform is enormous and growing.

But there is one caveat. While the facts I've presented are undeniable, the outcome is by no means inevitable. That depends entirely on each and every one of us.

CHAPTER 4

CHOOSING
THE MORE
EVOLVED PATH

WHILE THE SIGNS OF *IDIOCRACY* MAY BE ALL AROUND US, it's by no means a predetermined fate. It certainly does not have to be *your* fate. Not only do we have the ability to determine our own path, but we also have the potential to change the entire landscape for many others. That's the unique power of an entrepreneur, an innovator, a business leader. But that future—yours and ours—depends entirely on seeing the world as it really is and making the right decisions going forward.

Today, you have a choice to make: Follow the online social collective to mediocrity or break from the status quo and lead the way into the future. This chapter is about choosing where you go from here. And it begins with a story about how I made that same choice, long ago.

YOU ARE NOT A ZOMBIE

Lincoln High School, my *alma mater*, had an English teacher named Mrs. Greenfield, a middle-aged woman whose idea of a good time was to curl up in bed with a good book and a cup of hot chocolate. She once had the class read a short novella called *Anthem* by Ayn Rand. While the choice of material was initially unpopular with the class, Mrs. Greenfield gave us the option of reading Rand's *The Fountainhead* instead. That book topped out at about a thousand pages, so *Anthem* it was.

Anthem is a dark story set in a future world where everyone is an indistinguishable member of a social collective. Individuality is a thing of the past, and the word *I* has been eliminated from the language. You might call it an Orwellian society, but the book preceded *1984* by more than a decade, so it was quite controversial in its time.

The novella is a lot like *Idiocracy* but without the humor. And while English was about my least favorite subject, I was a big fan of science fiction and had no trouble digesting the book in short order.

While I found *Anthem* intriguing and the ending dramatic—the book's hero and heroine discover old books with the words *I* and *ego*, completely overturning their worldview—it would prove to be a gateway book to Rand's life-changing *Atlas Shrugged*, which I read years later along with *The Fountainhead*.

Although I had become a voracious reader by then, I'd never been so profoundly inspired by a book as I was by *Atlas Shrugged*. Having grown up in the Soviet Union, Rand despised socialism and collectivism. And the way her lead characters manifest her deeply held belief in the power of the individual to change the world resonated with a long-held, if immature, notion that I was somehow special or unique.

I bring this up here because, if you distill the book down to its core concept, Rand was celebrating the greatness of the entrepreneur—those who hold personal accountability above all else, compete honestly and fairly on their own merits, and answer to no one but themselves and their own high standards of what it means to be a successful businessperson.

She also links the ideal of individual greatness to the pure simplicity of innovation, business relationships, and free-market capitalism, which together ultimately triumph over the mediocrity and bureaucracy of the social collective that threatens to overrun the nation.

More than anything I'd read before or since, the powerful insights and lead characters of Rand's masterpiece informed my view of the working world and what it might take to become an accomplished business leader. Not only has Rand's philosophy figured prominently in my success, but I also value those same principles to this day.

All that said, there is a catch, and it's a big one. Today's world is a lot like the one Rand constructed, but in a far more twisted and perverted way than even she could have predicted.

Clearly, we are behaving more like a social collective every day. And rampant political correctness, overemphasis on diversity and inclusion, de-emphasis on individual performance, and increasingly socialistic economic policies are threatening to turn the modern world into a Randian nightmare full of mindless bureaucratic zombies that think and act alike, when they think and act at all.

And the great irony is that Millennials and the rest of the content-generating, crowdsourcing social media horde delude themselves into believing they're destined to be entrepreneurs and business leaders while marching in lockstep to the deafening drumbeat of the social collective. That, by definition, is the opposite of entrepreneurialism.

Not only are social collectives made up of mindless drones, they're poor drones, at that. In an adaptation of his groundbreaking book *You Are Not a Gadget*, internet and virtual reality pioneer Jaron Lanier does a masterful job of exposing the inherent flaws behind today's *open* and *sharing* online utopia. He explains how Web 2.0 enables a handful of aggregators like Google and Facebook to get richer while the social collective that generates the bulk of online content and services gets poorer. He also points out that digital collectivism and lack of free-market competition stifles innovation and leads inevitably to mediocrity.

I've actually heard quite a few technology CEOs admit that the modern high-tech industry concentrates wealth in the hands of a few while increasing the growing wealth gap. Web 2.0 is as big a factor in that outcome as any.

Now, don't get me wrong. I'm no Luddite. I'm not saying technology is bad. Nothing can be farther from the truth. I'm actually dictating this on an iPhone. I will be transcribing and editing on a MacBook Air. And later I will likely get a text or a call from my wife on her way home from work to see if I need her to pick up something for dinner. And then we'll watch a movie downloaded over a broadband network onto a DVR on an enormous flat-screen TV in Dolby Digital 7.1.

More important, I essentially grew up in the high-tech industry. Finding my way into that world was the best thing that ever happened to me, next to meeting my sainted wife, of course. My career has been a real blast—a wild, fun, harrowing, adventure-filled roller-coaster ride.

I would wholeheartedly recommend the high-tech industry as a great place to work to anyone who asks. The people are generally great and the opportunities nearly limitless, and you'll be hearing plenty of wonderful stories and lessons from my time in Silicon Valley and beyond throughout the book.

But none of that changes the realities of business and competitive markets. If you're still not convinced that, with rare exception, working as a Web 2.0, social media, or content marketing entrepreneur is synonymous with working for peanuts, I'm sure you will be by the end of the book.

For now, I'll just say that Lanier is absolutely right. So was Rand. And so was Judge, although he's probably more surprised to hear that than anyone. There is no entrepreneurialism, no innovation, no differentiation, and no success to be found in utopian notions or social collectives of any kind, whether it's the former Soviet Union, the present online culture, or the future world of *Idiocracy* or *Anthem*. That's the simple truth.

THE BLUE PILL OR THE RED PILL

I probably don't know you from Adam, but I bet I can say one thing about you with great certainty: There will be times in your life when you suspect you may have taken a wrong turn and ended up on the wrong path.

Maybe you realize you hate your job and are just plain fed up with being miserable. Perhaps your goals aren't being met and you wonder if your plan is working. Or you've gotten some sort of wakeup call that caused you to look in the mirror and rethink things.

That's not bad news. That's good news. Every successful executive and business leader has gone through that at least once. Companies, too. Think of it as a rite of passage.

When that happens, you have two choices. If you saw the movie *The Matrix*, it's the same choice Morpheus offers Neo: The blue pill or the red pill. You can give in to fear, take the blue pill, and live a life of illusion or delusion, depending on how you look at it. Or, like Neo, you can be brave, swallow the red pill, open your eyes, embrace the painful truth of reality, and at least give yourself a fighting chance to rule your own destiny.

God knows, I've been there more than once. I've taken both pills and one thing's for sure—the blue one sucks. It only leads to what Henry David Thoreau was referring to when he wrote, "The mass of men lead lives of quiet desperation." The blue pill always leads to regret and sometimes to worse things. Either way, it's a bitter pill to swallow.

Of course, the red pill is no picnic, either. As they say, the truth hurts. But then, they also say the truth will set you free. Taking the red pill may be the beginning of a long and difficult road, but it will inevitably lead you to a better place for one simple reason: However things turn out, you will always know you made the right choice.

When you look at it in such black-and-white terms, the choice seems obvious. But it might surprise you to know how many people choose the blue pill—even top executives and business leaders—and sometimes more than once. That's what Thoreau figured out during his two years of solitude at Walden Pond. The reason people do that is a somewhat lengthy story that I suspect we'll get to later, but for now, let's just take it at face value.

Assume for the moment that you've decided to take the red pill. Good. There's actually a simple method for going down that road, and it's more or less the same for people and companies. In the corporate world, it's called *strategic planning*, but that term's gotten a bit of a bad rap, so let's not use it.

Instead, let's just say we're going to take a road trip from point A to point B. The principle behind planning the trip is simple. If you don't know where you are—your starting point—you don't have much chance of getting anywhere, right? And if you don't know where you're going, you certainly won't get there.

The first step is to look in the mirror and determine exactly what's going on. It sounds easy, but there's a catch. You've got to be completely and brutally honest with yourself, and that can be painful. You may see things that need to change about you, where you are in your journey, the path you're on, or where you want to go. Once you figure that out, you map out a plan to get from where you are to where you want to be. Sometimes that's an iterative process, but it's still not very complicated.

Interestingly enough, executives and management consultants use that exact same process for turning around troubled companies. I've used it for decades with companies big and small with great success, although there have been exceptions. Even after hearing the truth, some CEOs opt for the blue pill after all, preferring delusion to reality. Sadly, things always end badly for those leaders, and their companies never survive.

The good news is that you already took the red pill when you bought this book. In fact, you've already come part of the way to understanding what's going on and where you stand, aka point A. Next, we'll talk about where you want to go, aka point B. That's a personal decision for each of you to make, but let's get the ball rolling by putting the future in perspective.

We are not destined to become the losers portrayed in *Idiocracy*, nor are our progeny. The future is always in flux because it's influenced by the decisions each of us makes in the present. And at the risk of mixing movie metaphors, since we've agreed to take the red pill and see things for what they really are, our prospects for a bright future have just risen dramatically.

It's an issue of evolution (remember the limbic system?). And here's the thing. Evolution may have gotten us into this mess, but it can also get us out of it. The limbic system may have a powerful influence on our behavior, but we have evolved over the millions of years since we lived in caves. We can overrule our limbic systems. We are smarter than lab rats in a behavioral conditioning experiment. We can master the caveman inside us with the voice of reason, logical decision making, self-confidence and self-awareness, and strength of will and discipline.

The solution to the *Idiocracy* Effect, the spiral of silence, cultural conformity, Web 2.0, and the insidious drumbeat of the social collective is evolution. We have evolved. We have frontal lobes. All we have to do is use them, just as every great entrepreneur, innovator, executive, and business leader has done for centuries. Civilization has evolved. And those who choose to evolve—to go forward instead of backward—will become the entrepreneurs, the innovators, the executives, and the business leaders of a new generation.

The way evolution or natural selection works is pretty straightforward. Every so often, a genetic mutation occurs that benefits the organism in some vital way, making it more successful at passing along the trait to offspring. If the trait benefits the species, it ultimately moves civilization forward. In short, evolution occurs when mutations outperform the status quo and take over.

It's the same with innovation in business. People and their companies become successful by coming up with game-changing products, services, and ways of doing things that benefit customers in important ways. And if they're really beneficial to a large group of customers, they take over.

But to do that—to be the beneficial mutations of today and the success stories of tomorrow—you have to engage your higher-level brain functions and overcome the addictive tug of the social collective.

Just as with genetic mutations, breakthrough innovation always starts with a unique individual, not a collective. It always starts with a single person's idea, not groupthink. It always starts when unique individuals tap what's inside them instead of looking to others.

Entrepreneurship is about leading, not following, the herd. It's about doing what you think is right, not what everyone else is doing.

It's about going forward, not backward. And it's about getting out and experiencing the real business world, not talking and reading about it.

None of the successful businesspeople you seek to emulate wasted their precious time connecting or being social. They couldn't care less about their personal brand or self-improvement. They paid no attention to how many followers they had, how many hours they worked, or their work-life balance (or lack thereof).

They didn't follow other people's habits, rules, or paths. They had their own unique habits. They broke the rules. And they carved their own paths.

Founders and executives at companies like Apple and Qualcomm, FedEx and Virgin, Skype and WhatsApp, Uber and Airbnb didn't make it big by following the pack. They did it by finding a problem that needed to be solved, coming up with a solution that nobody had ever devised before, and then bringing it to market, one customer at a time.

Success comes from evolution, not devolution. It comes from individuals who shatter the status quo and invent new ways of doing things. It comes from entrepreneurs who think differently and act differently.

And even though we're seeing signs of it today, I for one reject the notion that *Idiocracy* is our future. I believe that all we need are a relatively few number of positive mutations by unique individuals who want to change the real world—not just be a drone in the virtual one—to keep civilization moving forward.

If you join me on this journey, there's no telling where it might lead. Point B may be different for each of you, but it's not sitting around blogging and tweeting like a billion undifferentiated devolved drones clicking buttons all day long like lab rats in a Skinner box. That's no way to live. And it's definitely no way to change the future and save us from *Idiocracy*.

The funny thing about this loony entrepreneurial craze is that, on any given media site, the most popular articles are inevitably about supposedly common traits, habits, and behavior among successful people. Here's the irony: The only thing they all really have in common is that they couldn't care less about that sort of nonsense. They didn't get to where they are by giving a crap about how anyone else does things. On the contrary, they became successful by thinking and acting differently. That's what real entrepreneurs do. Now that you've made the right choice and taken the red pill, let me show you how they do it.

PART II

THE
REAL
ENTREPRENEUR

CHAPTER 5

RULING
YOUR OWN
DESTINY

ONE THING I BET WE CAN ALL AGREE ON IS THAT EACH of us is solely responsible for how our lives turn out. That goes for just about every facet of our lives: our health, our happiness, and our careers. That may very well be the most important lesson of the past couple of decades.

We may be born with unique DNA into different circumstances, but we all start with the same clean slate, more or less. We all begin as infinitely elastic sponges thirsty for knowledge and experience. Beyond our upbringing, what happens next is entirely up to us. Our lives are mostly a function of our behavior and experience.

That's exactly what the Founding Fathers had in mind when they broke from the tyranny of England, wrote the Declaration of Independence, founded the United States of America, and named certain unalienable rights, including "life, liberty and the pursuit of happiness."

The part everyone seems to forget, however, is the amount of personal risk involved in that endeavor. The Founding Fathers actually put their lives on the line. Our risks may be a little less drastic, but they're risks just the same. We're all free to pursue the American Dream, but there are no guarantees in the outcome, and there are penalties for failure.

When you take control of your own destiny, you take on enormous risk and responsibility. You are, in a very real sense, putting yourself and your future on the line.

These days, entrepreneurship is being portrayed in a dangerously utopian light. The media—mainstream and social, reinforced by our own rhetoric—has glossed over and assumed a far too cavalier attitude toward risk. Popular culture has romanticized entrepreneurialism to the point where the downside doesn't seem real.

There is nothing romantic about being your own boss. Entrepreneurship is a risky business that's far from the utopian panacea it's been made out to be. Since every choice you make has an impact on the outcome, you should never make career decisions lightly. There are all sorts of trade-offs and factors to consider before determining where you go next. The following stories about my early encounters with the startup world will provide invaluable lessons to help you position your career for long-term success, just as they did mine.

TRUST YOUR GUT

After nearly a decade learning the ropes at two enormous technology corporations—Texas Instruments and NEC—I'd had about all I could take of being buried under layers of bureaucratic bullshit. It was time to step out and search for an opportunity where I could be a bigger fish in a smaller pond.

Soon enough I had an offer in hand to run three technology design centers across Southern California and Arizona. It was a director-level position and a big step up in terms of responsibility and compensation at a midsize public company where I could have a real impact. But before I could accept the offer, the phone rang. It was the hiring vice president I was already starting to think of as my new boss.

His message came as a shock. He and his boss, the president of the company, were leaving to lead a startup as vice president of engineering and CEO, respectively. And they wanted me to join them. I couldn't just shut the door on either opportunity. The following week I found myself at an industry conference in Las Vegas being pitched by both companies.

The new vice president at the midsize company reiterated the original offer and tried his best to give me the warm and fuzzies. But he was no match for the startup's new chief executive—a charismatic French guy who went on about the top-notch venture capitalists that were backing the company and the stock options we would all get. Then he put his hand on my shoulder, looked me straight in the eye, and said, "Steve, once you go startup, you never go back."

It never occurred to me at the time, but this was a guy who'd never actually worked at a startup, let alone *run* a startup. He had actually spent almost his entire career climbing the corporate ladder at large public companies, just as I had. Still, my head was spinning—and getting larger by the minute from all the attention—as I flew back to Southern California to discuss all this with my fiancée.

Of course, I ended up taking the startup job. After all, who could resist what sounded like a no-lose proposition—same position, same money, way more stock—there didn't seem to be a downside. And you've got to admit, it's pretty heady stuff to have a well-known, high-level executive blow that much smoke up your ass . . . with a French accent, no less.

That feeling lasted about a day into my first week of customer meetings. I figured I'd start out easy—with customers I knew and trusted. I told them not to pull any punches, and they didn't. They didn't just beat me up: It was downright ugly. They explained in eminently clear and logical terms why our concept would never work. The words of one customer in particular hit me like a brick to the head: "Tobak, you've been sold a bill of goods."

By the time the week was over, that sentiment was unanimous. And I was a mess. What the hell had I gotten myself into?

Long story short, after a few more weeks of the same I took the customer feedback to management. They didn't take it well. "What do they know?" they said. Let me tell you something: It's a bad sign when an executive says that about potential customers. A *really* bad sign.

Anyway, they gave me more data, an improved PowerPoint pitch, and a software demo, and sent me back out into the field. The result was the same: déjà vu all over again. But I was a pro. I didn't give up. I fought hard for months until a pivotal moment came that shattered my illusions about this startup and brought reality into razor-sharp focus.

We managed to get one large defense contractor to do some prototype testing of our technology. Of course, their end customer was the Department of Defense, and I knew from experience that the government was pretty free with other people's money, meaning taxpayers. Still, we were all excited to at least have something going on.

We had a big high-powered meeting in Los Angeles with both companies' top brass in attendance. Our CEO did his pitch, then one of our customers' executives got up and presented the results of their prototype testing. We were treated with slide after slide of data that absolutely undermined everything the Frenchman had just presented. Our technology truly flopped. Then our fearless leader did something I'd never seen an executive do before: He went absolutely ballistic.

I'd seen people go nuclear before, just not the chief executive of a company trying desperately to win over his first major customer. To say it was uncomfortable is a wild understatement. It was downright embarrassing. I wanted to crawl under the table and hide. They went back and forth for a while until finally, thankfully, the meeting broke up, one of the VPs showed us out, and my boss and our CEO went red-faced to their rental car to have it out.

I drove home and drank heavily.

The next day I told the story to my soon-to-be wife and, while drawing the inevitable conclusion that I'd made a terrible mistake, had my very first panic attack. When I was done hyperventilating, she said I should quit. I agreed. Seven months into my first startup experience, I resigned. And with all the humility I could muster I called the midsize company that had previously offered me a job but, as you might expect, they'd already filled the position I so cavalierly walked away from.

I learned two valuable lessons from that enormously painful and personally embarrassing experience. They may seem self-evident, but there's nothing like turning down a great opportunity and finding yourself suddenly unemployed to ensure that even the most obvious observations get through your thick skull and hit home so you never, ever forget. And I never have.

Lesson 1: Utopian Thinking Kills Companies and Careers

Even the smartest and most accomplished people on earth are subject to utopian thinking. Successful executives and VCs with decades of experience are all capable of convincing themselves and others that the sky isn't really blue and monkeys can fly. They can screw up just like everyone else, except that when *they* do, they tend to drag a lot of other people's jobs and money down with them.

That was the first of many, many times I would observe executives and business leaders who should know better make terrible decisions that impact countless people. And that leads to one of the most important axioms in life: "Past performance is no indication of future results." It's intended as a word of caution for investors, but it's as true of anything and anyone as it is of stocks and mutual funds.

If you call "Heads!" and flip a coin 20 times and it comes up heads each time, you might think you're on a roll. But even though you've called it correctly 20 times in a row, the odds of it coming up heads again on the next toss are still just 50/50. While real-world decisions are by no means pure luck, it's human nature to think that success leads to more success when in fact it doesn't.

In my experience, the opposite is true. Time and again I've seen successful executives and business leaders live in a delusional state of infallibility while their enormously oversized egos write checks that reality can't cash. That's certainly what happened with that ill-fated startup.

From that day forward, I never again trusted another human being—no matter how smart, accomplished, or successful—more than I trusted my own judgment. Yes, I listen to what they have to say. Then I listen to my gut and make my own decision. And that has served me well over the years.

Lesson 2: Entrepreneurship Is Risky Business

So is your career. When you come right down to it, business is risky business. There's a lot at stake. Actions have consequences. And while we're all too fond of drawing connections between risk and reward, we rarely talk about the far more common connection between risk and loss.

Just look at all the popular phrases: no pain, no gain; no risk, no reward; nothing ventured, nothing gained. And of course, that unforgettable line from the ultimate entrepreneur movie *Risky Business*, "Sometimes you gotta say 'What the fuck.'"

Granted, all those sayings are true, especially the last one. And I certainly don't mean to imply that risk taking is a bad thing. Nothing could be farther from the truth. More often than not, we're too risk-averse for our own good. That said, in *The Prince*, the great Renaissance philosopher and political realist Niccolò Machiavelli wrote, "[T]here is nothing more difficult to take in hand, more perilous to conduct, or more uncertain in its success, than to take the lead in the introduction of a new order of things."

In other words, there's a great deal of nuance behind smart decision making when it comes to risk. There are lots of shades of gray in between the black and white of extreme risk aversion and throwing caution to the wind. And there are grave risks to oversimplifying important life decisions.

For example, the common wisdom of the day is that you'll never get ahead working for *the man* in corporate America, so you should quit your job now and start your own gig or you'll end up broke and miserable. There's even a bestselling book with that as its premise.

That's got to be hands-down one of the top five dumbest things I've ever heard. I can think of few things more ludicrous or irresponsible to suggest. And yet people buy into that sort of sound-bite silliness every day.

I know hundreds, maybe thousands of deliriously happy, enormously fulfilled, highly accomplished, and successful people who've spent years, decades, or even their entire careers in the corporate world. Had it not been for his prior career working for others in the corporate world, the opportunistic guy who wrote that bestselling book never would have had the financial freedom or the practical business prowess to do anything on his own.

Even if you ultimately make the decision to start your own company, get one thing straight. The goal is certainly *not* to take enormous risks and assume everything will work out. The goal in business—even risky business—is to minimize risk by making smart decisions based on sound intelligence and experience. Failure may be a necessity of business life, and it can certainly be the source of great humility and wisdom—if you learn from it, that is—but it's not the goal. The goal is to win, not to lose. The goal is to succeed, not to fail.

I should know. I've failed plenty of times and it's never been pleasant, but that's as it should be. We learn lessons and become stronger because failure is so painful that we dare not repeat it. My first startup experience certainly wasn't my last, but the 25 years since have included two IPOs, a successful merger, and running marketing for the $2 billion company that acquired us. That's not a bad track record considering a universe of opportunities and all the would-be flops I didn't pursue.

I never would have achieved such strong career and business results if I hadn't gotten my hands dirty and learned that experience is the best teacher, to think for myself, and to trust no one but myself.

The point I'm trying to make is that the term *common wisdom* is an oxymoron. Wisdom is never common. It rarely comes from the mouths or the writing of others, and it never comes from popular groupthink. Wisdom comes primarily from your own experience, observations, thought process, and genuine instincts. It comes from inside you. And while there are people you'll come to trust and learn from in life, you're not likely to find them on Twitter, Facebook, or LinkedIn.

TRIAL BY FIRE

Life is a lot like an enormous tree with thousands of branches going off every which way. You choose to explore some branches while ending up on others by plain luck, good or bad. Some of us make our own luck by determining which branches may offer the best opportunities and preparing ourselves to take advantage when those opportunities present themselves.

In that sense, success is initially a game of trial and error that eventually leads to a game of successive approximation. Early on, you're pretty much just shooting in the dark trying to figure out what matters and what doesn't. And you make that determination by doing. You learn by trial and error. You learn from experience. You've been doing it your entire life.

I seriously doubt you'll remember this far back, but as a baby you were very efficient at determining what mattered most. You quickly learned that walking took you places you wanted to be and reaching got you things you wanted to have. You also learned that playing in the dirt and chewing on things you shouldn't have also mattered, but in a different way: Those activities brought parental attention, which was important for your survival.

Most things matter when your world is that small. But as you grow into adulthood, your world becomes much, much bigger. You learn that the world doesn't revolve around you, as you once thought, and the universe of possibilities becomes almost impossibly large. That's why, for adults, it's very important to determine what matters and what doesn't, and sooner rather than later.

The only way I know to whittle that universe of possibilities down—to a point where you're heading toward opportunities that are right for you and offer relatively high probabilities of success—is by getting out there and working.

That's exactly how some of the world's best-run businesses— firms like General Electric, Procter & Gamble, McKinsey, American Express, and IBM—breed thousands of leaders who go on to become the founders and CEOs of countless great companies, according to a 2007 article in *Fortune*. GE and P&G alone turned out Intuit founder Scott Cook, former Microsoft chief executive Steve Ballmer, AOL founder Steve Case, Boeing CEO Jim McNerney, ASK founding CEO Sandra Kurtzig, Home Depot chief Frank Blake, HP and former eBay CEO Meg Whitman, and countless other successful business leaders.

And while I didn't realize it at the time, I used exactly the same method throughout my career, by gaining experience and learning functional skills to round out my rough edges and prepare for executive leadership. That's where the game of successive approximation comes in. Once you have your eye on a target, you home in on it by filling in gaps in knowledge and experience.

After a decade of cutting my teeth on technology and management skills, I felt something important was missing. A big part of my job had long been standing up in front of dozens of potential customers and selling them on our technology capability. And while I was successful and comfortable in that role, I stood in awe of some of the sales reps I worked with. These were the people who called on customers, opened doors, built relationships, and created opportunities. They were master schmoozers, negotiators, and closers. This, I realized, was where the business rubber met the road. I had to develop those skills.

So when the seven-month startup snafu ended with a thud, I gave up a decade of engineering management experience to become a sales rep with a new firm headed up by the most seasoned sales guy I knew, Phil Richards. My folks thought I was nuts, but I knew it was the right call. Still, I had just a six-month guaranteed salary before going straight commission, so I had to quickly build my territory from zero to enough to pay the bills.

There's nothing like a trial by fire—not to mention a car payment and a mortgage on a townhome in Southern California—to light a fire under you. So I learned from the best, worked my butt off, and made things happen. When the dust settled on my first year, the manufacturers we represented voted me sales professional of the year.

To this day, 24 years later, I still have that plaque in my office to remind me of two things: what you can do when you set your mind to something and how taking that humble step back to learn a key missing skill set could open the gates to the executive ranks. I didn't have to wait very long for that to happen.

After trying and failing to start my own rep company, I was sitting in the makeshift office of my Redondo Beach home trying to figure out my next move when the phone rang. It was Gary Clow, the CEO of a fast-growing startup named Stac that I'd called on a few times. I'd really connected with him and his cofounders, and he was calling to offer me a job as director of worldwide sales and marketing in charge of Stac's hardware business, reporting directly to him. Of course I accepted.

The following year Stac went public, but the success didn't last. A gut-wrenching competitive and legal battle with Microsoft would doom the software part of the company, but it still managed to spin off the hardware business I had previously led into a far more valuable company named Hifn, which eventually went public as well.

By then, I had leveraged my newfound skills and experience as a global business executive into a career as vice president of marketing and sales with several well-known tech companies and another startup that in time would go public. Over the years I competed and did business with many of the world's technology giants and came to know a who's who of senior executives, VCs, and founders. And I eventually became CEO of a startup and cofounded a Silicon Valley-based management consulting firm that I run to this day.

But I doubt any of that would have happened had I not learned early on to take risk and failure seriously, trust my own judgment, focus on what matters, and develop and hone the skills I would need to be successful. I also learned that you occasionally have to swallow your pride and take a step backward to eventually move forward. And sometimes life has a way of making that decision for you—whether you like it or not.

CHAPTER 6

YOU ARE NOT A PRODUCT

S OME SAY THAT DOING THE SAME THING AGAIN AND AGAIN and expecting a different result is the definition of insanity. I'm not sure if it means you're crazy, but it's certainly no way to get ahead. Sometimes, the only way to move forward is to figure out what's holding you back and deal with it. The problem may stem from your own limitations or external factors, but the solution always involves you doing something differently. After all, your actions are the only things you can control.

That process of determining what's not working and changing it is one every successful entrepreneur, executive, and business leader learns. We do it over and over throughout our careers, every time we hit a wall. Sometimes it's difficult or painful, but if you have high aspirations in life, it's something you need to get used to. This is how it works.

THE GOOD NEWS IS, YOU'RE FIRED

The one thing I left out of the Stac story from the previous chapter is that it wasn't my decision to leave the company and move on to bigger and better things. I was fired. Sure, they were nice about it and made the termination part of a mass layoff, but the truth is I was fired because I went head-to-head with the CEO over the company's direction and had become a toxic pain in the butt who was seen as more trouble than he was worth.

It was small consolation that I had lasted longer than others—the company had always been a revolving door for sales and marketing executives—and that my original plan to spin off the hardware business turned out to be the right strategy. It was a humiliating experience nonetheless. Not to mention that I was once again unemployed and, while the exit package was generous, had just four months to find an executive-level job during a bad recession.

That was when it dawned on me that self-motivated, accomplishment-oriented people with aggressive goals and high expectations could be their own worst enemy. I had certainly become mine. The details are unimportant, but suffice to say I had pushed too hard and taken my job and myself way too seriously. The result wasn't pretty, at home or at work. And I had nobody but myself to blame.

As failures go, this was way worse than my first startup experience. This time it was personal. I took it hard, and I took it to heart. I looked in the mirror and didn't like what I saw. I thought, "What good is a successful career if it makes you and everyone around you miserable?" Besides, my attitude and behavior were ultimately self-destructive. It was time to make some changes, to lighten up and let go. So in between contract work and hitting the help-wanted classifieds of every California newspaper I could get my hands on (we did it old school back in '93), I got some much-needed R&R at the beach. That Zen time really paid off.

Just as our bank account approached zero, I came upon an ad for director of marketing at a fast-growing Bay Area chip company that had just gone public. What really got me excited about OPTi is that I knew this company. I'd met with two of the founders at their Sunnyvale headquarters about a year before, and, to my recollection, it was a good meeting. So I called the sales rep who made that connection, got him to walk my resume in, and after a few interviews, landed the job. It was time for the Tobaks to head up the coast to Silicon Valley.

As it turns out, getting fired from Stac was the best thing that could have happened to me, but only because I took it for what it was. I didn't try to sugarcoat it or blame someone else. I took the feedback to heart, took a good hard look at myself, learned from the experience, and became a better person and a more capable executive as a result.

In business, as in life, understanding what's holding you back and keeping you from achieving your goals is one of the most powerful tools at your disposal. And while we all search for answers to life's defeats, the truth can only be found by looking inside ourselves.

I know lots of similar stories to my own, but none is more moving than the one Steve Jobs told at his now famous 2005 Stanford University commencement speech.

Jobs talked about the devastating loss of being ousted from Apple, a publicly humiliating event that was precipitated by his toxic management style. "I didn't see it then," Jobs said, "but it turned out that getting fired from Apple was the best thing that could have ever happened to me."

What followed was a period of soul-searching and transformation that led Jobs to the woman he would spend the rest of his life with. It also led to the founding of the enormously successful animation film studio Pixar. And it ultimately led to his return to Apple and what is undoubtedly the greatest turnaround story in the history of corporate America.

Jobs went on to say, "I'm pretty sure none of this would have happened if I hadn't been fired from Apple. It was awful-tasting medicine, but I guess the patient needed it. Sometimes life hits you in the head with a brick. Don't lose faith."

As it is with life, your career is a long journey without a well-defined destination. You depend on those major inflection points, those wakeup calls, those bricks to the head, to tell you that your current path isn't right for you. But it's up to you to learn and grow from the experience, and use the opportunity to find a new path.

Jobs put it this way: "You've got to find what you love. And that is as true for your work as it is for your lovers. Your work is going to fill a large part of your life, and the only way to be truly satisfied is to do what you believe is great work. And the only way to do great work is to love what you do. If you haven't found it yet, keep looking. Don't settle. As with all matters of the heart, you'll know when you find it."

Losing your job is a great loss. It's humiliating and painful. And it's not unusual, at least at first, to feel anger and resentment, to blame others for what happened to you. Just don't let the process end there. Once you get past the pain and the rage, take a long, hard look in the mirror and be honest with yourself about what you see.

In time, you'll look back and realize that, in losing something important to you, you found something even more important: an opportunity to gain insight into yourself and find a better, truer path, a path that leads to happiness and fulfillment.

As jazz great Miles Davis said, "When you hit a wrong note, it's the next note that makes it good or bad."

YOUR PRODUCT IS YOUR BRAND

Life is a lot like a roller-coaster ride. It goes up, it goes down. Sometimes it's terrifying, but with the right attitude and some courage, you'll mostly enjoy the ride and end up with a big smile on your face.

The same is true of companies (yes, they do have life spans, just like people). Careers too. They never go straight up and to the right without a hitch. Instead, they more closely resemble stock market charts. There are plenty of challenges and hurdles to overcome. We create some of those obstacles for ourselves, while others are external. Whatever the source, the only way to go forward is to figure out what's holding us back.

The social media world is doing just that. It's filling our Twitter feeds, LinkedIn accounts, and ultimately our heads with one insidious fad and destructive myth after another. If you want to evolve, if you want to make it in this world, if you want to have any chance of achieving your goals, you have to see all that popular nonsense for what it is and, more important, how it's holding you back.

It's time for a little tough love. It may be awful-tasting medicine but the patient needs it, as a great entrepreneur once said. Our culture's obsession with self-improvement, positive psychology, personal productivity, emotional intelligence, employee engagement, inspirational quotes and stories, the habits of the wealthy, and being happy all the time is holding us back. It's holding you back.

And this may feel like a real brick to the head, but you absolutely need to hear it: The same is true of personal branding, blogging, and social networking. The vast majority of what you do online is not only a complete waste of time, but it's also keeping you from doing what really matters—what will enable you to someday become a successful entrepreneur and business leader.

In the business world we call that *opportunity cost:* In this case, it means spending time on activities that will not benefit you, which prevents you from being exposed to new opportunities—opportunities that pass you by while you're otherwise engaged in nonsense.

You only have one life. If you spend it chasing the wrong things, you'll never get anywhere.

Take personal branding, for example. The first time I heard the term was when the executive editor at CBS Interactive tried to sell me on doing video and radio spots in addition to my blog, which was already taking up way too much time. Skeptical, I asked him, "Are you guys going to pay me for that?"

He shook his head, smiled patronizingly, and replied, "Just think of it as building your personal brand," he said, "the brand that is you, Steve Tobak." Thinking back on it, nothing that guy ever said to me made any sense. Not a word turned out to be true. And he didn't last long in that job, which didn't surprise me one bit.

In any case, let's try a thought experiment. Let's say I just dropped out of the sky with no experience whatsoever. Who would hire me to advise them on their business strategy? What media company would pay me to write commentary and, even if they did, who would read it?

Nobody, nobody, and nobody, that's who. I have no useful expertise, knowledge, or advice to offer them. From the customer's perspective—which is, incidentally, the only one that matters—I have no value proposition.

But wait. By today's logic, I could create a nifty personal brand—an online persona that positions me as a business writer and consultant. I could create a professional-looking website, write a blog, optimize the site so I come up high in Google searches, and promote myself all over social media.

But it would be pure BS. And any customer with half a brain would realize before long that I had absolutely nothing valuable to offer. Instead, she would go out and hire one of the thousands of consultants who actually know what they're doing. Likewise, media companies have lots of commentators they can hire, and readers have lots of content to choose from.

Not only that, anyone who did make the mistake of hiring me or reading my blog would soon know I was an incompetent charlatan with no expertise. In time, my reputation in the real world wouldn't be worth squat. And that would be that.

Now let's get back to the real world. The real me has decades of experience in technology, business, marketing, and executive management. That's why people read what I write and hire me as a management consultant. And I deliver the goods. As a result, I have a great reputation and a strong brand. But that brand reputation is not a cause; it's an effect. And the only thing I did to get it was to do great work.

I didn't create that brand; I earned it by providing unique capabilities to clients and genuine insights to readers based on real knowledge and experience. I wasn't successful because I built a brand. I have a brand because I was good at what I did. And the minute I stop offering clients great advice and readers insightful commentary, they'll be gone, along with my reputation.

A brand is a result. Sure, a company can create and market a brand identity. We call that a brand promise or platform. But if that company's products and services don't deliver on that promise in real life, its brand will be worthless and the company will ultimately fail.

A brand is an aggregate of all the interactions customers have with you, your company, your products, and your services. On that list, you are by far the least important. Your products and services matter more by orders of magnitude.

Contrary to popular belief, you are not a product. And your online persona is not a real brand or a value proposition that means anything to real customers. That's not how business works.

People hire you for what you can do for them and pay you for a product or service that benefits them or their business. It's not you they're paying for. Not really. And no matter how you portray yourself online, if you fail to deliver in the real world, your reputation and your brand will be worthless.

If you have talent or experience, that's one thing. But if you portray yourself to be a great actor, you'd better be able to demonstrate some acting ability at auditions or you won't get hired. If John Grisham hadn't had a long career as an attorney before he ever put pen to paper, he would not have become a great writer of legal thrillers. That's his brand now, but it came after the fact.

Whenever I explain how this works, someone inevitably brings up Mark Cuban or Donald Trump and says something like, "They promote themselves, and look how rich and famous they are." When I point out that they only started promoting themselves *after* achieving remarkable business success, not before, you can almost see the truth slowly dawning on them in their eyes.

Of course customer relationships matter. So does your reputation. They matter a lot. But it's been that way since the beginning of time— or at least since the snake sold Eve on the whole "take a bite of the apple from the tree of knowledge" thing. Look how that turned out. You know the snake's reputation wasn't worth dirt in the Garden of Eden after that.

Likewise, potential customers and employers will feel exactly the same way about you if you fail to deliver the goods. And there's no amount of blogging, tweeting, or posting that will change that. You can dress up your online persona all you like, but you'll just be putting lipstick on a snake.

Growing up in New York, I had a friend with a plaque on his wall that read, "If you can't dazzle them with brilliance, baffle them with bullshit." You know the guy never amounted to much. If that's how you want to make a living, be my guest. There's no shortage of snakes and snake oil salespeople out there, that's for sure. But I have a better idea. Build your brand the right way.

The Sonoma Wine Country School of Branding

A few weeks ago I visited Unti Vineyards, a boutique family-owned winery in Sonoma Valley I hadn't been to in years. It was great to see how much they'd grown. And while I'd previously gotten to know cofounders George Unti and his wife, Linda, this would be the first time I got to meet their son, Mick, who actually runs the place.

We got to talking about business philosophy, and Mick said how lucky he was to have a like-minded partner in his dad. For one thing, they agreed to focus on Italian and French Rhone varietals that were not well-known to American consumers, even though that was risky. And they were also in agreement about producing only wines with qualities they loved and could do justice to.

For example, Mick said he's often asked why they don't make Nebbiolo, a popular Italian varietal that's also known as Barolo and Barbaresco, depending on the region it's from. His answer was simple. "It's a notoriously finicky grape that's hard to grow and it would not do well here," he said. "I'm not going to put the Unti name on wine I'm not proud of."

That, in a nutshell, is why Unti has done so well. They found a niche they loved that set them apart from competitors. They built their brand and reputation on just that, a great product. No more, no less.

So how did these folks get to be so business savvy? They didn't just wake up one day and say, "Let's be wine entrepreneurs." George's parents were farmers, and he had a nearly 40-year career as an executive with Safeway. Mick spent many years in the wine business before cofounding the winery with his dad. And although Linda's not really that involved in the business, she's a former top communications executive with Visa and National Semiconductor.

These people had serious business chops before they embarked on this path. First they had successful careers. They gained valuable experience. They learned how to manage and how business works. And they learned about themselves. Then they started their own business and eventually made great products that customers love. Now they have a successful business . . . and brand. That's how it usually works.

BAD-TASTING MEDICINE

Without the advent of Web 2.0, personal blogs, and social networks, the personal branding fad could never have taken off. It would have amounted to little more than a narcissistic hobby, a self-indulgent trivial pursuit.

To say it's gotten a little out of hand has to be the mother of all understatements. It goes way beyond Generation Me. User-generated content is a phenomenon that crosses all demographics and borders.

Facebook has more than 1.3 billion monthly active users. There are more than 500 million tweets posted daily on Twitter. More than a billion users visit YouTube to watch hundreds of millions of hours of video every day. WordPress says more than 400 million people view more than 18 billion blog pages every month. And more than 120 million new blog posts and comments are added monthly.

Those are staggering numbers, but who posts all that stuff? Who are these people? Countless millions post online to promote themselves, build their brands, and grow their networks daily. They believe that activity is somehow beneficial to their business and their career. For many, it *is* their business and their career.

But do they really believe that, or is it just an excuse to feed their egos and online addiction? And for those who really believe it's beneficial, is it? For those who've made it their business, is it a viable business? Is it a real career that can make you happy and pay the bills? I know you think it is. I know the social media hordes say it is. But is it *really*?

Before we go any further, this might be a good time to remember why you swallowed the red pill. The whole "Be brave, be brutally honest, face reality, and embrace the truth no matter how painful it may be because the truth will set you free" thing from way back in Chapter 4?

Well, this may be another case of bad-tasting medicine, but it'll make you feel a lot better later. So here goes.

Posting online is like going to the beach in Los Angeles and pouring a bucket of ice into the ocean. At first, you can see some ripples in the water. If you stick your hand in, it might even feel a little cooler. But give it a few seconds, and it's as if nothing ever happened. Sure, there were some short-term localized effects. But did it really make a difference? Nope.

Social media is the same way. You probably have a relatively small circle of friends or followers who aren't busy, disciplined, or, let's face it, evolved enough to overrule the addictive tug of their limbic systems and cultural conformity. They have little business impact, and, as a result, their attention isn't worth much. As for those you want to reach, those you seek to influence—potential customers and hiring managers—there's simply too much noise for them to hear you. Besides, they're too busy working and making money in the real world.

As communication goes, social media is terribly inefficient. Think about it. When you talk to folks one-on-one, you have a chance of engaging them. It's not a slam dunk, mind you. People have lots of things on their minds, and what you say may be of little interest or low on their priority list. But at least you might make a real connection.

When you shout something in a packed arena at a football game— that's another story. Those nearby may hear what you say—sort of like those ripples from the ice cubes—but the chances of anyone who matters hearing you, like the coach or a player, are slim to none. And even if they do hear you, chances are they couldn't care less.

I wish I could say that posting online is about as efficient as shouting in a crowded football stadium, but it's actually much worse than that. We passed the point of communication overload years ago. We are all constantly bombarded with tweets, status updates, posts, emails, videos, comments, and messages. Very little of it appeals to us, even if it does somehow manage to get above all the noise. And the odds of it making a real connection that might materially impact your business is about the same as someone in Tokyo noticing the ripples from your California ice cubes.

That also explains why it's nearly impossible to be successful as a social media or content marketer. All you're really doing is helping users and businesses deliver buckets of ice cubes to the ocean.

Let me give you a real world example. I've been writing commentary—some pretty engaging and insightful content, or so I hear—for some of the most highly visible websites on earth since 2007. I've written more than a thousand articles, all of which were posted on the usual social media sites and provided a link back to my consulting firm's website. Millions of unique viewers have read them. After all that, the impact on my consulting business has been minimal. The vast majority of my clients are by word-of-mouth or Google searches that hit my website—where I don't blog, by the way.

So why do it? Simple. I've already had a long and successful career. Now I want to give back by sharing what I've learned, as a legacy of sorts. And I love to write; the truth is, I like it way more than consulting. But if I were just starting out, this is not what I'd be doing. I'd be doing the same thing I did thirty-something years ago: working my way up the corporate ladder in the high-tech industry, gaining experience, earning my chops, and getting exposure to real opportunities in the business world.

Don't get me wrong: Social media has a purpose, especially for certain professionals. If you're a celebrity or a member of the media, Twitter and Facebook *are* important. If you're a recruiter, so is LinkedIn. And all of us have to have a profile there. LinkedIn is your resume, more or less. But for the vast majority, spending a lot of time blogging, tweeting, and posting on those sites won't count for much. Sure, you'll get hits, but converting them into real opportunities or business is another matter entirely.

I occasionally use social networks to make a connection or two, but I've rarely found it useful in terms of actual results. Networking is important—building relationships with people in the real world, that is. Until you connect with people in person, they're unlikely to lift a finger to help you. The value of social networking is way, way overblown. To me it's a lot like chasing people who don't want to have anything to do with you. And if they do, *you* don't want to have anything to do with *them*. It reminds me of the J. Geils song "Love Stinks": "You love her but she loves him/And he loves somebody else, you just can't win."

I know some say that stuff is important for your career, so let me tell you what hiring managers are really looking for in up-and-comers. They're looking for a good fit. They're looking for go-getters they can count on to do the job well with little supervision. They're looking for people whose knowledge, experience, and personal qualities demonstrate that. And sooner or later, they'll figure out if you really are who you represent yourself to be.

Now let me back all that up with some data, a few examples, and by posing a simple question: If social media is such a powerful business tool, why don't the most successful companies and their CEOs use it?

The vast majority of Fortune 500 chief executives have absolutely no social media presence whatsoever, according to a joint CEO. com and Domo study from 2013. About a quarter have LinkedIn accounts—which makes sense, since it's actually a business network— while about 7 percent are on Facebook and 5 percent use Twitter. And few actually use those networks actively, which prompts the question: In an increasingly connected world, why are top executives so disconnected?

For one thing, the business case isn't credible. That's right, I said it. I committed social media heresy. Feel free to blast me on Twitter, for all it matters. But everything I've read that says otherwise is entirely anecdotal and inconclusive. Contrary to popular groupthink in the social media collective, followers and page views don't translate to return on investment. They simply don't. That leap of faith might be good enough for the self-interested companies that do the surveys and the social media marketers who post and tweet all sorts of nonsense on the subject, but it isn't good enough for the executives who make critical business decisions on a daily basis, and it shouldn't be good enough for you.

In the meantime, executives have better things to do, like running their companies, making great products, beating the competition, and winning customers—who, incidentally, also have better things to do.

Nevertheless, even hardened and disciplined corporate bigwigs will eventually succumb to the hordes of PR, HR, and IR professionals who insist the world will end if they don't share their wisdom on LinkedIn or engage customers and employees on Twitter.

But before they actually start banging on the keyboard, this is what seasoned veterans do. Immediately after asking their communications pros, "What's the benefit?", they inevitably ask a follow-up question: "What's the downside?"

More powerful people have shot themselves in the foot by shooting off their mouths and saying what they shouldn't than any other method of self-destruction. Contrary to popular doctrine, more communication is not necessarily better communication. It just increases the chances of doing more harm than good.

For one thing, it's getting trickier every day to walk that ultrafine line between political correctness and putting just the wrong emphasis on the wrong word and offending some activist, who then decides to use your following against you in a social media campaign to boycott your products and get all your advertisers to jump ship.

With the whole web watching and no way to take it back once Google indexes every tweet or post, C-level executives—especially of public companies—know they'd better be sure that every word is reviewed, edited, scrubbed clean, and approved by their entire staff.

In which case, we're right back to where we started before this whole social media thing began: It's just another PR channel. And where's the fun in that? Where's the openness? Where's the engagement? More important, what's the point?

Nevertheless, some executives insist on venturing into the uncharted online world without their PR handlers' help. They learn the hard way that such self-indulgence can do far more harm than good to your reputation, your career, and your company. There are serious hazards to being too social in the age of social media.

I could rattle off dozens of stories, but here are just a few off the top of my head:

▸ After pleading guilty to one misdemeanor count each of battery and domestic violence against his girlfriend in 2014, RadiumOne's famously flamboyant CEO, Gurbaksh Chahal, just couldn't let it go. Instead of admitting he screwed up, apologizing, and letting things settle down, the egotistical executive took to social media with long rants and tirades that painted himself as the victim and lashed out at everyone, including his girlfriend, police, prosecutors, the media, and his board of directors. For that, he was fired from the company he founded.

▸ Former PayPal president David Marcus sent a scathing company-wide email slamming some employees for not using the mobile payment app he helped develop, for forgetting their passwords, and, of all things, for *not* hacking into Coke machines that don't accept PayPal, as some of the company's more impassioned employees apparently did. The caustic diatribe got a lot of social media attention, and a few months later Marcus was gone amidst rumors that he had been fired. While parent company eBay denied the rumors, Marcus ended up as Facebook's VP of messaging, clearly a step down.

▸ Not to pick on PayPal, but two months after joining the company as director of strategy, Rakesh Agrawal unleashed a bizarre and mostly incoherent tirade on Twitter that began at 1 a.m. and went on into the wee hours of the morning. He called the company's vice president of global communications a "useless middle manager" and "a piece of shit." Hours later, the company tweeted that Rakesh "is no longer with the company."

▸ Former Hewlett-Packard vice president of engineering Scott McClellan foolishly shared previously unreleased details of the company's cloud computing strategy on his public LinkedIn profile, tipping off competitors to confidential information that should have remained under wraps. I don't know if that cost him his job, but after spending his entire 26-year career at HP,

McClellan took a demotion to work for Red Hat, a much smaller company.

▸ And who can forget Justine Sacco, the PR executive who posted this on Twitter before boarding a flight to South Africa: "Going to Africa. Hope I don't get AIDS. Just kidding. I'm white!" The tweet went viral and, by the time her flight landed, half the world thought Sacco was a raging racist. She was fired a couple of days later. Why'd she do it? Outrageous tweets got her attention. That one sure did. For the rest of her life, that's probably all you'll see if you Google her name.

Besides the risk, there's another very good reason why top executives don't waste their time on social media. They have no time to waste. They have no time for anything except what really matters. That's why busy executives have so painstakingly managed every moment of their precious day since the beginning of time.

There may be a 4-hour workweek for the social media entrepreneurs who call themselves CEOs while blogging in their pajamas, but for the real deal, if it's a choice between adding to an 80-hour workweek or spending a few hours with their family, that's a no-brainer—if they want to keep their family happy, that is.

For the record, I'm not saying companies should not invest in social media as part of their overall communications and customer support strategy. Of course they should. I'm also not saying companies don't benefit from making certain executives available to the media and promoting them as thought leaders. To that extent, social media is simply another PR or sales support channel.

But it's not some sort of business utopia for you to build a career or a business around. Even if you're the second coming of Mark Zuckerberg or Larry Page and come up with the world's next great app or search engine, you should be spending your time on product development, not posting, tweeting, and networking online.

If personal branding, social networking, content generation, and all that goes with it is a big part of your life, if you think you can build some sort of entrepreneurial career on top of that foundation, the sooner you realize you're building a house of cards, the better. It's holding you back from making something of yourself.

Don't be in a hurry to call yourself an entrepreneur or a CEO until you have a real business or startup developing a real product. After all, your reputation isn't built on a title, a Twitter handle, a LinkedIn profile, or a bunch of blog posts. It's built on actions, not words. It's built on experience, capability, accountability, and credibility. It's built on business savvy and smart decision making. It's built on developing and selling great products customers love.

It's time to put on your adult clothes and get out in the real world where the customers, careers, and opportunities are. That's where you'll find your true passion: what you love to do, and what you can do better than anyone else. That's where you'll make a real name for yourself. That's where you'll build your real reputation.

CHAPTER 7

ALL THAT GLITTERS IS NOT GOLD

NEARLY ALL THE HIGHLY SUCCESSFUL ENTREPRENEURS I've known have one thing in common: They're driven by a compelling need to prove themselves. That's no coincidence. Not only is that compulsion often self-fulfilling, but it also provides critical insight into the makeup of some of the world's greatest business leaders and what it takes to become one.

It must have been about 20 years ago that, after speaking at a small conference in Pebble Beach, California, I stuck around to catch the keynote by a little-known entrepreneur from Japan named Masayoshi Son. The speaker choice surprised me. After all, Japan was known for industrial conglomerates, not high-tech startups.

As it turned out, Son's software distribution company, SoftBank, had been on a buying spree, acquiring the Ziff-Davis Publishing Company and 17 computer trade shows, including the industry's biggest, Comdex, which I had just attended in Las Vegas. SoftBank had also gained a controlling stake in internet portal Yahoo! Clearly this guy was on a roll, and I was curious to hear what he had to say.

I was not disappointed. Having done a great deal of business in Japan over the years, I had a pretty good handle on the culture and had built plenty of relationships. But I'd never met anyone like Son. Although his company was hardly known outside the island nation, his plan was for SoftBank to become a global player in the computer industry and the world's leading provider of "digital information infrastructure."

I was astounded by his aggressiveness, his competitiveness, and the grandiosity of his vision. We met briefly afterward. He was a short guy, even compared to me, but that just made him seem all the more impressive, like a high-tech Napoleon (in a good way). I walked away thinking the guy was a force to be reckoned with.

Sure enough, what Son has since accomplished with the company he founded goes light-years beyond even his own lofty aspirations.

Today, SoftBank is a global telecommunications and internet powerhouse with annual revenues of about $60 billion. And Son is the richest man in Japan, with a personal net worth of more than $16 billion. In addition to Yahoo!, Son was an early investor in E-Trade and China's Alibaba Group. And in 2013 he acquired 70 percent of Sprint Nextel for $20 billion.

Knowing what a competitive risk taker Son turned out to be, you would never guess that he grew up in poverty. After his family emigrated from Korea, the young Masa—as his friends call him— lived in an illegal shack on the Japanese island of Kyushu. His parents adopted a Japanese surname to hide their Korean heritage and avoid discrimination in the more or less ethnically homogenous country.

As a teenager, Son was obsessed with overcoming his humble beginnings and becoming a successful businessman. He developed plans to start his own business, becoming fixated on Den Fujita, an entrepreneur who brought the first McDonald's franchise to Japan and grew McDonald's Japan into a 3,800-restaurant chain, according to a 1999 profile in *Forbes*.

After more or less stalking his idol over a period of months, Son landed a meeting with Fujita, who encouraged him to go to America—which Son did. He moved to Berkeley, got a degree in economics, and became enthralled with the technology industry. At 24, he returned to Japan to start SoftBank, and the rest is history. But it's doubtful Son would have turned out to be such a wildly successful maverick if he hadn't grown up with little more than a chip on his shoulder and a compelling need to prove himself.

The backgrounds of great business leaders are full of stories just like that one. It's no coincidence that so many started with so little.

Jack Ma, chairman and founder of ecommerce giant Alibaba, grew up poor in communist China. As a youth he biked to a nearby hotel and guided foreigners around the city just to learn and practice the English language. That worked for him: Ma was actually an English teacher before becoming fascinated with the internet.

During the dotcom boom of 1999, Ma persuaded a group of friends to pool $60,000 to found what is now one of the world's most powerful companies. In 2014 Alibaba had the biggest IPO in history, fetching $25 billion at a valuation exceeding $200 billion. And like his friend Masa in Japan, Ma is now the richest man in China.

It always makes me laugh to hear people talk about "big telecom," as if companies like Verizon and AT&T started life as corporate behemoths and their CEOs just dropped out of the sky into cushy corner office chairs. Nothing could be farther from the truth.

Former Verizon chief executive Ivan Seidenberg hails from a working-class family in the Bronx. He fought in Vietnam and began his career as a cable splicer right out of high school. Seidenberg then earned two degrees at night while working his way up the corporate ladder, eventually turning a regional Baby Bell into the nation's most valuable telecom company and one of the world's most powerful brands.

Growing up under adverse conditions and learning to survive and adapt by relying on their own instincts and street smarts are remarkably common themes among those who beat the odds and made it big in the business world. The battle may begin in a competitive inner-city environment or a tough home life, but it certainly doesn't end there.

As a product of the streets of New York, I should know. It was definitely a tough place to grow up. We were packed into thousands of tiny apartments like rats in a cage. No wonder we always hung out on the street (or shopping centers, basketball courts, playgrounds)—we went wherever there was space.

So many of the kids I grew up with were characters, and we competed for everything from girls and friends to laughs and attention. We fought to stand out and to fit in. We competed for positions on sports teams and academic honors. After graduating from the streets of New York City, everything in life seemed so much easier.

Don't get me wrong; I had some edgy tendencies that needed rounding out. I tend to see life as a zero-sum game, so I'm always on, always looking out for threats and advantages. And you may have noticed by now that I'm a little more sardonic and irreverent than the average person. But nothing has played a bigger role in what I've achieved throughout my career than the stress and adversity I faced growing up.

That's where my zest for knowledge and experience comes from. My fascination with people and what motivates them to behave the way they do. My relentless drive to accomplish great things and pursue a fulfilling life. The childlike belief that dreams can come true and that somewhere in me is the power to make that happen.

It's no coincidence that, of 23 secondary schools that have produced two or more Nobel laureates, nine are in the Big Apple. My high school alone accounts for three, not to mention dozens of famous business leaders, scientists, athletes, musicians, authors, and actors.

Goldman Sachs chief executive Lloyd Blankfein grew up not far from where I did. And his dad was a postal worker, just as mine was. Starbucks founder and CEO Howard Schultz lived in public housing in the Canarsie section of Brooklyn. He was the first person in his family to go to college.

Indeed, the culture we grew up in played a big role in how we turned out. My parents didn't have much, but they worked hard to put food on the table and a roof over our heads without ever taking a handout. They pushed my brother and me hard in school because they wanted us to have a better life than they did. And they instilled in us a powerful work ethic.

Although we grew up in a dangerous neighborhood, we were allowed to venture out on our own and play. We were encouraged to take risks and reach for the stars. That's how we learned valuable lessons that taught us self-reliance, helped us gain self-confidence, and shaped our character.

We didn't have much, but it didn't take long for us to learn that, if we wanted more out of life, we had to make it happen on our own. That's why none of us have a sense of entitlement—that we're inherently owed something we didn't work for and don't deserve. That concept simply doesn't exist in a competitive world where nothing comes easy and everything has to be earned.

Adversity. Friction. Stress. Competition. Those four factors are entirely responsible for natural selection and evolution. They're how all species survive and thrive.

Those same factors gave rise to the United States of America. They're responsible for spawning freedom, liberty, and democracy. And they didn't just give rise to free market capitalism. They govern how competitive markets work.

The corporate cultures of highly successful technology companies such as Apple, Oracle, and Intel are known to be demanding, stressful, competitive places. That's precisely why employees thrive there.

It's no secret that Steve Jobs and Oracle founder Larry Ellison were both adopted by working-class families. Intel patriarch Andy Grove grew up under Nazi occupation and later escaped communist-controlled Hungary to emigrate to America. All three executives were famously tough on employees.

Those same four factors are responsible for the strength and success of everyone and everything from entrepreneurs and companies to nations and entire species. If that's true, and it most certainly is, then how do we reconcile that with the popular dogma of today's culture?

We keep hearing about the evils of stress, meritocracy, and competitive corporate culture. Everyone's supposed to get the same treatment these days. Everyone's supposed to be equal. Everyone's supposed to be a winner. It's a happy-go-lucky, win-win world.

Everyone wants to be positive, happy, and inspired all the time. Everyone is only supposed to focus on their strengths, never their weaknesses. Our leaders are all supposed to be enlightened, emotionally intelligent, engaging, optimistic, and above all, politically correct. And everyone should be included, except of course those who don't conform to that remarkably utopian notion of life on earth.

If adversity, friction, stress, and competition are actually good, then how *do* we explain all those popular memes? We don't because they're simply not true. They have no basis in science, in management, in business, or in reality, for that matter.

They're just a collection of myths and fads spawned by self-serving shysters and pseudo-academics out to make a buck. And they're perpetuated by a conforming online social collective, as we've discussed at length.

While they may seem harmless, those popular memes that now pass for common wisdom are anything but. And they're having a profound influence on far too many of us—and not in a good way.

The problem is that cultural conformity, as we know all too well, is highly contagious. Nobody's immune to the popular crazes perpetuated by the social media crowd, not even those in leadership positions.

THINK HAPPY THOUGHTS

If you buy into all the popular hype, emotional intelligence improves just about everything from leadership performance and business results to work stress and personal happiness. But much of that is a load of pseudoscientific nonsense that's been largely disproven.

As the University of Pennsylvania's Wharton School of Business professor Adam Grant explains at length in a 2014 article in *The Atlantic*, comprehensive published studies have shown no significant correlation between emotional intelligence and performance for the vast majority of job functions. The sole metric—emotional quotient (EQ)—is based on self-reporting and self-testing that's neither objective nor scientific. It's fatally flawed and in no way predictive of leadership performance or business success.

Besides, there is no one-size-fits-all model or set of characteristics for executives and business leaders. Even if reading a book, taking a test, going to a seminar, or getting some coaching made you more self-aware, it wouldn't necessarily lead to behavioral change. That can take years of hard work and reinforcement. To suggest otherwise is utopian nonsense.

In reality, a leader's ability to manipulate and control his own emotions and the emotions of others has a significant dark side that's associated with narcissistic or psychopathic behavior. Suffice to say there's a lot more to this concept than meets the eye, and it's certainly not the panacea it's been made out to be. And yet emotional intelligence has somehow become the latest leadership fad du jour. How did that happen?

Well, this is America, where popular spells opportunity and opportunity spells money. Thousands of self-interested opportunists have taken advantage of the hype surrounding emotional intelligence, positive psychology, and other fads to enrich themselves by pushing books, seminars, and other garbage.

I recently came across a couple of psychologists-turned-consultants who had written a book and a bunch of popular articles spewing enough feel-good nonsense on emotional intelligence to make Sigmund Freud jump out of his grave and beg for Prozac. Their Ph.D.s came from the California School of Professional Psychology. Never heard of it? Join the club.

According to *U.S. News*, as of 2013, none of its campuses ranked among the 200-plus psychology graduate schools in North America, and their mean exam (EPPP) scores also rank among the lowest in the nation. And yet the school is fully accredited and turns out more psychologists than all the graduate schools in California combined. Half the state's practicing psychologists got their degrees there.

Today the nation is flooded with executive coaches, life coaches, speakers, and consultants with bestselling books, blogs, seminars, training programs, and certificates from schools like that. This brings us to the latest popular and surprisingly destructive craze: happiness coaches. Sorry to be a buzz kill, but you can't coach happiness. Reality works through cause and effect. Actions lead to consequences. And happiness is not an action; it's a consequence. It's not a cause; it's an effect.

Look at it this way. Each of us is a complex creature with unique characteristics and a lifetime of experience that influences our behavior and decisions. How we feel at any given moment—happy, sad, surprised, afraid—is a consequence of that. It's the result of a lifetime of factors. You can't directly manipulate them, and you shouldn't even if you could. It's important to pay attention to what your emotions are telling you.

Your feelings provide important information about what's going on inside and around you. They're like signposts on your journey through life. Sadness and fear are not bad emotions, any more than happiness and joy are good ones. They all provide critical information. And although they're sometimes beneath the surface, they matter just as much as conscious thought, if not more.

Listening to your feelings is called self-awareness. Obviously, there are times when you need to control your emotions, but constantly manipulating them or pretending they're different than they really are is not a good idea.

Look, everyone has problems. Everyone confronts personal challenges and professional hurdles. Everyone faces pain and tragedy. But sweeping real issues under a rug of disingenuous positive thinking keeps you from accurately assessing situations, making smart decisions, and taking effective actions. It stops you from facing your problems and dealing with them. Simply put, it's delusional.

I can say pretty much the same thing about our culture's obsession with motivational speakers and inspirational stories and quotations. Inspiration doesn't come from outside you. It comes from inside. It comes from your emotions, your passion. That's what drives you. That's what inspires you.

If your work doesn't inspire you, if you constantly have to be pumped up by what others say and write, that probably means you haven't yet found a career that resonates with you. Keep looking. You'll find it someday. But don't sweep those dissatisfied feelings under a rug of happy thoughts.

If you want to make the best of your life, here's how you do it: Be aware of what's going on inside and around you. Face that reality and deal with it as openly and honestly as you can. Make decisions. Take action. Rinse and repeat. If you do that, you have a better chance of waking up happy tomorrow.

Adversity. Friction. Stress. Competition. It's tough stuff, no doubt. But it's part of all our lives. Nobody has it easy. And if they do, they're not likely to become highly successful entrepreneurs and business leaders like Masayoshi Son, Jack Ma, and Ivan Seidenberg.

Look, we're all flesh and blood humans. We all laugh and cry. There is no happiness without sadness. No pleasure without pain. No victory without defeat. No success without failure. No life without death. There is a yin and yang, a natural balance to all living things.

Think about it. Without problems there would be no innovative solutions. Together, they build confidence and character. They create strong, self-reliant individuals with the courage to take big risks, tackle tough challenges, and accomplish great things. They produce real entrepreneurs.

All that glitters is not gold, and all that is gold does not glitter.

CHAPTER 8

MAKING
YOUR
OWN LUCK

LOOKING BACK ON IT, EVERY PIVOTAL EVENT IN MY LIFE happened seemingly at random. These events were never planned or well thought out. And had I not been present and willing to trust my gut and go for it, none of those events would have happened. In hindsight, we tend to view positive life-changing experiences as if we just happened to be in the right place at the right time, but that's not how it works in real time.

First, you're making a conscious decision to put yourself out there. Second, you're taking a risk because you have no idea if what you're doing is a good idea until long after the fact. So you have to make the right call without knowing how it will turn out.

For example, when I was at OPTi, I saw an opportunity to advance my career by building strong relationships with the microprocessor companies we partnered with. Instead of waiting around for something to happen, I created an opportunity and ultimately landed my first vice president job at Cyrix.

That's called *making your own luck*. Think of it as equal parts luck, risk taking, and decision making. Successful entrepreneurs and executives make their own luck. And they do it by embracing the chaos of the real world.

The natural world always tends toward increasing randomness. That's just basic physics—the second law of thermodynamics, to be exact. Meanwhile, biological organisms attempt to fight the chaos of the physical world by organizing themselves into cells and more complex organisms. The creation of organizations is actually the same process at work.

So you can think of organisms and organizations as being anti-chaotic. And that, by definition, means they favor the status quo. Meanwhile, to create positive change and move things forward, you need a little disruption. And therein lies the rub.

As we've already discussed, it takes genetic mutations to advance a species and breakthrough innovation to advance a company or an industry. Likewise, if you want to make your own luck, you have to be open to where life might take you, trust your instincts, and go for it. In short, you have to embrace the chaos of the real world.

While many everyday things are within your control, *inflection points*, or the big make-or-break events that change your life, are not, at least not completely. They usually involve letting go, giving up the illusion of control, and accepting the chaos. Anyone involved with startups and how products go viral will tell you that.

It's easy to look back at innovations like TiVo, Uber, and FedEx and think of their breakout success as foregone conclusions, but that's simply not the case. While their creators certainly had vision, they had no idea their products would change the way so many people live and work. And yet they had the guts to throw themselves into their ideas with abandon.

One of the biggest problems I see in the entrepreneurial community is that people are trying to be too controlling. They're distracting themselves with minutiae, losing sight of the big picture, and potentially missing out on what's important—namely, those inflection points.

Consider our culture's crazy obsession with personal development. Spending your time in a relentless pursuit of self-improvement is the best way I know of to miss out on all life's big make-or-break moments.

If Richard Branson had been concerned with personal development, there would be no Virgin Group. Does a guy who starts out selling records and then rolls the dice—getting into everything from airlines and aerospace to mobile phones and soft drinks—seem like he's trying to better himself? Don't be ridiculous. Branson doesn't play small ball; he swings for the fences.

Besides, those focused on improving themselves don't work 100-hour weeks developing SpaceX rockets and Tesla electric cars like Elon Musk, who's actually chief executive of both companies. They don't disrupt the global taxi industry, as Uber founding CEO Travis Kalanick did. And they don't come up with crazy notions like same-day delivery—and actually make it happen—as Fred Smith did when he founded FedEx.

Honestly, folks, wasting your time looking for ways to improve yourself will only accomplish one thing: keeping you occupied with silly details while real opportunities pass you by. That's not the way to find your passion in life, come up with breakthrough ideas, or experience life-changing events. It's certainly not the way to become a successful entrepreneur.

I'm not saying it's all about luck or that any of this is easy. You still have to connect the dots and make smart choices or all the opportunities in the world won't amount to beans. And there absolutely are things you can do to improve your odds of being in the right place at the right time.

Spend your time on things that matter—focus on the big picture and the long run instead of giving in to instant gratification. Step outside your comfort zone and face your darkest fears. Put your butt on the line and take big risks instead of following the path of least resistance and falling into a safety net.

Most of all, have the courage to carve your own path instead of giving in to the status quo or popular groupthink. That's how real entrepreneurs make their own luck.

OPPORTUNITY MEETS DESPERATION

Very few people lead charmed lives. Careers, even great ones, almost never shoot straight up and to the right. As we've observed before, they behave a lot like roller coasters. And if you take a snapshot at any point in time, the ride may very well look as if it's going to crash.

That does happen. I'm not talking about hurdles or obstacles—I'm talking about colossal flops. Crushing defeat. Devastating loss. It happens, and a lot more often than any of us would like.

Show me a great entrepreneur, and I'll show you someone who has experienced disaster. It comes with the territory. That's because successful people don't do things halfway. They're not timid. They go all in, take huge risks, and fight like hell to win. And sometimes they lose big.

I've lost ridiculously high-paying jobs and small fortunes in the stock market. I've lost a battle to turn around a high-tech startup and was forced to lay off dozens of people. If there's something really good, you name it; I've lost it.

To say those experiences were unpleasant would be a ridiculous understatement. They were gut-wrenching. And the public failures were humiliating. They tested my strength, my will, and my self-confidence. And yet I still managed to get up, brush myself off, and bounce back stronger than before.

The funny thing is, great opportunities always seem to pop up when things can't get any worse. Successful people are known for always managing to snatch victory from the jaws of defeat. That's because for them—as for me—luck is not when opportunity meets preparation but when opportunity meets desperation.

Think about it. How open are you to taking big risks when you're on top of the world? How willing are you to pull the plug when things are going gangbusters? How receptive are you to doing something scary when you have everything to lose? That's right, not very.

On the other hand, if you feel your very survival is at stake, that's when you're most open to new ideas. When defeat is staring you right in the face, that's when you're most receptive to change. When you feel hopeless, that's when you get into the "I'll try anything, I've got nothing to lose" mindset.

That's why addicts usually have to bottom out before they can recover. Because that's what it takes for them to give up control, let go, and give in to the chaos. That's when they become brave. That's when they're willing to try anything, even quitting.

That's also why necessity is the mother of invention. It's why when the going gets tough, the tough get going. And it's why many if not most of our greatest companies rose from the ashes of financial distress or macroeconomic crises, as occurred during the fallout of the dotcom bust.

I once read that two-thirds of the Dow Industrial Average was formed during recession or in the Great Depression. I've no doubt that's true.

Life offers two distinct paths for each of us. The first is the path of least resistance: Get a job, show up, collect your paycheck, rinse and repeat. The second path is the risky one: Take chances, face enormous challenges, suffer terrible defeat, rise up even stronger than before, and someday, make it big.

If you choose the latter path, I can say one thing for sure: There will be desperate times. But contrary to what you might think, those are precious times. When you're desperate, when you feel you have nothing to lose, when you're most open to opportunity and change, that's when great ventures are born. That's when disruptive innovation is most likely to occur. That's when unique individuals who think different can rise out of chaos to change the world.

CHAPTER 9

THE REAL SECRET TO PERSONAL PRODUCTIVITY

IT'S NO SECRET THAT ARTICLES AND BOOKS WITH TITLES LIKE *How to Be a Better Procrastinator* and *What the Most Successful People Do Before Breakfast* annoy the hell out of me. Actually, it's not their content or authors I have a problem with, but our culture's apparently enormous and insatiable demand for solutions to nonexistent problems.

I don't know how it became everyone's goal in life to squeeze every second of every minute of every day and become some sort of productivity ninja robot, but I really can't think of anything more inhuman and, ironically, more unproductive.

Not only am I not a morning person, I'm pretty sure I've never had an intelligent thought before noon. I'm hopelessly disorganized. I don't make lists or have daily plans. I've never had a file system that works. My inbox hasn't been cleaned up in a decade. And my office looks like it was hit by a tornado. A boss once told me that walking into my office made him physically ill. True story.

I'm also a terrible procrastinator. I honestly can't remember ever doing something today I could get away with putting off until tomorrow. And I'm incredibly lazy when it comes to doing things I really don't want to do. I guess the hope is I'll die before I ever have to get to them.

If all that makes me unproductive, so be it. But by any measure, that hasn't stopped me from being relatively happy and surprisingly successful. So how do you reconcile that with the popular dogma about personal productivity and time management?

You might think I'm successful in spite of my unproductive ways, but there is a distinct possibility that I've been successful because of them. The truth is, I find it all pointless. Why worry about being productive when life offers so much opportunity, so much to experience, and so much to do?

I would argue that, if you want to accomplish great things, you should focus on doing just that. Quit wasting your time in search of nonexistent quick fixes. Figure out what you want to do and just do it.

I know everyone always complains about there not being enough time in a day. They have too many things going on, too many irons in the fire, or too many commitments. They're too busy or spread too thin.

One word: bullshit.

You don't have too much to do. Productivity and time management are not your problem. You just have to be disciplined about setting priorities, focusing on what's important, and letting go of what isn't.

DO ONLY WHAT MATTERS

Let me explain how this works. When there's something you really want to achieve, you find a way. Example: this book.

When I signed the deal to write this fine piece of literature, I knew what I signed up for. Six months, one manuscript, 300 pages. End of story. Well, that's not exactly the *whole* story. There's a lot of other stuff that goes into developing and marketing a book. The issue was that I already had a job. As you know, I'm a management consultant and columnist. And no, I don't delegate that stuff. My clients hire *me*, not some MBA. And every word published under my name is my own. So how was I going to pull this off?

First, let's be clear. Writing this book was very near and dear to my heart. I'm passionate about it. I'm also passionate about earning a living, paying the bills, and not giving my wife yet another reason to divorce me (trust me—it's a long, long list). So I knew what my goals were. And I never let anything stand between me and my goals. Ever.

Second, I did the math: 300 pages in five months equals 60 pages a month. Yes, I had six months, but I still wanted to get it done in five. You know how you pack an extra pair of underwear for a trip, just in case? Same thing. Anyway, that's about 15 pages a week. I figured that's three days of work, including outlines, research, rewrites, and all that. So I compressed all my other work into three and a half days and left Sunday afternoons to watch football or otherwise screw around.

I wasn't religious about that schedule; I got more done some weeks than others. I just knew I had to stay reasonably on track, so if I fell a little behind one week, that meant working longer hours the next.

And of course I took some breaks. I woke up this morning and decided to take the dogs for a run in the rain. I needed it. They needed it. More important, my wife needed me out of the house. So I'll work a little later tonight. No big deal. I also make dinner a few nights a week. I love to cook. It's fun. It's also how I relax. The wine doesn't hurt either.

Those are my priorities: Work to pay the bills, write the book, exercise, take care of the various creatures in my life, relax, and have fun . . . and watch football. As for everything else, if it's not an emergency, it can wait six months.

At this point, I'm about a third of the way through the manuscript. So far, so good. Can I keep this pace up indefinitely? No way. Not at my age. But I can do it for six months. If you're reading this, I must have finished it, so I guess the plan worked. Hallelujah.

The point is I've used this same philosophy throughout my career. I used it as a young engineer aspiring to become a manager, as a manager working to become an executive, as an executive double- and triple-booked in meetings and traveling a few hundred thousand miles a year, and as a small-business owner. It hasn't failed me yet.

As unproductive as I am, at least by all the popular notions of the day, I've somehow managed to accomplish everything I set out to do and have a good time doing it. I have seven rules to keep me on track.

Rule 1: Focus On Your Goals and Priorities

If you're not clear on what your goals are, you have no chance of achieving them. Yogi Berra once said, "If you don't know where you're going, you might not get there." He was a master of the understatement. Goals are big things you want to achieve with your life. Priorities are things you have to get done either to help you achieve your goals, pay the bills, or keep your family safe and comfortable. You must focus on your goals and priorities. And unless you're the head of manufacturing at Toyota, productivity should not be one of them.

Rule 2: Know Yourself

Yahoo! CEO and former Google executive Marissa Mayer is a famously insane workaholic who says she averages 90-hour weeks packed with 60 meetings. She once said that avoiding burnout is about "knowing yourself well enough to know what it is you're giving up that makes you resentful" and "finding your rhythm." That's what enables her to work so hard. Same here. I know what I need, and I make sure I get it.

Rule 3: Always Get the Job Done

I have always had a powerful work ethic that guides my decisions on what is and is not OK to do. I'm a reasonably smart, effective, and hard-working guy by nature, but when I'm paid to do a job, my priority is always to get it done and do it better than anyone on earth. People always talk about exceeding the expectations of their boss or customer. That never crosses my mind. My expectations have always been higher.

Rule 4: Love Your Work

If you enjoy your work, long hours come easily. You can work tirelessly for extended periods of time on long-term projects without feeling like you're missing out on something. And there's nothing wrong with making it as fun as you can. On nice days I work outdoors. If I've got a tight deadline, I'll have a second cappuccino to provide a boost. If I'm working at night, I have a glass of wine or two. Work shouldn't have to be painful. Make it easy on yourself.

Rule 5: Be Flexible, Adaptive, and Creative

One of the great misconceptions about entrepreneurialism is that you're your own boss. Wrong. We serve our customers, our investors, and in a way, our employees. Those are your stakeholders. And if you're always there for them by being flexible, adaptive, and creative—by having a "sure, no problem" attitude even when you have no idea how you're going to do something—they'll reciprocate and cut you some slack when you need it.

Rule 6: Work When You Have To, Not When You Don't

I've commuted across the country, taking weekly red-eye flights for more than a year. I've gotten on a plane, flown to Tokyo for a dinner meeting with an important customer, and flown right back that night. That just comes with the territory. But I only work hard when I have to, not when I don't. As long as you do what you need to do when it counts, you can take time off and screw around when it doesn't.

Rule 7: Take Care of Yourself

This is the part that seems to confuse people. They think that by managing every nanosecond of their time, they'll maintain some bizarre sort of balance. They gobble down fast-food meals, stress out, lose sleep, and run themselves into the ground in the name of productivity. That's just nuts. You should be able to eat right, sleep right, get exercise, and take good care of yourself without stressing over how much you got done before breakfast. Burned-out stress monsters are not healthy. I doubt if they're very productive, either.

PRIORITIES, FOCUS, AND DISCIPLINE

Somewhere between dreaming about Tim Ferriss' *4-Hour Workweek* and the reality that you're becoming a 24/7 workaholic is an elusive concept called *work-life balance*.

When you ask people how they're doing, you're likely to get a one-word answer: "Busy." Nobody's got time to breathe, let alone time to take a walk in the park, get a little exercise, or cook a decent meal. Everyone's swamped. Busy seems to be the bane of our existence these days. And work-life balance is our holy grail.

Why should that come as a surprise? In a world where everyone feels so overworked, overwhelmed, overcommitted, and overstressed, it's only natural that we would want to work less and enjoy life more, right?

But what if none of that were true?

What if we're not really as overworked as we think we are?

What if we have just as much leisure time as we've always had?

What if some of us actually like or even love to work?

What if this seemingly elusive work-life balance is entirely within our control? What if it's not an elusive concept at all but a simple matter of personal choice?

This will no doubt come as a shock, but the image of the overworked and overstretched American is a complete myth. We actually have far more leisure or spare time today than at any time in recorded history, and that cuts across nearly every category and demographic, according to a 2006 article in *The Economist*.

The folks who do this kind of research have all sorts of fascinating reasons for what is clearly an enormous disconnect between our perception and reality, but let's cut through all that and get right down to business, shall we?

The problem is a combination of misguided priorities, addiction to instant gratification and distraction, and lack of focus and discipline.

We spend way too much time doing what doesn't matter and not nearly enough time focusing on what does. And that's by choice.

We constantly complain about living in a world where we have to be on 24/7, but the truth is we stay connected because we want to.

Nobody's holding a gun to your head to answer a call or text when you're supposed to be sleeping, playing with your kids, or having dinner with your better half. Nobody makes you reply to tweets and emails when you should be focused on getting something done. So why do you do it? You love the attention. It makes you feel important. It makes you feel special.

And guess what? Companies know that and leverage it, if they're smart. By providing flexible work conditions, allowing people to work and conference from home, and buying them smartphones and notebook computers, they're getting something in return: more of your time and attention when you're not at work.

Sure, executives, professionals, and business leaders work long hours—I always have—but, again, that's a matter of choice. If you want to accomplish big things, you have to shoulder big responsibility, and that usually means working long and hard. That's why they make the big bucks. That's how it works.

Besides, folks like me have a tool set that seems to elude most people these days: priorities, focus, and discipline. We're disciplined about focusing on our priorities and shutting out the noise. We always do what needs to be done, but for everything else, we have a saying: "Tomorrow's another day."

Now, let's talk about the real time wasters in our lives: social media and personal blogging. As we discussed in Chapter 6, the vast majority of time we spend on Facebook, Twitter, and LinkedIn is wasted. So is the time we spend blogging and reading all that useless user-generated online content. So are the hours of watching 200 cable channels and YouTube videos, playing with our game consoles and smartphone apps, and shopping for all the stuff everyone thinks they have to own these days.

Americans now spend an average of five hours a day online plus five hours a day watching TV. If you want to be far more successful than the average American, you simply can't get away with that. If you want to make it big in this world, you're going to have to resist that tug. You're going to have to be disciplined about focusing on your priorities.

For every successful entrepreneur and executive I know, work comes first. It's what they live for. They're not freewheeling, fun-loving people who live for the weekend. They live to do what they love, and that's work. Granted, they don't work *all* the time. They have families and friends. But they never think about work-life balance because they know what their goals and priorities are, and they know what they have to do and what they have to sacrifice to achieve them.

I'd be willing to bet that just about every famous entrepreneur you've ever heard of who achieved great things fits that description. Steve Jobs, Bill Gates, Larry Page, Mark Zuckerberg, Larry Ellison, Sandra Kurtzig, Elon Musk—they all worked their tails off making their companies successful because that's what those kinds of people do.

Now, some who choose the entrepreneurial route don't feel that way. They don't want to work that hard. They don't think they should have to sacrifice. Others feel as if they're working constantly and never getting ahead. They aren't comfortable merging their home and work lives together and just don't know how or where to draw the line.

Those, I suspect, are the people who read lots of books, blogs, and articles and attend seminars, workshops, and speeches in search of some sort of solution to their dilemma. If you fit that description—and I certainly don't fault you if you do—the rest of the chapter is for you.

First, let's be clear. In thirtysomething years, I've never known a single person—entrepreneur, executive, manager, engineer, small-business owner, you name it—who made a good living working less than 40 or 50 hours a week. And I don't know anyone who made it big working less than 50 or 60 hours a week. And many of them worked a whole lot more.

We all have our own peculiar ways of managing our work lives, but none of it will help you break the laws of physics or economics. By all means, work smart. But unless you figure out how to clone yourself, you've still got to do the work—and a lot of it if you want a lot in return. You get out of life what you put in.

As for those who want to work less and enjoy their personal lives more, I don't blame you, but I wouldn't quit my day job just yet. And if you still think you can make it big as an entrepreneur without having to work hard, you can always come up with a catchy sound bite and market it to the gullible masses as the secret to success. That's certainly worked before.

Now, if you're among those who can't seem to figure out why you're working all the time and not getting anywhere, don't lose faith. Read on. In all likelihood, we'll hit on your problem and provide a solution sometime before the end of Part III. If not, contact me and I'll help you out, on the house. No kidding.

To summarize, here's my theory on living a fulfilling life while avoiding a life full of regret:

If you work too hard and completely miss out on life, you'll be miserable. If you have too much fun and don't make enough money, the result's the same. Somewhere in between is an optimum point where you work hard enough, make enough money, and still have a good time. That point is different for everyone. It's highly subjective, but it does exist. It mostly depends on your goals.

If your goal is to have a fulfilling career and a rich family life, you should be able to pull that off. If, on the other hand, you really want to make it big, you're going to have to sacrifice on the personal side. And if your goal is to party hard, work as little as possible, and just skate by, that's fine too; but don't expect to park a Ferrari at your mansion.

Look at it this way. Life is full of tradeoffs, and, for the most part, you're in control. If you focus on doing only what matters and are reasonably disciplined about your priorities, you should never have to concern yourself with nonsense like personal productivity.

CHAPTER 10

COMPETENCIES FOR A CHANGING WORLD

A FEW YEARS BACK, A COLLEAGUE SENT ME A LINK TO A 2009 video by a visiting professor of political psychology at the Harvard Graduate School of Education. The talk was about five competencies we should teach students to help them adapt to a changing world, which were:

1. Managing ambiguity
2. Agency and responsibility
3. Finding and sustaining community
4. Managing emotion
5. Managing technological change

What struck me about the video was how strongly I disagreed with much of what the good professor had to say, and I'm quite sure she would feel the same about my opinions on the subject. I suspect that's equally true of our views on politics, economics, and culture. After all, we see the world from completely different perspectives: she from academia, and me from the business world.

The point is, there is nothing objective about the way each of us views the world. We all see things through our own inherently subjective filters. It's as true of professors and professionals as it is of you and me. The sooner you learn to question everything you hear and read regardless of its source, the better. That includes both the professor's work and mine.

That said, we certainly agree on one thing: The world is changing, and that means we need to adapt. But adaptation is a response to a competitive environment. That's as true in business and academia as it is in biology and society. We all live and work in a highly competitive world. So we don't just want to react to a changing world; we want to shape it. We don't just want to survive as indistinguishable members of the herd; we want to be out in front, leading the pack. Here, in my view, are five competencies you will need to develop if you want to adapt, thrive, and distinguish yourself in this new world.

CRITICAL THINKING

When you question assumptions, claims, and viewpoints instead of just accepting them as gospel, as in "A Harvard professor (or a business leader, for that matter) said it online, so it must be true," that's called critical thinking. It's fundamental to smart decision making. And that, in turn, is key to being successful at just about anything.

The concept dates back thousands of years to Socrates' and Buddha's teachings. If you naturally question conventional wisdom, challenge the status quo, and avoid collectivism and groupthink, you're in good company. They're all facets of the same concept.

Unfortunately, the web has been overrun with user-generated content full of miracle cures, quick fixes, fads, pseudoscience, and downright lies. Anything that seems eye-catching gets picked up by hundreds of bloggers and retweeted all over the web. In short, the vast majority of online content is complete bullshit.

Lately it seems that people have forgotten how to think logically. Maybe they overindulged in the past and are trying to cut down. Maybe it's a new fad, the *No Critical Thinking* diet. Maybe everyone's just too busy talking, texting, and tweeting to be bothered with a little thing like rational thought. Or maybe we're all so doped up on dopamine and serotonin from our gadget and social media addictions that our brains just don't work right anymore.

As continuously bombarded with content and sound bites as we are, our ability to question what's real and what isn't, to reason logically and not generalize from a single data point, to understand causal relationships, is more critical today than ever before.

For example, there's a 2007 book called *How to Change the World: Social Entrepreneurs and the Power of New Ideas* that has an Amazon page with some interesting facts from author David Bornstein, including this one: "97 percent of Generation Y are looking for work that allows them 'to have an impact on the world,' according to a Harris Poll."

Bornstein also provides a long list of famous business leaders investing a great deal of time and money on social entrepreneurship, including Bill Gates, Warren Buffett, eBay founder Pierre Omidyar, Google founders Sergey Brin and Larry Page, and venture capitalists William Draper and John Doerr.

What's missing from the book's marketing material is the causal link between these entrepreneurs' business and social activities. *First* they spent years, even decades, founding and building wildly successful companies. *Then* they made their fortunes. *Then, and only then*, they became social entrepreneurs. The equation would not work in reverse. In other words, without their breakout business success, there would be no money to impact social causes.

Not to pick on this particular book, but it's a perfect example of the same sort of lack of common sense cause and effect I often come across in discourse on the subject of social entrepreneurship. So many young would-be entrepreneurs are putting social causes ahead of or concurrent with traditional business and career goals: They're either not getting, not understanding, or choosing to ignore the critical causality in the equation. I believe that's reflected in the Harris Poll data.

Question everything, especially common doctrine. Listen to those who challenge your own and popularly held beliefs. Resist the pressure to view things in black and white or "us vs. them" terms. Learn to see the world in shades of gray and from different angles, viewpoints, and perspectives.

And instead of attending a motivational speech or leadership seminar by some shyster, take a philosophy class. I hear Socrates is making a comeback.

FOCUS AND DISCIPLINE

We passed the point of information and communication overload long ago. Even highly focused overachievers who should know better sit down to work only to find that, a few tweets, texts, and emails later, half the day is gone and all the work remains.

Focus and discipline have always been critical to success in just about any field, but these days, managing distraction has become harder and harder for even the most disciplined among us. That's not likely to change any time soon.

The problem goes far beyond lost time. Distraction compromises our decision making and erodes our effectiveness. Nobody's immune, not even executives and political leaders.

I remember when BlackBerry smartphones first came out. Every board meeting had two or three VCs and executives thumbing away at the things. That was just the beginning. Today our obsession with smartphones and other gadgets is completely out of control.

Senator John McCain was actually photographed playing poker on his iPhone during a Senate committee hearing on whether the U.S. should use military force in response to Syria's use of chemical weapons on its people. Not exactly what I would call a trivial matter. Yet there he was, totally distracted.

Even seasoned executives are learning—the hard way—that they have to be more disciplined than ever. In 2014, Uber senior vice president Emil Michael let an online tech journalist's persistent sensationalist attacks on the company get so under his skin that he did something *really* dumb. He reportedly floated the idea of hiring a team to dig up personal dirt on the press and "give the media a taste of its own medicine."

He didn't say it in private. He said it at a high-profile media soiree that was supposed to help fix the uber-aggressive and PR-challenged company's bad reputation. The dinner included Uber's Kalanick, publisher Arianna Huffington, iHeartMedia CEO Bob Pittman, and BuzzFeed editor-in-chief Ben Smith, who ran with the story. The news set off a firestorm that did far more damage to the company's reputation than anything the journalist in question had written.

Every company has its public detractors in the media and beyond. Executives have long known to just let that sort of thing go. But today, everyone's voice is amplified by social media and the blogosphere. And the pressure to pay attention and respond is enormous.

Now, more than ever, you have to learn how to manage distraction and shut out the noise without shutting yourself off from what really matters. This is not easy. But if you're too distracted and undisciplined to focus on what's critical, you can't get things done. And if you can't get things done, somebody else will.

BEING HUMAN

In a very real sense, we are becoming virtual images of our real-world selves. That would be fine if those personas replicated the real us. Unfortunately, they rarely do. Instead, they're carefully constructed avatars that reflect social norms, popular themes, and wishful thinking. The information we share is filtered and purified.

More and more we behave like sound bites personified—virtual actors portraying cardboard characters in a two-dimensional digital world.

And the temptation to hide behind our creations is so strong that we're becoming more isolated, less comfortable in our own skin, and awkward in the physical presence of others. That's why we prefer texting, messaging, and posting to talking on the phone, meeting face to face, or speaking to a group.

In many ways we are becoming desocialized, like the proverbial children brought up by wild animals or dogs that never get to play or interact with others. We spend enormous amounts of time building our online networks and personal brands without realizing that we're just blasting gigabytes of superficial sound bites and links at each other. We share lots of data that way, but all the social cues, emotional subtleties, body language, and intuitive inferences are lost.

In reality, social networking isn't even fractionally effective when compared with a simple real-time discussion or face-to-face meeting. Besides the loss of enormous amounts of "human" information, you're not really connecting on an emotional level, so the bond is far weaker. That's why one relationship with a person in the real world is worth a thousand virtual connections.

Business is built on real communication and real relationships. Running a business is about motivating investors to provide capital, customers to buy products, and employees to work their tails off for you. Every business transaction ultimately has a human being at both ends.

Now more than ever, we need a renewed sense of humility and genuine self-awareness to remind us that we're flesh-and-blood humans, that we're not always the insanely great business leaders, managers, entrepreneurs, partners, and parents that we hold ourselves out to be in the virtual world.

In a world of indistinguishable online lemmings, where everyone tries to be different in superficial ways and, in so doing, ends up behaving exactly like everyone else, those who strive to remain unique individuals will have a big advantage. Instead of hiding behind your social media avatar and personal brand, have the courage to be your genuine self. Forget your social network and build relationships in the real world. Listen to what people have to say and trust your instincts. That's the only way to genuinely relate, make connections, and understand people.

Be human.

GETTING THINGS DONE

The idea that successful entrepreneurs and business leaders are typically driven by high ideals and lofty aspirations is a myth. None of the highly accomplished executives I've known got where they are by walking around with their heads in the clouds. They got there by putting one foot in front of the other and getting the job done.

If they're not motivated by grandiose dreams, then what does drive these people? Some are driven by the need to prove themselves and do great work. Some are highly competitive and want to win big at everything they do. Others are passionate about innovating and developing products customers need. Then, of course, there's the need to put food on the table and a roof over their family's heads.

Whatever the reason, successful entrepreneurs have the ability to focus and motivate people to work together toward a common goal. They have a strong sense of personal responsibility, accountability, and work ethic. They are born troubleshooters and problem solvers. And adversity, obstacles, and risks do not deter them. On the contrary, they energize them.

They don't do things in half measures or hedge their bets, at least not when they're getting started. They don't typically mince words or worry about work-life balance. They know what their goals and priorities are. They know that business is not about them but about their customers. They know it's not what you say or write that counts but what you do. They know what they want to get done, and that's exactly what they do. They deliver the goods, get the job done, and satisfy the needs of their stakeholders, no matter what.

Success always looks preordained after the fact, but nothing could be farther from the truth. When you look at companies as diverse as Uber, GrubHub, WhatsApp, and Alibaba, they disrupted their respective industries in more or less the same way: by noticing a problem that needed to be solved and making it happen.

Take Uber, for example. It started with a question: Why isn't there an app to get someone to take me from point A to point B? To a user, it seems so easy. It's just an app. You tell it where you are and where you want to go, pick an option, and, voila, a car shows up to take you there.

But that seamless and reliable user experience required a complete top-down reimagining of how people get from one place to another when they don't have a vehicle. Not to mention the software development, logistics deployment, and rapid recruiting and operations ramp-up in dozens of cities around the world.

Sure, it's groundbreaking, but in a "Why didn't I think of that? It's so obvious" or "How did we ever live without it?" sort of way reminiscent of FedEx and TiVo. In reality, it was the enormous amount of behind-the-scenes and under-the-hood work that made the end result seem so simple and intuitive.

The same applies to other must-have apps and businesses. GrubHub's founders wondered why there's no one-stop website for ordering takeout food. WhatsApp's Jan Koum and Brian Acton wanted a simple messaging app that didn't store messages, collect user data, or bombard users with ads, games, and gimmicks. Alibaba's Jack Ma wondered if ecommerce could connect a billion Chinese people to the products they wanted to buy and sell without brick-and-mortar infrastructure.

Sure, some of those problems seem immensely complicated or downright impossible to solve. But if you ask the right question and define the problem in just the right way, you have the beginning of a disruptive product. Then it comes down to getting the job done. And that's where the rubber meets the road. The founders of those companies were people of action.

The other day, a reader scoffed at a column on what it really takes for startups to be successful. He said ideas are all you need. The problem, of course, is that *everyone* has ideas. We have more ideas, rhetoric, debate, conversations, analysis, studies, theories, and research than ever before. We have more grandiose ideals and lofty aspirations than ever before. We have more entitled people who think they deserve what they haven't worked for than ever before. We have more rules and regulations than ever before. And those trends are likely to continue.

It's never been more challenging to get things done. What we need are people of action who are driven to make things happen and get the job done. That's a competency that will be in greater demand as time goes on.

COMPETITIVE SPIRIT

Ecommerce and the rise of the global economy have opened the business world's competitive floodgates. New competitors are arising on every front as technology lowers the barriers to entry and more and more companies cross over into each other's lanes. Meanwhile, we're de-emphasizing competitive spirit and individual achievement in our schools. As we level the playing field, the motivation to compete and win is being bred out of society. We're beginning to see competition as a bad thing.

That's creating an interesting dichotomy, a *competition gap*, if you will. Clearly, the situation presents both challenge and opportunity. On the one hand, the competition is brutal. It's rough out there. On the other hand, if you're highly driven to compete and win, you've got a leg up on most of the young people entering the workforce. And that gap is only going to widen over time.

Markets are essentially *zero-sum games*, meaning market share is somewhat constrained. I know economists say markets are elastic; they grow over time. That's true at a macro level, but at a micro level every business transaction generally has one winner and multiple losers. Just one person gets to fill a job opening. Promotions and raises are limited. In a very real sense, you are always competing in the real world.

But that doesn't mean it's a bad thing.

One product, company, or candidate beating out another on their merits is an honorable thing. It's no disgrace to lose, either. That's how we learn to improve and do better next time. Competition is how new technologies replace old ones, how startup companies become corporate giants, and how good performers become great ones. It's also how species and civilizations advance and decline.

Some companies manage to survive despite playing nice with the competition, but that's the rare exception, not the rule. While it's true that you can *segment the market*—carve out your own specific domain—your competitors don't always see it the same way. Take chip giant Intel, for example. When I was at OPTi, Intel was a partner. It made microprocessors while we made peripheral chipsets to go with it. For strategic reasons, Intel decided to enter our market. We weren't prepared, Intel crushed us, and that was that. For all intents and purposes, OPTi is no more. But that's not the end of the story.

Seeing the writing on the wall, I jumped to Intel competitor Cyrix, which was founded by two industry executives, Jerry Rogers and Tom Brightman. These guys essentially wanted to take on mighty Intel and kick its butt, Texas style. The company's Dallas headquarters had an atrium with a marble tombstone bearing an epitaph that tells you everything you need to know about their competitiveness: Intel Inside, RIP.

Cyrix was profitable early on, went public in six years, developed highly sophisticated chips that competed with Intel's best on a fraction of the budget, and was ultimately acquired by National Semiconductor. More important, its novel designs and competition with Intel helped to cut the price of PCs in half.

Intel proved to be just as competitive, though, chasing Cyrix into the entry-level category, effectively squashing National's dreams. C'est la vie in competitive markets. Intel's then-chief executive, Andy Grove, had a famous mantra, "Only the paranoid survive." It's that competitive spirit that has made Intel the top semiconductor company in the world for going on 23 years now.

The point is, many if not most great companies are founded and led by fierce competitors. Besides Intel's Grove, there's Gates, Jobs, Ellison, and more. Google aggressively pursued Apple into the smartphone business, even as then-CEO Eric Schmidt sat on Apple's board. Uber's Kalanick takes a lot of heat for his competitiveness, but in just five years he's built a company that's now valued at $41 billion. That's astonishing by any standard.

Competitive market savvy is key to business success. And competitive spirit, the relentless drive to win, is a critical success factor that will only increase in value as the competition gap grows.

Keep in mind, these are learned behaviors, not innate qualities. Granted, some of us were raised in environments that taught us the virtues of such behavior, but that doesn't mean you're forever locked out if you weren't. In time, you can learn to adapt and develop these abilities through experience. And that, in turn, will give you a long-term competitive advantage in a changing world.

CHAPTER 11

FINDING POINT B

THERE'S SO MUCH CONTENT ON THE SUBJECT OF determining your career path that if I were just starting out in the working world, I wouldn't know where to start. For every article or book that says one thing, there's another that says exactly the opposite. That should be your first clue that maybe you're looking for your career path in all the wrong places.

One of the most important insights to come out of Steve Jobs' Stanford speech we discussed in Chapter 6 was the realization that "to do great work," you have to "love what you do." In identifying career paths as "matters of the heart," Jobs may have done more for the plight of those wearily searching for their true calling than anyone since Dick Bolles of *What Color Is Your Parachute?* fame.

LOOKING FOR A CAREER IN ALL THE WRONG PLACES

One of the great mysteries of the universe is how, among the billions of people on this enormous planet, we somehow manage to find our one true love, get married, and live happily ever after, just like in a fairy tale.

Come on now, you didn't think I was serious, did you? The search for a mate is all about evolutionary biology and instinct, courtesy of your limbic and endocrine systems. It begins when your hormones start to kick in, accelerates with that first kiss, and, for some, ends with a ring and a ceremony. For others, the search doesn't end until they finally stop kicking. It's a process.

Some of us find the one we want to spend our days and nights with relatively early in life. Most don't. Some never do. Not to be cold and calculating about such a sensitive subject, but that distribution probably fits a pretty traditional bell curve.

Your career follows more or less the same pattern. Instead of hormones, the process begins the first time you're asked, "What do you want to be when you grow up?" Instead of a first kiss, you get your first taste of the working world when you land your first job. And so on.

Some of us find a career we love fairly early in life, some never do, and the rest of us fall somewhere in between—in the fat part of the bell curve. Again, it's a process. There's nothing mystical or magical about it.

You can buy into the whole "one true love" or "one true path" thing—that you're fated to be with one particular person or do one particular job—if you like. I've got no skin in that game. The process is still the same.

I'm just here to help you find a career you can love and cherish. A career that will bring you happiness and success. If you want to believe it's *the one*, be my guest. If you want to go for two or more, I'm cool with that too. Just so you know, Steve Jobs had two careers. Bill Gates is on his second. So am I.

In fact, I started out wanting to be a cowboy when I grew up. Then I wanted to be a fireman. Then an astronaut, an NHL defenseman, and a rock star. What I actually became was a high-tech marketing and sales executive, and then a management consultant. Today, all I can think about is getting this damn book done . . . and becoming a bestselling author, of course.

The point is, figuring out where you want to go in your career, aka the much discussed point B from Chapter 4, is not a be-all and end-all proposition that you have to come up with just once in your life. It's only natural for it to change as you experience the world and discover new opportunities you never knew existed.

Think of it as a road trip with several destinations, all of which are subject to change. Let's face it: There are a ridiculous number of variables and unknowns in this equation. It's mind-boggling, if you think about it. So don't. Don't dwell on it. And definitely don't make this any harder than it has to be.

What if I told you we could boil it down to a simple process that will work for your entire life, even as things change? What if I told you that everything you've ever read on the subject has it wrong, that you're looking for career love in all the wrong places?

You're probably wondering how it can be simple when there are so many questions to answer:

Should you follow your passion or follow the money? How do you decide what your passion is, and how do you know when you've found it? And shouldn't you be involved in some bigger cause to help people?

Should you get a real job, quit your job and become an entrepreneur, or try to do both at the same time? Is corporate America really evil? Will you really end up broke and miserable working for someone else?

Everyone says you should take risks, but how much risk is too much? Should you go big right out of the gate or start small? Everyone says failure is OK, but how do you know when it's time to quit and try something different?

So many questions, so little time.

First, let's dispense with the concept of time. I know people say life is short, but in my experience that's entirely untrue. In reality, life is a lot longer than you think. And when it comes to finding love—

human or career—that common misconception can really screw things up for you. The Supremes sang "You Can't Hurry Love." They were right.

Look, I know we live in an information society where everyone thinks they can find all the answers to all their questions online, but when it comes to matters of the heart (even if that is just a metaphor for biochemistry and survival instincts), trust me when I tell you there are no answers there. And the worst thing you can do is put all sorts of pressure on yourself to try to figure everything out all at once. That's not how it works.

There are few if any things in life as important as your family, friends, health, and career. And if you're willing to trust any of them to something you read in a popular blog or a book written for a generic audience, you're making a big mistake.

Yes, I know *this* is a book, but I'm not telling you what to do or even how to do it. I'm just showing you how the real world works to help you navigate the journey. The rest is entirely up to you.

Most self-proclaimed career experts either tell you what they think you should do or provide some sort of toolset or intellectual exercise for figuring it out. Neither approach makes a bit of sense. For one thing, when it comes to matters of the heart, you should know by now that nobody can tell you what to do. You have to figure it out for yourself.

Toolsets and exercises are also the wrong way to go. There's an episode of the TV show *Friends* called "The One With the List," in which Ross can't figure out if he should be with Rachel or Julie, so he makes a list of their pros and cons. When Rachel sees the list, she goes ballistic, and rightly so. You can't intellectualize something as emotional as falling in love—with a person or a career.

The only real way to figure out what you want to be when you grow up is through experience. That's how the right path for you will unfold, regardless of how many destinations are on it. That's where you'll find all the answers to all your questions. It isn't mystical or magical, but experience is beautiful. And it really does work wonders—for everyone.

Understand that life is a marathon, not a sprint. And while it's good to have goals and plans, one of the great epiphanies in life is the realization that reaching a destination isn't nearly as important as the journey. After all, we all do end up in the same place, n'est-ce pas?

So don't be in such a rush to find answers or get somewhere. Relax, settle down, take a deep breath, and stay with me while I explain how all this works.

How do the vast majority of highly successful entrepreneurs find passion, innovation, and opportunity? How do they ultimately make their millions and their mark on the world? They don't do it by reading books or blogs or overthinking it. They do it by getting out into the world, getting their hands dirty, and getting to work. Whether you know you want to be an entrepreneur or you're not sure, that's always the best way to go: Get experience.

Maybe this is heresy in the era of the entrepreneur, but you can have an exciting, fulfilling, and lucrative career by starting out with a great company that grooms up-and-comers for success or making it big as an *intrapreneur* with a startup or two. Millions of people do. I did.

In any case, getting out into the working world is the best way to expose yourself to new ideas and opportunities, meet and learn from a lot of really smart people, and figure out what you actually love to do. It's the best way to learn how to manage people and run a business. And it's the best way to gain practical knowledge and develop skills that are essential to making it on your own. Not only that, you get paid doing it.

As you know, I joined a big high-tech company right out of school. Frankly, I didn't know there were any other options. But it gave me a solid foundation in business fundamentals, management skills, and operating processes that were critical to my subsequent success in startups and high-growth companies. It paid off big-time later in my career, when it mattered most. If I knew then what I know now, I still wouldn't change a thing.

It's easier to do anything after you know how it works. Until you've done it, you have no basis to appreciate just how many factors go into building a successful business. It's very hard and very risky. So many things have to go right, especially in today's brutally competitive global markets. Sure, you can learn from trial and error, but as with anything, you'll be better equipped to take on the challenge after you've seen how it works a few times.

Then there's the one thing nobody ever thinks of: What if you're actually successful as an entrepreneur? What if you beat the odds and whatever crazy idea you've concocted goes viral or becomes a hot product? You'll soon find yourself running a business and an organization with, well, with what tools? Remember that big companies are just small companies that were successful, but if you don't know what you're doing, that's not likely to happen.

And what about all those questions you had a few pages ago? The best way I know to answer them is through experience. When I got out of school I had a couple of degrees but no real idea of what I wanted to do or what I'd be best suited to do. But the tech industry opened up a universe of opportunities. It's how I learned what I loved to do and how I met all the people who would open so many doors for me down the road.

The problem with going it alone right off the bat is that you never gain exposure to a wide range of markets, companies, and job functions. And you'll forever have a narrow perspective and limited career potential. Ironically, you'll develop a broader network and gain more exposure to startup opportunities working at an established company.

Most important, the corporate world is where I learned how to be an effective senior executive and how to run a company. Everything I know about management and leadership and all the insights I use in my consulting practice and writing come from real-world experience. I learned invaluable lessons from hundreds of experienced executives. I learned about people: how to motivate them, organize them, galvanize a team, and create a whole that's greater than the sum of its parts. And I learned how to be an effective communicator and develop what I'm told is a powerful executive presence.

It taught me everything I know about finance and operations. I took a few classes toward an MBA, but I was learning so much more and so much faster on the job that I quit. Instead of getting a business degree, I put my energy into climbing the corporate ladder, learning how companies operate, learning about P&L and balance sheets.

It's where I learned about marketing: Corporate and product positioning, value proposition, competitive positioning, market segmentation, promotion strategy, how to make a big splash on a shoestring budget, and what it really takes to enter an established market and gain market share over entrenched competitors. Those are all key concepts for any business owner. You'll learn them far more effectively on the job than from books.

I may have learned some of the basics of selling in a small rep firm, but I learned how to build a sales force, sell myself, negotiate, and do business with dozens of multinational and international companies like Samsung, Toshiba, IBM, and Microsoft in the corporate world.

It's also how I learned to raise capital and developed a network of VCs. I participated in two IPOs, helped to raise several rounds of funding, and acquired a Rolodex full of angel investors, venture capital firms, research analysts, private equity companies, and investment bankers. You can't put a price on that.

If there's a raging hunger inside you that can only be fulfilled by doing your own thing, if you think you've got a shot at becoming the next Richard Branson or Mark Zuckerberg, by all means, go for it. Be my guest. But if you first learn the ropes, build a foundation, and gain some exposure, you'll be better equipped to answer all those questions, make smart career decisions, and achieve lasting success.

ENTREPRENEURIAL MYTHOLOGY

The entrepreneurial world has always been about challenging the status quo and questioning conventional wisdom in search of new and better ways of doing things. That's what gave rise to America, and, in one way or another, that's what gave rise to every great American company.

After all, if you're just going to follow the pack and do what everyone else is doing, you may as well just go out and get a job working for someone else.

That's why nothing raises the hairs on the back of my neck more than everyone moving in lockstep to the same drumbeat. When a thousand shrill voices tell you to do the same thing, that's a sure sign of groupthink. It's also a good time to get some earplugs and do some of that critical thinking you learned about in Chapter 10.

Today, there is a pervasive and nearly deafening mantra insisting that each and every one of you should quit your job and become an entrepreneur. The popular crowd says you should drop everything and do it today. The social collective says that every day you wait brings you closer to a life of poverty and regret.

But that's simply not true. As we just discussed, the idea that you can't have a fulfilling career, be remarkably happy, and even get rich working for someone else is perhaps the most ludicrous, disingenuous, and irresponsible myth I've ever heard, and I've heard a lot.

Don't get me wrong: Entrepreneurship can be incredibly rewarding. Starting your own business may be the best decision you ever make—but it's not for everyone. There's a lot to consider before you take the plunge or decide on a career path, starting with a few myths that are very much in need of exposure.

Myth 1: Entrepreneurship Is the Only Way to Get Rich

This is a complete fabrication.

Granted, the richest people in America are mostly entrepreneurs or members of entrepreneurial families, and half of America's millionaires are self-employed. But that doesn't mean they were *always* self-employed. Many of them worked for companies before striking out on their own, as we discussed before.

Besides, that list also includes talented entertainers and professionals like doctors and lawyers. And most of America's self-employed millionaires also tend to live well below their means and invest their money, which has an enormous impact on their net worth.

Then there's the other half of America's millionaires who are *not* self-employed. Hundreds of companies such as Microsoft, Intel, Google, Apple, and Facebook created hundreds of thousands of millionaires.

The truth is, there's no data or logic to support the premise that any given person has a better chance of making more money or getting rich by being self-employed. And the notion that it's a simple either-or proposition is a fallacy. You can do both.

Myth 2: Follow Your Passion or a Cause, Not the Money

This is another myth born of oversimplification.

Some people discover what they love to do, make a living at it, and find fulfillment. Others do what they're good at, achieve financial success, and that frees them to pursue their passion. Still others pursue a passion or a cause with no market, go broke, and wind up having to do work they don't enjoy to make ends meet.

While you'll probably have a better chance of being happy and successful if you enjoy what you do for a living, there are lots of other factors that determine whether you can pull it off. Passion alone won't pay the bills.

Just because you're into food doesn't mean you should open a restaurant. It's a highly competitive business with an extremely high failure rate. And maybe you want to help others, but you're going to have a hard time doing anyone any good unless you help yourself first.

Passion and money are both important. You shouldn't choose one or the other.

Myth 3: Entrepreneurship Is More Fulfilling and Will Make You Happier

Just about everyone enjoys doing great work they can be proud of. And you can do that working for a big company, a small company, or your own company. Fulfillment has absolutely nothing to do with business ownership. If you want to manage, lead, or run a business, you're better off learning the ropes in a good company before starting your own.

And the last time I checked, the question of what makes a person happy is pretty subjective. Most people are actually happier without the headaches, risks, burdens, hurdles, and uncertainty of having to own and run their own company.

A lot of people worry too much about what the popular crowd says they should be doing. I think that's what's making everyone feel guilty and less happy . . . but it shouldn't.

Myth 4: Entrepreneurs Have More Freedom, Less Stress, and No Bosses

If you run your own business, there's a good chance you work 24/7 and wear all sorts of hats you're not necessarily comfortable with. Work often becomes your life. And the financial burden can be enormous. There's nothing wrong with that, but not everyone feels more freedom and control and less stress that way. Many have the opposite response.

Besides, everyone has bosses. Depending on the size and type of company, entrepreneurs may have to answer to a board of directors, customers, and investors, not to mention federal, state, and municipal regulators and bureaucrats. Trust me, they can all be pretty bossy.

I often hear people say, "Sure, there are issues, but at least I get to do it on my own terms." I've actually heard homeless street people say exactly the same thing.

Myth 5: Corporate America Is Evil

Every corporation—even giants like Apple and Walmart—began as somebody's startup or small business. That's right, a ginormous corporate behemoth is really just a small business that did really well. So why is entrepreneurship cool, while corporate America is evil? It doesn't make a whole lot of sense, does it?

I remember one of the mantras of the Occupy Wall Street movement was, "Corporations are not people." Oh, yes, they are. They are run and staffed entirely by people. Every action they take and decision they make is by and for people. Their investors and customers are all people or companies that are themselves made up entirely of people. There is no distinction. Period.

I had a fabulous career working for and with companies big and small in the high-tech and related industries. So have thousands of people I've known over the years. As for companies, organizations, and governments that behave badly, it's their leadership that's the problem . . . just as it is with individuals. It's the same thing.

Myth 6: Technology Destroyed All the Jobs

Ever since the Industrial Revolution we've worried about machines taking our jobs and technology taking over our lives. While outsourcing, offshoring, and technology have without a doubt changed the job market—particularly with respect to manufacturing—the popular mantra that there are no jobs is simply untrue. But that never stopped anyone from fearmongering.

If technology is destroying jobs, how do we explain the most lucrative and fastest-growing industry on the planet, technology? If people can't find a job, chances are they lack in-demand skills and education. If anything, I think our families and educational system have done a poor job of keeping up with the changing market.

There's also little doubt that the two big post-millennial recessions had a major impact on a growing gap between productivity and employment and the decline of median household income in the U.S. But, as we discussed in Part I, that time frame also coincides with the advent of Web 2.0 and the distressingly low labor participation rate among Millennials.

The problem is, instead of building real companies and making a living, they're slugging it out with the rest of the digital collective: blogging, tweeting, and personal branding their way to poverty and ending up boomeranging back to their parents or falling into a growing government safety net.

Contrary to popular belief, technology is not destroying jobs. That's a ludicrous theory and a convenient excuse for a sluggish economy and a government that's anything but business-friendly. But the more we behave like drones in a digital hive, the poorer we become. And that's entirely by individual choice.

Don't buy into popular myths. What you do with your career is your own business. Make it your business to make informed decisions. Do what's right for you, when it's right for you. Have faith in yourself. Follow your own path. Everything will work out fine.

KNOW YOURSELF, FACE YOUR FEAR, FOLLOW YOUR HEART

At some point in your journey from point A to point B, you will look back and say, "I wish I knew then what I know now."

Truth be told, I'm not the kind of guy who does that a lot. Long ago, a friend told me, "Never look back. You can go crazy wondering 'What if?'" I've never forgotten his advice and, to this day, I rarely look back.

But it doesn't come up much because, for various reasons, I've always followed the path that seemed right to me. I took risks when I needed to and didn't let fear get in my way. As a result, I've spent a good part of my life outside my comfort zone and terrified, which I highly recommend.

That said, of course everyone has regrets, and I'm no different. I've regretted things I did and, just as important, things I didn't do. To help you minimize those bitter moments, here's some advice to make your own journey of discovery perhaps a little less regretful.

Always take the first step, especially if it sounds exciting or scary. Of course you can't know in advance whether you're moving in the right direction, but if an opportunity arises and you don't take that first step, if you don't go for it, if you don't say, "OK, let's rock," you'll never know what you might have missed.

Learn to say yes . . . a lot.

For example, the hands-down best piece of advice I ever got was when my girlfriend's father—the chairman of a high-tech startup on Long Island—told me that digital electronics were going to be the future. That was 1977. I don't know why, but I believed him, probably because it sounded exciting, I had nothing better going on at the time, and I had nothing to lose. I wasted no time going back to college, getting a master's degree in electrical engineering, and finding my way to the high-tech industry. Clearly, that was the right path.

It was thrilling and terrifying at the same time. And that's exactly how it *should* feel. If it sounds exciting or scary, that's your heart telling you something. Listen. And find a way to do it. While you're at it, observe people. Business is all about people. If you get people, you'll kill it out there. If you're a people person, then friendships and relationships will come naturally to you. If not, you might want to work on that a bit. I'm not saying you can't be successful if you're introverted. Of course you can. But every opportunity involves a person.

That same girlfriend's father asked me if I wanted to take a ride and see what his startup was like. I could have said no. Luckily, I didn't.

It's also a good idea to be geographically mobile. Most of the people I grew up with never left and never went anywhere in life. If that was their choice, fine. But I bet many would do it differently if they could.

I always went where the opportunities took me. My first job after grad school was in Dallas. It was no picnic being a Yankee in the South, but Texas Instruments offered the best opportunity, so that's where I went. I subsequently moved from Dallas to Orange County to Los Angeles to Silicon Valley back to Dallas and back to Silicon Valley again. I've commuted to work halfway across the country on a weekly basis and racked up millions of air miles to so many different countries I'd wake up in hotel rooms with no idea where I was. Was it worth it? Hell, yes!

Don't let geographic boundaries stand in the way of your path. Come to think of it, don't let *any* boundaries stand in the way of your path.

One more thing. If it isn't working, try something different. It's not always easy to know if what you're doing isn't working, but if you're miserable and you would rather be anywhere doing anything but where you are and what you're doing, it's time for a change. Don't wait. If you're not sure, trust your gut.

Regret is the most tragic thing in life. The best way to avoid it is to know yourself, face your fear, and follow your heart wherever it takes you. And quit looking for answers. You'll find them all in time on your journey to point B, C, or D.

PART III

THE
REAL
BUSINESS

CHAPTER 12

STARTUP = ENTREPRENEUR + VENTURE CAPITAL

SOMETIME IN THE 1990S A VC USED THE WORD "entrepreneur" to describe the CEOs of his portfolio companies. I'd been in the tech industry for more than a decade—and had even worked in several startups—but, strangely enough, I had never heard that word come out of anyone's mouth before.

I don't know why, but when that VC said the word, it sounded ostentatious, as if to describe royalty or inspire awe. I couldn't imagine ever using it in actual conversation.

Nevertheless, it is a key variable in the equation that describes how the tech industry works:

Startup = Entrepreneur + Venture Capital

Granted, universities like Stanford and Caltech play a big role, as do research institutes such as PARC and Stanford Research Institute (now SRI), but that single equation explains the modern technology revolution to a tee. No wonder that word sounded so reverent coming from the mouth of a VC. He was describing the other half of the equation that defined his world. I won't go quite as far as saying the entrepreneur-VC pair is as powerful as hydrogen and oxygen or man and woman, but in terms of the business world, it's definitely in the ballpark.

Things sure have changed.

Today the word *entrepreneur* is so overused, the concept so overhyped it's come to be almost meaningless. It's used to describe an occupation, a mindset, a generation, and a cultural movement. But in reality it's none of those things.

Entrepreneur is not a job title or a function. It has no organizational meaning. It's not a state of mind, as so many *wantrepreneurs* seem to think. And the generation and cultural movement it's used to describe are entirely mythical, as we learned in Chapter 2.

So what is it? That's what we're here to find out: what it really means to be an entrepreneur and, just as important, what it takes to start, grow, and run a business . . . because that's what real entrepreneurs do.

FIRST, LOSE THE LABEL

According to my go-to online dictionary, Merriam-Webster, an entrepreneur is "a person who starts a business and is willing to risk loss in order to make money" or "one who organizes, manages, and assumes the risks of a business or enterprise." That is what it means. Note the keywords. If you don't *risk loss to make money* or *assume the risks of a business*, you're not an entrepreneur.

The great irony of the entrepreneurial fad—and yes, it is a fad in every sense of the word—is that the very act of using the term before it's earned is likely to be self-defeating.

Here's a little-known secret about entrepreneurs. I've worked alongside dozens, maybe hundreds of successful startup founders and CEOs. And in all those years I never heard a single one call himself or herself an "entrepreneur." Not one. Want to know why? Because to them, it's nothing but a label. They had jobs to do. They had companies to run and products and services to deliver to their customers on behalf of their stakeholders. That's what they did full time and that's what they thought about 24/7. Bill Gates was chief executive of Microsoft. Andy Grove was CEO of Intel. Those were their jobs.

There are two kinds of people in this world: those who talk and those who do. You can talk about what you do, but if the doing doesn't come first, you're just a blowhard.

For example, I was an executive officer of two or three public companies. For a time I was CEO of a well-funded startup. I've been involved in two IPOs and the merger of two public companies. My contact list is full of big names from venture capital, investment banking, and private equity. And I've run my own company for more than a decade.

And you know what? I still don't consider myself to be an entrepreneur. But if I were the sort of person who got hung up on trite labels, I wouldn't be much use to my consulting clients, or the companies I worked for over the years, because a label is not a job.

Just to be clear, I'm not saying job titles aren't important. I think they're very important—if they're real occupations and not conjured up out of thin air. For example:

▸ If you're an engineering manager, you have to deliver products on time and on budget, and they had better work or heads will roll, starting with your own.

▸ If you're the head of marketing, you've got to launch great products that delight customers and ensure they beat the competition and become market leaders.

▸ If you're an executive officer of a public corporation, that's a very big responsibility you have to take seriously, because thousands of customers, employees, and shareholders depend on you.

Those are some of the jobs I held for the first two decades of my career. And that's how I gained the knowledge, skills, and insights to do what I do today. By doing my job.

The word entrepreneur may mean a lot of things to a lot of people these days, but it's not a job function. It's not even a job title. It's just a label. And focusing on a label will keep you from finding your passion and achieving great things.

It takes a lot of time and effort to figure out what you love doing— what you can do better than anyone else. It's not just a label—it's a job, an area of expertise, an innovative capability. And it doesn't just jump out at you and shout, "Here I am!" You have to go out and find it. And that can only come from experience.

That experience comes through developing real expertise, learning a trade, figuring out how business really works, understanding your customers' problems, negotiating deals with real companies, becoming an effective manager, and gaining exposure to the business world— things you simply can't get sitting in your room with a laptop.

Maybe the most important thing you learn from experience is what you don't know. It's one of the great ironies of life on earth. We all start out thinking we know it all. But the longer you're around and the more you learn, the more you come to realize how little you actually know, and I'm talking about both the outer world and your inner self.

But once you gain a certain amount of experience, you begin to see the world as it really is and yourself for who you really are. That's when you begin to gain a sense of humility and balance. That's when you begin to develop maturity and perspective. And those are very important qualities when it comes to building and running a successful business.

Had I decided to be an entrepreneur early in my career, I probably never would have gained the knowledge and insight to help so many entrepreneurs and executives. I doubt I ever would have found my passion or been so fortunate to help so many. How do I know that? After all these years, I know myself. I'm happy. I'm fulfilled. And I love what I do.

The world is full of infinite possibilities, but your career—and your life—is finite. There are loads of opportunities out there, but if you don't go out and look for them, you'll never find them and they'll never find you. It'll be as if they never existed, like far-off lands you'll never get to see.

You would not believe how many great companies would never have been born if their founders had focused on a label like "entrepreneurship" instead of going out and getting a job:

- ▶ While Steve Jobs and Steve Wozniak had been friends since high school, the pair worked together at Atari before founding Apple Computer with Ron Wayne, also an Atari alumnus. It was that exposure to the computer world and that experience of working on games together that set the two Steves on the right path.

- ▶ GrubHub was founded when a couple of software developers at Apartments.com were working on lookup searches for rental real estate. Hungry and frustrated at having to call a bunch of restaurants, Matt Maloney and Mike Evans wondered why there wasn't a one-stop shop for food delivery. That's when the light bulb went off in their heads.

- ▶ Not only did WhatsApp cofounders Jan Koum and Brian Acton work together at Yahoo!, but the $250,000 in seed funding that enabled them to launch the messaging app that Facebook bought for $19 billion came from five former Yahoo! friends.

- ▶ Howard Schultz was a marketing executive at a company that sold coffee beans in Seattle when a trip to Milan gave him the idea for espresso cafes just like the ones he saw on so many streets in Italy. His company's owners wouldn't go for the idea, but they funded Schultz's retail chain and sold him their brand—Starbucks.

The only way to bring opportunities to life is to go out and experience things. Do things. Learn things. Work. Meet people. Learn what they like to do and the problems they face every day. That's how you'll find what you want to do for a living. And I can tell you with great certainty that you won't find it by calling yourself an entrepreneur, especially when you're not.

THERE ARE ENTREPRENEURS AND THERE ARE *ENTREPRENEURS*

Some people become founders relatively early in life, and while there seem to be loads of twentysomething success stories like Maloney, Jobs, Gates, Page, and Zuckerberg, the truth is they're few and far between.

According to CB Insights, which tracks all sorts of data on venture-backed companies, the average founder is a former executive between the ages of 35 and 44. Those wunderkinds you always hear about are actually a rare breed. Regardless of their age and experience, I guarantee that no founders of successful startups just woke up one day, decided to call themselves entrepreneurs, and then sat around trying to figure out what they were going to do to live up to the label.

What they did was figured out what they like to do, came up with an idea or product with unique market potential, and then went out on their own and made it happen, usually with some help from people with money.

While it's a popular romantic notion that anyone with a MacBook and a blog can just create an entrepreneurial persona, I'm afraid that's not how it works. This is not Hollywood, and you are not an actor. (If you are, you definitely bought the wrong book.) Calling yourself an entrepreneur doesn't make you one any more than wearing a black mock turtleneck and blue jeans makes you Steve Jobs.

As a wise VC whose name escapes me once said, "There are entrepreneurs and there are *Entrepreneurs*." What does that mean? I'll tell you what it means to me.

If you say you're human, you know that's a fact. If you call yourself a man or a woman, that's also pretty darn factual. But if you call yourself an engineer, an artist, an auto mechanic, or a doctor, you'd better have some real basis for saying it or you're not going to have many happy customers or patients.

And while "entrepreneur" may not be a job description, there are very real requirements for being one. Not to dash your hopes and dreams, but it's not for everyone, and many of you probably aren't cut out for it. And the sooner you realize you're not going to be the second coming of Mark Zuckerberg, the better.

Look, it's great to reach for the stars. As Robert Browning said, "A man's reach should exceed his grasp." But that doesn't mean you can achieve something simply by reaching for it. That's not how the real world works. In the real world, there are entrepreneurs and there are *Entrepreneurs*. The latter have demonstrated they have what it takes by actually doing it. The former have not and therefore don't deserve the label, at least not yet.

So while there is no one-size-fits-all model for real entrepreneurs, there are a number of common themes. It's not a laundry list of attributes or qualities, but more about their behavior and motivation. What makes them unique is what they do and, just as important, what they don't do. Becoming a real entrepreneur is certainly not preordained, but it's not a cakewalk either. This, in my experience, is what sets real entrepreneurs apart from the crowd.

They Are Driven By Passion

Of the seven deadly sins, pride is generally considered to be the original and the source of all the others. Similarly, passion is the primary source of all the behaviors that make entrepreneurs successful. Their passion for their work is at their very core. It's what motivates and inspires them. It's what sets them apart.

That's what makes finding what you love to do, what makes you obsessive and crazed with excitement, so critical to becoming a successful entrepreneur. It's what drives you to work 24/7 and not give a crap that the rest of your life has gone to hell. It's what keeps you going when everyone says you're nuts. It's what occupies your mind every waking moment and keeps you hungry and focused on accomplishing that one thing.

One of the greatest, wealthiest, and most prolific entrepreneurs of all time, Howard Hughes was a true renaissance man who was wildly successful in a diverse range of industries from entertainment and real estate to aerospace and oil exploration. He was also a lifelong obsessive-compulsive.

Steve Jobs was a card-carrying control freak, a maniacal micromanager who could never pay too much attention to the details of the companies and products he built. Had he been any other way, Apple would not be Apple today. Neither would Pixar be Pixar.

While they weren't as compulsive as Hughes and they didn't necessarily have Jobs' sense of aesthetics, nearly every great entrepreneur I can think of—Gates, Grove, Ellison, Kurtzig, Zuckerberg, Michael Dell, and a laundry list of those less famous—were all passionate about their work.

This phenomenon isn't just limited to businesspeople, either. For no logical reason, Albert Einstein was obsessed with light. He somehow knew in his gut that light was in some way special. It was that passion that drove him to imagine what it would be like to hitch a ride on a beam of light, and that's what led to the special theory of relativity, $E=MC^2$, and the nuclear age.

Whether it's a vision of the future, a problem that needs to be solved, a prophecy that must be fulfilled, a mystery that begs to be unraveled, or just something that's captured their attention for no apparent reason, it's their relentless focus on whatever drives them that enables entrepreneurs to forsake all else and do the impossible—or at least what others say can't be done.

The great irony is how many of these people become fabulously wealthy when money means so little to them. For them, money is just a means to an end. And since neither money nor anything else is much of a distraction, they can truly focus on what really matters: doing what motivates them, what they're passionate about, what nobody has ever done before.

If you find that you're always in need of motivation and inspiration, all that means is you haven't found what you love doing yet. Keep looking. Keep the faith. You'll find it.

They Let Nothing Stand in Their Way

Real entrepreneurs never think about work-life balance. They don't do a little of this and a little of that. They don't do things in half measures. When they hit on something they think is really cool and exciting, they go all in. They don't just dip their toes in the water. They jump in headfirst without a moment's thought about the rocks below.

They're mostly workaholics because their work comes first. It's what they live for. They're not freewheeling, fun-loving people who live for the weekend. They live to do what they love, and that's work. While everyone else complains about how much they have to work, successful entrepreneurs usually have to be pried away from it.

They don't take risks for the sake of taking risks. They just don't let anything stand in the way of what drives them. They pursue it come hell or high water. Risk just comes with the territory.

So does facing fear. Great entrepreneurs often appear to be fearless, but that's certainly not the case. They feel fear just like you and me. They just don't let it stop them from accomplishing what they set out to do. They don't let it stand in their way. They don't succumb to those voices in their heads—the ones that taunt you with everything that can go wrong. Their motivation, their passion, is simply strong enough to overcome their fear. Or maybe they just don't think about it.

These people are uniquely driven to get the job done, no matter the obstacles, and that's exactly what they do. It almost makes you feel sorry for competitors that go up against them. They're definitely at an enormous disadvantage.

They're on a Mission from God

When Dan Aykroyd as Elwood Blues said, "We're on a mission from God," with that deadpan delivery, you knew that nothing was going to stop the Blues Brothers from getting the band back together. Not a bunch of angry Winnebago-driving hillbillies with shotguns, Aretha Franklin as Matt Guitar Murphy's pissed-off wife, a high-speed car chase through a shopping mall, or what appeared to be the entire Chicago police force.

Great entrepreneurs often seem to be on a mission from God. When they speak about their vision or idea, you'd swear they've been possessed by some sort of demon that, instead of inciting chaos and mischief, inspires innovation and creation. There's definitely an aspect of fanaticism in their zeal for whatever has captured their imagination. And it's often fueled by an unnatural belief that they're special, an aspect that can become a self-fulfilling prophecy.

In his seminal book *Organizing Genius: The Secrets of Creative Collaboration*, five of Warren Bennis' 15 lessons of what he calls "Great Groups" are that they "see themselves as winning underdogs," "always have an enemy," "have blinders on," always have "a strong leader," and "think they are on a mission from God." One of the groups profiled in the book is Apple's first Macintosh design team, which Steve Jobs famously told their purpose was to "make a dent in the universe." And they did.

Bennis' observations are all consistent with the belief that the unique cultures of great companies can usually be traced to their founders. Is it any wonder that, more than any other notable contemporary company, Apple's culture is as distinct and cult-like as its products are iconic and groundbreaking? That, of course, is an extension of the legendary entrepreneur who cofounded the company, his exceptional ability to inspire and motivate people to do great work, and the much heralded reality distortion field that seemed to surround him wherever he went.

From Google and Zappos to Southwest Airlines and Trader Joe's, true entrepreneurs create company cultures in their own image.

They Follow No One

When you work with successful entrepreneurs on a daily basis, you begin to wonder what it takes to influence them. They always seem to march to the beat of a drum only they can hear. They follow no one.

To them, there is no such thing as conventional wisdom. They have no patience for the status quo. Tell them how things are done, have been done, or should be done, and you're likely to receive an intimidating stare or be summarily written off as a lost cause. Tell them that what they want done can't be done, and the next thing you know, you'll find yourself doing it.

They have no interest in what anyone else says or does. The word *popular* has no meaning to them. They're indifferent to social conventions and societal norms. They don't have personal brands, and they don't try to be what they're not. They're true to themselves and comfortable in their own skin. Dealing with them is relatively simple and straightforward: What you see is what you get.

They strongly identify with their passion, their company, and their products. And when it comes to anything related to their work, they have their own methods, their own way of doing things, and a certain behavioral DNA that guides their process.

They are generally business-savvy, very quick on the uptake, and born troubleshooters and problem solvers. They're not particularly patient, they don't mince words, and they don't typically suffer fools lightly. They are confident and competent. They are decision makers, not consensus builders. They listen to others, but in the end, they only trust their own gut.

But they can be influenced. They may draw you into a prolonged and heated debate over a key issue, but the moment it dawns on them that you're right, they'll turn around and become the wind at your back. And they always have mentors. Behind every great entrepreneur is at least one great mentor. A real one, not a virtual one.

True entrepreneurs carve their own unique path. They're the makers of their own destiny. And they shape the world we live in.

If you learn nothing else from this book, know that entrepreneurship is absolutely not a state of mind. It has nothing to do with beliefs or even traits. It's entirely about behavior. It's about starting a business and risking loss to make money. It's about organizing and managing a company with real products, customers, and employees. And until you accomplish that, it's a good idea to lose the labels and get to work.

If these four behaviors don't fit you perfectly, don't panic. It doesn't mean you can't own a franchise or two, a dry-cleaning business, or a restaurant. It doesn't mean you can't be self-employed or a small-business owner. But if you want to do great things, if you want to be a real entrepreneur who starts, runs, and grows a successful, thriving business, you've certainly got your work cut out for you. And it starts here.

CHAPTER 13

STARTUP 101: THINK LIKE A VC

YEARS AGO I GOT AN UNEXPECTED CALL FROM A CFO I'd worked with in the past named Doug Norby. Doug has had a long and distinguished career as a senior executive and board director with various technology companies, but unknown to me when we worked together, he was once president and COO of Lucasfilm, the Bay Area film studio known for the Star Wars and Indiana Jones movies.

It turned out that Doug's favorite nephew, Mark Anderson, was running the physical effects division of Industrial Light & Magic, which had recently spun off as an independent company named Kerner Optical, just as Pixar had done years before. Kerner had developed some disruptive 3D technology for movies and other applications and needed some help on the business side.

The following week, Anderson, now president of the company, took me on a breathtaking tour of the studios and stages where the special effects for so many historic sci-fi and action films had been developed and filmed. But what really blew me away were their breakthroughs in 3D technology that were sure to revolutionize the way movies were made and viewed.

That was the good news. The bad news was that the company was mired in debt, in desperate need of capital, and organized like a jigsaw puzzle of different business entities. It was a dysfunctional nightmare I knew no reputable VC would touch, so I recommended a top-down corporate restructuring to facilitate outside funding. Anderson agreed.

Unfortunately, the relatively inexperienced executive let himself get bogged down by the company's day-to-day management and money woes and, to my knowledge, never actually got around to the restructuring it so desperately needed to break out of its tailspin. A young entrepreneur named Eric Edmeades acquired a majority stake in the company and bought it some time, but I doubt he knew what he was getting himself into. Less than two years later, the company filed for Chapter 7 protection, and its assets were ordered liquidated by a bankruptcy court.

Here you had a decades-old organization with next-generation technology and contracts to do physical effects for big movie franchises like *Pirates of the Caribbean*, *Transformers*, *Harry Potter*, and *Iron Man*. And just five years after a management buyout, the whole thing unraveled and ended up on its own cutting room floor.

While that's a sad ending to a once-storied company, it also stands as a powerful example of just how easy it is to screw up a business, even one that has everything going for it: a great reputation, talented people, plenty of customers, and bright prospects for the future.

I know it's hard to believe, but I see this sort of thing happen all the time. And yet there are millions of would-be entrepreneurs who think building a business is easy. It's not. But we can certainly improve your chances of success by teaching you how to think like a VC.

NEVER TELL ME THE ODDS

Not to douse your dreams with facts, but the vast majority of startups fail, and most small businesses never make it to the break-even point.

Even if you're the kind of person who loves to quote Han Solo's famous line from *The Empire Strikes Back*, "Never tell me the odds," I can tell you one thing with great certainty: The less you know about what it really takes to start, build, and grow a successful business, the longer your odds of founding one of the few that actually make it. While your chances are far better than the odds of "successfully navigating an asteroid field," which C-3PO quotes as "3,720 to 1" in the movie, the analogy is not as far-fetched as you'd think. Company founders often say their jobs are about averting one catastrophe after another, and those are the successful ones.

According to data from thousands of companies analyzed by Shikhar Ghosh of Harvard Business School in 2012, three-quarters of venture-backed companies don't return on investor's capital, and 95 percent fail to meet their revenue and break-even targets. These may be some sobering stats, but I'm sure they're better failure rates than those of non-venture-backed companies.

You've probably read an article or two quoting U.S. Bureau of Labor Statistics data that only half of small businesses fail in the first five years. An optimist might see that glass as half full, but that would be a big mistake. Just because you stay in business doesn't mean you're making money and paying the bills. If you dig a little deeper, you learn that just 39 percent make a profit over their lifetime, even fewer actually make a living at it—meaning it pays all their personal bills—and fewer still make enough to retire on.

Some might think the answer is to have multiple businesses or maybe keep your day job, but that inevitably reduces your focus and the odds of success even further. That's no solution, at least not to me. I'm not trying to discourage you from founding a startup or owning a small business; I just want to give you the best odds of succeeding. And one of the biggest problems entrepreneurs face is that they live and work in a vacuum. It's all too easy to get so wrapped up in your vision that you lose perspective. That's actually one of the key benefits of getting out and pitching some VCs who know your market: They give you feedback and, if they decide to cut you a check, that at least validates your strategy.

I was once describing a business strategy to a well-known VC I worked with. I knew it had some holes in it. It was, after all, a work in progress. Sure enough, he told me it sounded like an old cartoon he'd seen of two scientists at a blackboard filled with equations. Right in the middle it said, "Then a miracle occurs . . ."

Some gaps are to be expected when you're building out your strategy, but often, what startups leave to be fleshed out later—little things like low-cost materials, availability of components, and infrastructure—become showstoppers down the road. Good VCs will always point out those gaps—and make sure you address them.

Most businesses fail for the most obvious reason: They run out of cash. For every founder who manages to bootstrap a startup, there are dozens or even hundreds that blow it because they don't want to give up a piece of the pie, they don't budget properly, they don't plan for how long it takes to raise rounds of funding, their burn rate is too high, or some combination thereof. VCs have a vested interest in ensuring that doesn't happen. That's their job.

The failure mode that really ticks me off is when entrepreneurs listen to bad advice from the wrong people. With all the hype over entrepreneurship, the quantity of information has gone way up while the quality has gone way down. That means entrepreneurs are getting lots of bad advice from unqualified sources. And when they actually get good advice that conflicts with what they've been told, they don't recognize it for what it is.

The founder of one promising startup I got involved with a couple of years back was getting so much conflicting advice from so many different people it stopped her dead in her tracks. Instead of getting out and raising seed money to demonstrate her concept, she became convinced that she had to do it on her own. She slipped further and further into debt and, to my knowledge, never launched a company that I think had a very good chance of making it. That sort of thing happens far too often these days.

Regardless of how you fund your company, it pays to think like a VC. The problem is, if you ask ten of them how they pick winners, evaluate business opportunities, and avoid the most treacherous pitfalls, you'll get ten different answers. But I've been around so long and worked with so many accomplished venture capitalists and entrepreneurs that I've boiled it down to four key questions you have to answer.

WHAT PROBLEM ARE YOU SOLVING?

An employee of a company I was working with once approached me about an invention he had no idea how to market. This man had invented the perfect paper clip. No, I'm not kidding. He had analyzed all the different styles of paper clips, found that each one was flawed, and come up with a clever new design.

I checked it out. Sure enough, this had to be the most perfect paper clip in the world.

Unfortunately, I was pretty sure there were no office workers sitting at their desks cursing their paper clips because they didn't work well enough. Nobody on earth saw this as a problem that needed to be solved. That's the problem with inventors: They come up with brilliant concepts that nobody needs or even wants. They devise elegant solutions to nonexistent problems. And they think that if they build it, customers will come.

When you question the wisdom of this approach, they say customers don't always know what they want until you show it to them. That may be true, but don't expect a VC to cough up a few million bucks on that principle alone.

Hundreds of investors have passed on what turned out to be incredibly disruptive technologies and products, but those are rare events. If you've got something cool you really believe in, by all means, shop it around and don't give up easily. If it's relatively cheap to do, then do it. Just know that you're shooting for the moon.

All things being equal, you're always better off coming up with a solid problem statement, a critical market need, or what VCs call a *customer pain point*. And whatever you do, don't confuse that with a cause or purpose. They're not the same.

Mark Zuckerberg didn't have some high and mighty purpose to Facebook, and it certainly didn't take very long to develop and launch it. But I would still argue that he had a problem statement: It bugged him that there was no website for comparing the looks of women on campus. For him, that was a problem, and he solved it. Look how that turned out.

Uber's a great example of a disruptive company with a pretty clear problem statement (my words, not theirs): You can never get a cab when you need one. Why isn't there an app for that?

Some problem statements are so big they seem daunting. Alibaba's was like that. China had a billion potential consumers and producers, but the nation lacked critical infrastructure for buying and selling merchandise. Who knew you could solve that enormous problem with an ecommerce site or two? Now Alibaba is one of the most valuable companies in the world.

Problem statements work for existing companies developing new products as well. Apple's executives have a novel way of envisioning new gadgets: They use themselves as focus groups. They think about what they would love to be able to do but can't, and then they come up with the simplest and most elegant way of doing it. In the absence of a Steve Jobs, however, it helps to have a team of very smart and savvy people to bounce ideas around. Besides, few companies have the kind of research and development resources Apple has at their disposal.

Solutions can also be very tricky. Most entrepreneurs come up with concepts, not complete products. That's fine as long as you understand the difference. Ideas and inventions may be fascinating to you, but consumers and businesses usually buy complete products they can actually use. There is a world of difference. And you need to plan to get from one to the other without needing a miracle in the middle.

The hands-down most critical aspect of solving a customer problem is that the solution needs to be far better than what's already out there. To do that, you must understand the competitive market.

HOW WILL YOU BEAT THE COMPETITION?

I'm always hearing from people who want to be entrepreneurs so badly that they rack their brains trying to come up with ideas for services and products. Besides not having a clear problem statement, they can never tell me why their solution, whatever it is, is going to beat the competition. The really sad thing is that they don't seem to think it matters.

If all you can come up with is a me-too product or service that's been done to death, you're just going to end up slugging it out with everyone and his brother on price. That's no way to make a living unless you don't mind eating out of dumpsters for the rest of your life.

Granted, markets aren't entirely zero-sum games. They can be elastic and grow over time, at least at a macro level. But as we've already discussed, every transaction still has just one winner and a bunch of losers. And if you don't have a solution that's better than the competition in some material way, you're sure to end up on the losing end of that equation.

There's a simple reason VCs like to say you have to come up with something ten times better than anything out there. People are creatures of habit, and they don't like change. So there's a cost associated with getting them to switch. That goes for consumers and businesses alike.

Even if your solution uses existing infrastructure—like an app for Apple iOS or Google Android—the *switching cost* may be low, but so are the barriers to entry. In other words, it may be easy for you to develop a product and enter the market, but it's just as easy for competitors to do the same. It's a double-edged sword.

And if your solution requires that customers do things differently— different sales channel, manufacturing methods, materials, whatever— you'd better have a damn good reason for them to make that leap. And while most budding entrepreneurs know the importance of differentiation, far too many don't really understand what it means. *Differentiation* and *different* are not the same.

Take Cake, for example. Not the food: the alternative rock band from Sacramento. When you hear Vince DiFiore's trumpet and singer John McCrea's conversational voice and clever lyrics, you instantly know it's them. And it clicks. Cake is unique in a way that delights fans and differentiates the group from its contemporaries.

Differentiation means different in some material or meaningful way from the customer's point of view. Differentiation is in the eye of the beholder, and the beholder is not you. If the customer doesn't perceive a unique value proposition, I don't care what it is, what it's made of, how it looks, how you make it, or what you call it, it won't sell.

A couple of years ago, I was approached by a former employee who had come up with an invention that made a new type of touch screen feasible. But at best, this new technology was only marginally better than what was already out there. In other words, it wasn't compelling enough for customers to switch.

Consumers and companies only change how they do things, what they buy, and whom they buy it from with good reason. If your reason isn't compelling, they won't switch.

Existing technology or old ways of doing things have an inherent advantage. It's called inertia. In addition to customer switching cost, competitors with existing solutions don't give up easily. History is full of examples from pen and paper to disk drives and CMOS chip technology. There are barriers to toppling the status quo, and sometimes old-school solutions and the powerful companies that market them hang on far longer than anyone would expect.

Another significant phenomenon that trips up entrepreneurs is that markets are not static. They change, often in unexpected ways. They're complex, have lots of moving parts, and are therefore hard to predict. Nevertheless, you've got to try. You've got to think ahead. As the great Wayne Gretzky is said to have opined, "I skate to where the puck is going to be, not where it has been."

You've got to understand the market if you hope to gain a significant share of it. You've got to intimately know your competitors if you hope to beat them. And if you are seeking significant capital, VCs need to see a significant market opportunity. They don't risk millions for a two or three times return on capital. They want to see a 20 or 30 times return. That means at least a $100 million to $1 billion market size, depending on its growth potential and the share you can credibly expect to get.

DO YOU HAVE THE RIGHT TEAM?

You may have heard that the most important thing VCs look at when they evaluate a startup is the team. That's true, but the reasons may not be as obvious as you'd think.

Business is all about people. I could say business is about understanding what motivates people and building lasting relationships with them, but that's like saying art is about paint and a canvas. There's a bit more to it than that.

If they're going to get in bed with you, so to speak, investors want to dig pretty deep to find out what really makes you tick. They don't just want to know your capabilities. They want to know who you are, how adaptable you are, what motivates you, and how you'll act in a crisis. They want to know your true colors before they write you a check.

VCs will never admit to this, but that's one of the reasons it takes so long to get funded. Time may not be on your side, but it's on theirs. Obviously they don't want to risk losing anything critical, like your market window, but the longer they observe you under different conditions, the better.

Of course, they want to know you're a strong leader with a solid team that can do the job. They want to know all about your team, their background, and why they're uniquely qualified to run your venture and deliver its solution to market. They want to know if there are any significant holes and how you plan to fill them. They want to know how effectively you can scale to meet the goals of your business plan.

But just as important, they want to know if you're a smart decision maker. They want to know how flexible and capable you are at pivoting if and when your plans don't pan out. They want to know if you have what it takes to survive through all the inevitable hurdles you'll face because, more often than not, that's what startup success comes down to.

Lots of entrepreneurs are simply not in it for the long run or for the right reasons. Some founders just can't get along. Still others are out to make a quick buck and aren't committed to the business. And some management teams simply fall apart when the initial strategy fails, as it so often does.

There are also basics of project management and building and motivating a team that every founder has to learn to successfully run a venture. I see startups all the time with founders who have no idea how to hire, manage, and retain talented people. Many have gaping holes where key capabilities need to be. It doesn't bode well for them.

If you think you have what it takes to run a startup, get ready to work 24/7 and wear all sorts of hats. Make sure everyone you hire is motivated to do the same. It comes with the territory. If that workaholic energy level isn't there, chances are you're not going to make it.

And all those things VCs want to know about you and your team? You need to know them too . . . about yourself. It's a good idea to take a long, hard look in the mirror before you take the plunge.

DO YOU HAVE A CREDIBLE BUSINESS PLAN?

Would you like to know a little secret of the business world? Very few people are born business wizards. No, I'm not trying to be funny. I know nobody's actually born that way. What I mean is, I don't know too many people who actually get excited about income statements, balance sheets, and capitalization plans. And I'm no exception.

While I may have an aptitude for math and a head for numbers, my great love growing up was science, and later, technology. And yet that wasn't enough to make it in the startup world.

I hadn't yet discovered the wonders of marketing when I landed that job at Stac, the one we talked about back in Chapter 5. At 34, I suddenly found myself on the executive management team of a fast-growing startup on a fast track to an IPO. That's when I saw the writing on the wall. Actually, it was on the cover of a book Stac's CEO Clow tossed at me one day in his office after I'd said something that revealed just how little I knew about finance and operations.

The book was called *What Every Manager Needs to Know About Finance* edited by Hubert D. Vos. I read it in a day, and that's when it first dawned on me that running a company was all about business and money. And, since that's what I wanted to do for a living, I needed to learn how it all worked. So I did.

The point is, if you want to run a business, you've got to understand how a business works. It has to be about more than just your great idea or product. Finance, raising capital, marketing, operations, they all go hand in hand. So when I say the words *business plan*, I don't want you to roll your eyes or get scared. It doesn't have to be 20 pages of spreadsheets. You just need a reasonable idea of how to get your business to the point where its growth is somewhat self-sustaining. And to do that, you have to make sure you always have enough money in the bank. You've got to do the math.

I know I said it before, but it's worth repeating: The absolute number one failure mode for startups and small businesses is to run out of cash. There was a time when you could bootstrap a company, but markets are so hypercompetitive these days it's much harder than it used to be. I'm not a big fan of Kickstarter or any other type of crowdfunding, either. If you can't sell at least one or two professional investors on your idea, you're probably not ready for prime time.

The sad truth is most companies that contact me for advice have no chance of making it because they tried to bootstrap it, are already short on cash, and have backed themselves into a corner with no time left to raise capital. Starting a business is like entering a poker game: Even if you're good, luck may not be on your side. So even if you make the right bets, you've got to have enough of a war chest to fund a few risks and keep you in the game over the long haul.

You can and certainly should raise rounds of funding as you go, but you can't just do it on the fly. It can take at least six months to raise money, so you've got to make sure your capital pipeline is synchronized with your business growth. It's also important to achieve business milestones before each round so your valuation continues to increase and you're always parting with less equity each time you raise capital.

That's why you need to have a plan that essentially consists of three things, in order:

1. Go-to-market plan, including market share assumptions, phases, and milestones

2. Expense and revenue plan that rolls up to a multiyear income statement

3. Capitalization plan that keeps the pipeline full of cash to pay the bills and fund growth

If this all seems like Greek to you and you'd rather get a colonoscopy than even think about it, then you understand exactly why most startups fail and most small businesses never end up making money. Their founders love what they do and think they can get by without understanding the business side.

As I sat down to write this chapter, I actually started making a list of startups I'd heard from over the years that fit that description. It's a long, long list that includes every type of company you can think of, from baking and moviemaking to internet TV and app development. They either came to me too late or just didn't want to listen. And they all failed.

I simply can't overstate how important it is for you to get this. And while your first instinct may be to farm out what you're not into, the more hands-on you are with your business, the better your odds of making it. Don't get me wrong—I'm not saying you have to do your own bookkeeping. But a startup CEO or business owner who can't read an income statement or a balance sheet is just asking for trouble.

Look, it's not easy starting and growing a business. If it were, every startup would succeed. But we live in an era of unprecedented global competition. The internet may have leveled the playing field and made it easy to get started, but that's also why there's so much competition for the same limited ad dollars, page views, expense budgets, and sets of eyeballs.

I don't care how inspired or passionate you are. Like it or not, there are laws of physics, finance, and human nature your ego simply cannot overcome. By all means, do what you love. Reach for the stars. But if you don't keep your feet planted firmly on the ground, you're just going to end up floating away. And trust me when I tell you there are no customers up there in the clouds. Just a lot of hot air and water vapor.

That's why you should think like a VC as you build your business. Imagine you've got to pitch them and make sure you've got your bases covered. Even if you plan to self-fund or raise seed capital from friends and family, get out and pitch some VCs anyway, and listen carefully to what they say. Just keep in mind that they tend to be very polite, so you've sometimes got to read between the lines to get what they're really saying.

Perhaps the most important advice I can give you is this: If your first venture fails, it's worth spending time to understand what went wrong. That's the only way you're going to improve the odds of making it next time. And, yes, there will be a next time. That isn't rocket science. It's just Startup 101.

CHAPTER 14

BUSINESS IS
ALL ABOUT
RELATIONSHIPS

THE WORD *RELATIONSHIP* USUALLY CONJURES UP IMAGES OF loved ones: friends, family members, and significant others. I'm probably the last person you'd want to get that sort of relationship advice from. But business relationships are another story, and they are arguably just as important as personal ones.

If you ask ten entrepreneurs for the key to business success, you'll likely get ten different answers. I'm sure at least one would say it's all about the product, and that's true—that is a key factor. It's just not *the* key factor.

The key to business success is winning and keeping customers. And product innovation aside, the biggest factor in winning and keeping customers is relationships. The world's greatest business minds, from Peter Drucker and Mark McCormack to Regis McKenna and Theodore Levitt, have all said the same thing in one way or another, and they're right.

Unfortunately, you, my friends, have all been sold a bill of goods. You've been told over and over that building your personal brand, growing your online social network, improving your productivity, identifying and enhancing your strengths, and engaging your employees, among other things, will make you successful. They won't.

No matter what you do for a living or aspire to become, none of those fads du jour will have a material impact on how things turn out for you or your business. But building relationships with people in the real world will.

There's a reason why CEOs consistently say their network is their most important professional asset. It's unfortunate that the word *network* has become synonymous with online social network, because that's not what CEOs mean. They mean their *real* network—the people they actually know and work with every day.

Here's how it works.

The higher you climb up the corporate ladder, the higher the stakes, the bigger the deals, and the more important everything becomes. With so much on the line, the people you want to do any kind of significant business with want to look you in the eye, get to know you, and see how you behave before committing. They have to know you're who you say you are and will do what you say you'll do before they can feel confident that you'll deliver. Credibility breeds trust, but you have to earn it first. And vice versa.

Even with ecommerce, most transactions are still between two human beings. Think about it. Every significant B2C and B2B transaction still involves a buyer and a seller, not to mention all the channel development and pre- and post-sales support. And the best product doesn't necessarily win. Buyer behavior is mostly subjective, and relationships are a big factor. In a service business, they're the biggest factor, hands down.

There's a lot of risk associated with bad business deals, and relationships go a long way toward diminishing that risk. In addition, companies have to stay lean these days, and that means having fewer, stronger relationships. That's why manufacturers minimize their number of vendors, suppliers, and components. It's more cost-effective that way.

It may be easier than ever to work and communicate virtually, but all that does is level the playing field, meaning there's nothing to distinguish a relationship in the virtual world. There's no real connection, no real bond, and when push comes to shove—as it so often does in business—you can't expect online connections to do anything special or go the extra mile for you, or you for them.

Personal relationships create a level of engagement, intimacy, credibility, and trust that simply doesn't exist in the virtual world. I would easily take one strong relationship in the real world over 1,000 social media friends, fans, or followers. Maybe even 10,000.

PEOPLE PEOPLE

You'd be surprised to know just how many business relationships you have. We don't even think about it because they're so intricately infused into nearly every aspect of our lives. Accountants, lawyers, doctors, dentists, brokers, insurance agents, auto and home repair professionals, delivery people, utility service people—it's a long list.

To all these people, you're a customer. You matter.

When it comes to your livelihood, business relationships get even more involved. At work you have a boss or two, coworkers, and staff. If you own a business or run a company, you have employees, investors, vendors, and customers. You have IT, HR, benefits, and finance people.

You don't just do business with all these people. You relate to them on all sorts of different levels—more than you realize. And how you engage and interact with them has a surprisingly significant impact on your career and business. Any one of these people can change your life. And in all likelihood, many of them will over the long haul. They've certainly changed mine.

If you recall from Chapter 5, I learned how to sell at a rep firm owned by a phenomenal salesman named Phil Richards. That was actually the first time I worked from home. I got a bunch of furniture from Ikea and used the second bedroom of our Redondo Beach townhome as my office. I had a PC, a printer, and a fax machine, but the hands-down most important thing in that office was the telephone.

I had just gotten off the phone with a product manager from a chip company we represented when I looked up to see my wife in the doorway. I had no idea how long she'd been there, but she had a disapproving look on her face. You know, the one that makes you feel like you've done something wrong.

"What's the matter?" I asked.

"Aren't you supposed to be working?" she said.

"I *am* working," I replied, maybe a little more defensively than I'd intended.

"No, you're not," she said. "I heard you. You were just bullshitting."

"Well, yeah," I said. "Like I said, I'm working."

She just turned and walked away, shaking her head. At that point, I'm sure she was having second thoughts about my switch from engineering management to sales. She just didn't get that schmoozing was a really important part of relationship building . . . and the job.

When I'd come home from a long day of calling on customers, she'd ask, "Did you book anything?" I knew she was just giving me a hard time, but it drove me nuts. Selling custom-designed semiconductors in multimillion-dollar deals to big companies like Hughes and Xerox took a lot of time, work, and, yes, relationship building.

There's actually a very good reason we call it relationship *building*. You don't go out and *obtain* or *acquire* relationships. You *build* them. You *develop* them. Building and developing anything of substantial value takes time, effort, and commitment.

The longer the relationship, the stronger the relationship, the more valuable the relationship. That's an axiom you should never forget.

Many years later, after my long climb up the corporate ladder, Phil and I reconnected. He had sold his rep company and was interviewing to be the sales veep at a public company and needed a reference, which I was all-too-happy to provide. He got the job.

After that we stayed in touch and, when it came time to return the favor, Phil hooked me up with two opportunities. One was with his running buddy, Bruce McWilliams, who also happened to be the newly appointed CEO of a late-stage startup I mentioned in Chapter 1, Tessera. Tessera turned out to be a great fit as well as a financial bonanza when the company finally went public years later. Bruce also became a good friend and a long-term consulting client.

That story spanned 20 years, so thoughts of quid pro quo obviously never crossed my or Phil's mind. We were just doing what came naturally to us. I'm a people person. So is Phil. We're people people.

I like getting to know people. I like helping them. I like sharing ideas and joking around. I like building relationships. To me, relationships are not a means to an end. I was just having fun and doing my job. But you can't argue with the results. Looking back, those relationships I spent years building had a far greater impact on my career than any other factor.

Relationships are just like watching grass grow. You can't see anything happening, but one day you wake up to a beautiful lawn. If you have no patience for that sort of thing, you'll never be successful in business, at least not over the long haul.

WHY I LIKE GOING TO THE DENTIST

I broke a crown over the holidays and got to visit my dentist, Lisa.

That's right, I just said something that sounded a lot like I was looking forward to seeing my dentist. No, I'm not a masochist. I've just been seeing her for as far back as I can remember. She and her husband, also a dentist, actually bought the practice from my previous dentist. He was referred to me way back in the 1990s by my administrative assistant at OPTi. He's her dad.

If that sounds a bit incestuous, that's sort of the point. I have relationships with these people. That's why I stick with my dentist. I like her, and I like doing business with her. She's good, fair, and reasonable. I like her husband, too, and I've known their staff for more than two decades now. I trust them all. Why would I switch? The same goes for many of my personal and business relationships.

I've been working with the same accountant for 20 years. Steve says I'm high-maintenance, but he hasn't dumped me yet. He also says he's going to retire in a few years. I'm sure he's looking forward to it, but I'm not.

My State Farm agent recently retired. We'd been together since I first stepped foot in California back in 1987. I'm pretty bummed about it.

I go back at least a decade with my auto mechanic Rick, and Heidi, who cuts my hair. Sure, all these folks are very good at what they do, and I guess I'm a good customer, but that doesn't mean we haven't had our ups and downs. But you know, relationships can survive the occasional bump in the road. We're all willing to put up with a few mistakes or idiosyncrasies for people we like, trust, and have history with.

Customers can become very attached to people they feel a connection with. All things being equal, we will always do business with those we like, respect, and trust. And we will not switch. That's because business relationships are important to us. They matter. They matter a lot.

ENGAGE WITH PURPOSE

Have you ever met someone wealthy or famous and come away thinking, wow, he's just like a regular guy? Nearly all the highly successful businesspeople I've known come across that way. The thing is, they're not regular guys. They just appear that way.

I'm not saying they put on a façade. It's more that, while they can be quite charming and disarming, there's a lot more going on under the hood than you realize.

While all these people have distinguishing characteristics, there are advantages to not wearing success on your sleeve. Since business is all about building relationships and information is power, for lack of a better term, you don't want everyone around you putting their guard up. That's why you need to let your guard down, at least somewhat.

Still, there's far more to that process than meets the eye.

Before we go any further, I want to make one important point. We may live in an era of unprecedented access to information, but the internet leveled the playing field for everyone. Since everyone has access to the same information, it presents absolutely no competitive advantage.

In other words, critical information you can use to advance your business will almost always come from people in the real world. That's another value add for relationships.

So any time you meet a person, that's an opportunity to learn about her, what motivates her, and what she knows about others. It's an opportunity to gain information about her company and products that not everyone knows. It's an opportunity to gain a competitive advantage and make smarter, better informed decisions. And, of course, it's an opportunity to build a relationship.

Those who've been around the block don't give up important information easily. But they're more likely to do so if there's a level of engagement, openness, and trust in the relationship. So savvy businesspeople let their guard down a bit so information can flow readily in their direction. They may ask leading questions to fill in the blanks and get to know you better. That's all part of the process of determining who you are and how you fit into the scheme of things.

It may seem informal, but they're building a picture of you in their minds. And make no mistake, information does not flow back the other way unless they want it to. They may give up a little to get more in return, but successful businesspeople rarely give up more than they have to or intend to.

Over the years I've had the good fortune to observe and learn from some notable venture capitalists and entrepreneurs who sat on the boards of the companies where I worked. There was Bill Davidow of Mohr Davidow Ventures, L.J. Sevin of Sevin Rosen Funds, Adobe cofounder Chuck Geschke, Benchmark Capital's Bruce Dunlevie, Berry Cash of InterWest Partners, and the incomparable politician Jack Kemp, to name a few.

They all came across as regular guys (except Kemp, but he's a special case we'll get to later). They were all comfortable in their own skin and didn't take themselves too seriously. They were always generous with their time and advice. And they were all confident, competent, and consistent. These were solid, grounded people who knew themselves well.

But I could definitely discern a big shift in demeanor as I transitioned from an unknown quantity to a trusted associate who sat in the boardroom as part of the leadership team. That's no accident. There's a notable progression in how these people engage with others, gain information, and build relationships.

When I first met Davidow, for example, it was in his office. I was being considered for senior veep of worldwide marketing at Rambus, a publicly traded technology company where he was chairman. It's typical for CEOs to bounce their choice for a key executive position off an appropriate board director or two.

Davidow wasn't always a VC; he has a Ph.D. in electrical engineering and was the marketing and sales genius behind the launch of Intel's vaunted x86 microprocessors that have since dominated the personal computer industry. In other words, Davidow was an integral part of a leadership team that spawned an empire.

Although my resume was nothing to sneeze at, I still found myself a bit in awe of the legend who literally wrote the book on *Marketing High Technology*. Our first one-on-one began with the usual chitchat about people and places where our paths may have crossed, that sort of thing.

Davidow was charming and disarming; I probably was too. That's not to make it sound contrived; it does tend to come naturally when you've been doing it as long as we have. But I'm guessing he wanted to get me to lower my guard and reveal who I really was and how my mind worked, and I wanted him to see me as a comrade rather than an interview candidate. His plan worked—mine, not so much.

One moment we were talking like old friends; the next moment the grilling began. Nevertheless, this wasn't my first interview, so everything went well. He got to see the real me, and I got the job.

Our next one-on-one was much different. We met for lunch at a Palo Alto sushi restaurant, and as he walked in, I remember thinking,

"Damn, he's in really good shape for his age." I'm not exactly a fitness nut, but I'm a runner, and I thought we might have that in common. Besides, I'd just had knee surgery and still had quite a bit of swelling and discomfort, so it was on my mind. I said, "You know, you look great, Bill. How do you stay in shape?"

He looked at me with a wry smile and said, "Steve, you have no idea how much work it takes to look this good at my age." That, I remember thinking, is the real Bill Davidow. That sort of endearing, self-deprecating humor reminded me of something Warren Buffett once said: "I buy expensive suits. They just look cheap on me."

Clearly our relationship had changed, and that was significant. My purpose for the lunch was to share my thoughts on the company's strategic direction and a plan to address it in the context of a rebranding effort. At a minimum, I wanted his feedback, but I also thought his support would be very good to have.

At the next board meeting, I watched as one of our top executives pitched an acquisition and Davidow shot it down because, as he put it, our corporate strategy was unclear so there was no way to determine if the acquisition made sense or not.

I learned two things from my lunch with our chairman and the subsequent board meeting. First, I was right to learn what his thoughts were and seek his support. He was certainly a force to be reckoned with in the boardroom. Second, we were clearly on the same page.

At the following board meeting, I pitched my plan, got it approved, and six months later, a new corporate strategy emerged from the effort.

I believe that was also the meeting where Geschke shared the terrifying story of how he'd been kidnapped at gunpoint and held for ransom for a week. It was his wife's courage to bring in the authorities that enabled the FBI to catch the kidnappers and possibly save Geschke's life. It was a deeply emotional story, but he wanted us to take physical security seriously, so he told it.

That may seem an unrelated point, but it's not. If you view engaging others and building relationships as a gratuitous means to an end, you're not being entirely genuine and you won't be very effective at it, or as effective as you can be. But that doesn't mean you should always walk around with your guard down and your heart on your sleeve, either.

There's a time and place to seek information and a time and place to share openly, but it's not always obvious which is which. While this might sound like a counterintuitive, it's not always best to approach a casual one-on-one casually or a formal board meeting formally.

In business, the ability to build relationships can lead to opportunity, information, power, and competitive advantage. It's good to be a people person, but learn how and when to use it and engage others with purpose.

RELATIONSHIPS, TEXAS STYLE

I didn't mention the late, great Jack Kemp to namedrop, but for a purpose. The NFL star and politician extraordinaire sat on the board of Cyrix, the Dallas-based microprocessor maker where I cut my teeth as a marketing veep, as we discussed in Chapter 10. It's also where I learned some of the most powerful relationship lessons of my career.

It was a tradition for Cyrix to host annual strategy off-sites, usually in Santa Fe, New Mexico, where our chairman, Berry Cash, had a second home. These were relatively intimate multiday events with maybe 11 or 12 of us, and the first one I attended was soon after joining the company.

On the first day, one of our executives pitched a controversial strategy that would have us making our own personal computers and essentially competing with our customers. When he was finished, we went around the room, as was customary, to hear everyone's opinion. When it got around to L.J.—one of the most successful VCs at the time—he thought about it for a moment and said, "I don't know," in his characteristic Louisiana drawl. "This whole thing just makes my butt pucker."

That broke the tension in the room. I was grateful because I was next, and, as the new guy, I wasn't looking forward to being the sole negatron in the room. I just said, "I agree with L.J."

That night we had cocktails and dinner at Berry's house and I saw something I'd never seen before: a world-class politician work a room.

Kemp was a big guy, but his personality was enormous. He was bigger than life. The remarkable thing is that none of it was fake. He was the real deal. He actually took the time to get to know me.

A few months later I attended a speech he gave to a small-business group in Dallas. As he entered the room he stopped where I was standing with another Cyrix exec, flashed a big smile, flipped up my tie, and said, "Nice tie, Tobak. Breaking out the spring wardrobe?"

I'm not sure what impressed me more: how casual he was, his sense of humor, or that he remembered my name.

Kemp wasn't *just* a relationship guy, either. He was a fierce advocate for small-business America. His speech that day was so motivating and got me so pumped full of adrenaline that all I wanted to do afterward was go out and kick some competitive ass.

Speaking of which, Cyrix competed head-on with the biggest semiconductor company in the world that dominated the PC industry, Intel. The Santa Clara chip giant had orders of magnitude more capital and resources than we did, but that didn't stop our engineers from designing state-of-the-art processors that competed with Intel's best.

Likewise, I knew I was going to have to fight lean and mean and capitalize on every opportunity to win over customers and the media on a tiny budget, but that too came down to relationships.

Our founding chief executive, Jerry Rogers, was a raucous, outspoken guy who had no love for the media, didn't trust customers, and considered everything related to marketing and sales to be a necessary evil. He commonly made over-the-top claims and used the press to set unrealistic performance and delivery targets that drove our engineers crazy. As a result, the company had lost much of its credibility and developed a somewhat bad reputation.

Still, Rogers' technical competency and competitive determination had gotten the company to that point, and he deserves credit for realizing that, in some ways, he was doing more harm than good. My job was to insert myself between him and the outside world, repair the relationships that had been burned, repair our negative brand image, and win back customers. So that's what I set out to do.

I worked closely with our engineering and sales teams, hired a top-notch PR agency, courted key infrastructure partners, and went to work on influential analysts and pundits. Besides a great deal of strategy and positioning, turning things around mostly came down to identifying and meeting with key constituents and building trust and credibility through long-term relationships.

After seeing a key Microsoft executive named Carl Stork present at an industry conference, I decided to sit at his table for dinner. After all, he was the man responsible for working with microprocessor companies, including ours. We got to know each other a bit, and then, at an evening mixer at another conference, I ran into him again. We sat together during the conference and had dinner and drinks with some others the following evening. We seemed to develop a real connection.

To make a long story short, I flew to Redmond, Washington, on several occasions for meetings with Stork and others at Microsoft, and when I did, he and I would sometimes catch a Seattle Mariners game, since he was one of the team owners. Of course I genuinely liked hanging out with Carl, but our relationship also led to greater cooperation between our companies that paid off in many ways.

Likewise, I met with key analysts, media pundits, and journalists wherever and whenever I could. Besides bringing them into the fold on our technology and product plans, we would sometimes go out for dinner and drinks or attend parties at industry trade shows. That blossomed into many more connections and relationships. You can see where this is going.

As Cyrix's engineers executed on our technology and product plans, we eventually built our credibility back to where it deserved to be, and everyone who mattered began warming up to us again. Our press and analyst coverage turned from negative to positive, we were better aligned with infrastructure partners, and our customer relationships began to improve as well.

Perhaps the most powerful evidence that we had turned things around came when, on two separate occasions, researchers thought they'd discovered a bug in our microprocessors. That might have quickly turned into a PR catastrophe and thousands of returns, but, thanks to our solid relationships with Microsoft and the media, we kept it from happening. In one case we issued a software patch and in another we traced the problem to another chipset on the motherboard.

In both cases our relationships helped us mitigate a crisis.

Nevertheless, Cyrix was plagued by poor decision making that took our operating results deep into the red. Rogers was eventually asked to resign, and the board appointed CFO Jay Swent to run the company.

What Swent lacked in technical ability, he more than made up for in business savvy and operating smarts. He was no Jack Kemp, but he did have a healthy sense of humor and respect for everyone who worked for him. We developed a solid relationship, and I don't think I've ever loved my job as much or felt more motivated before or since.

Most important, we partnered with Compaq to launch the world's first sub-$1,000 personal computer and launched the WebPAD—the first internet tablet that, while admittedly clumsy and bulky, was 13 years ahead of Apple's iPad. Those launches were huge industry milestones and front-page news around the world.

After successfully repositioning the company as a leader in low-cost computing, we were acquired by National Semiconductor, a remarkable outcome considering we were nearly bankrupt a year earlier.

While Rogers' demise might come across as an indictment of the kind of hard-driving, hyper-competitive, "ends justify the means" leadership style we often see in high-tech founders, it's not. If he were not exactly the way he was, there never would have been a Cyrix to begin with.

Among the many lessons I learned at Cyrix, none was more paramount than the importance of relationships in business. No person is an island, and no company goes straight up and to the right. When you hit those inevitable hurdles and pitfalls on the road to point B, you will need relationships to carry you through.

YOU'RE NOT AS INTROVERTED AS YOU THINK

At this point I would hope you're convinced that building relationships is important. If you're an extrovert, you're probably feeling pretty good. If not, you're probably feeling a bit uncomfortable. You may even be wondering if this relationship-building thing is something you're born with or a set of skills you can learn and develop.

Well, I've got good news for introverts and perhaps a bit of a damper for the rest of you. Relationships have absolutely nothing to do with any of that. There are just three things you need to know.

First, while some aspects of your personality may be genetic, you're still born with an enormous sponge called a brain. As such, most of your behavior is learned and you do have the ability to change it, even if it feels ingrained or forces you outside your comfort zone. Don't lock yourself into a box of your own making.

Second, your success is to a great extent based on how you interact with others. If that penetrates the gray matter and resonates with you on an emotional level, you'll be more aware of your behavior, more motivated to engage with stakeholders, and more open to listening to what matters to them.

Third, remember this isn't about falling in love or becoming best friends (even though I've used those analogies to help illustrate some points). It's about connecting with others on a level you're both comfortable with. It can be all about business, or maybe you'll find something else in common. The important thing is to be genuine and try to be open and responsive to others' wants and needs. And if you want someone to drop their guard, drop yours first.

Being somewhat introverted didn't stop L.J., Carl, Jay, or hundreds of other entrepreneurs, executives, and business leaders I've known over the years from building great relationships and becoming remarkably successful. In my experience, business engagement transcends those kinds of generalizations.

As we discussed in Part I, humans are made to connect with others. Our limbic systems reward us for it. It's no coincidence that business is about people and people are about relationships. Just remember it's relationships with people in the real world you're after, not virtual relationships with avatars in cyberspace. Keep it real. That's the key.

CHAPTER 15

DESTIGMATIZING SALES

I F SOMEBODY HAD TOLD ME YEARS AGO THAT AN ENTIRE generation of entrepreneurs would be trying to learn how to sell from writers, researchers, and consultants who've never sold a product or managed a sales force in their lives—whose only real experience in business is selling books, seminars, and speaking engagements—I wouldn't have believed it.

And yet, here we are. The blogosphere and bookstores are full of content from what I can only describe as self-serving shysters with a tight sound bite and an inspirational story that they use to sucker small-business owners into coughing up their money and buying into a gimmick.

So let me start by telling you there is no magic to selling. It's just a critical business function that, for better or worse, has gotten a bad rap. So I'm going to destigmatize it, shatter some popular myths, and share some useful insights learned the hard way, on the job.

After all, selling isn't rocket science; it's just a skill set, honed through experience. There's simply not that much to it, at least in terms of what you can learn from a book. Most of it's pretty intuitive because it's consistent with behavior you've learned over the course of your life, although you may not realize it.

The most important thing you need to know is the one thing I keep saying over and over, and it's worth repeating: Businesses exist for just one purpose, to win and keep customers. And while sales is but one aspect of making that happen (we'll discuss the others in subsequent chapters), it is where the rubber meets the road. Here's how real sales leaders build long-term relationships with key customers in competitive markets.

YOU'RE NOT SELLING USED CARS

I remember the day I called my parents to tell them I was transitioning into sales after a decade in engineering management. There was dead silence on the phone, and then my dad said, "You mean like a car salesman?"

"No, Dad," I said, "I'm going to sell semiconductor chips."

"What's the difference?" he asked.

Again silence, but this time it was mine. Not only did I not know the answer, but I'd also been wondering the same thing myself.

It turns out there's an enormous difference.

We all have an image of a salesperson as a fast-talking shyster who will stop at nothing to close a deal, which is usually selling you something you don't need for more than you can afford.

Today, more than a quarter century after that phone call, I see sales in a completely different light: as the fulfillment of a successful business relationship—providing products customers want at a price they are willing to pay. Both parties should be satisfied. If they're not, you're doing something wrong.

This is how sales interactions should go, at least in my mind. First ask questions and listen to determine the customer's needs. Then figure out if you have a product that's right for them, and, if so, tell them about it. Finally I think about the big picture, the customer's long-term strategic value, and whether it represents an opportunity worth pursuing in terms of time and resources. Contrary to what you might think, a transaction should be the farthest thing from your mind. That comes later.

Obviously there are all sorts of nuances depending on the type of product, whether the customer's a consumer or a large corporation, and whether it's a one-time deal or a long-term strategic relationship with large potential. Nevertheless, a deal either makes sense or it doesn't. And if it doesn't make sense for you or the customer, it shouldn't happen. Period. If a deal does make sense, then it's your job to win the business or build a relationship and win long-term, as the case may be.

If you're uncomfortable with selling—if you feel the need to be aggressive, pushy, or coercive—then something's wrong. You either learned from one of those posers I mentioned earlier, are selling the wrong products to the wrong customers, or are in the wrong business entirely. Not to make it sound overly simplistic, but for the most part, good business is usually a win-win affair, more or less. At least it should be.

And if you're selling an undifferentiated product based solely on price or silly sales tactics, I think you should quit and find a better job. End of story.

SELLING IS A MARATHON, NOT A SPRINT

Selling is a process—an often long and arduous one. The bigger the opportunity, the more strategic the relationship, the longer it takes to make something happen, and the more committed to the effort you need to be to win over the long haul.

If you think about it, that's exactly as it should be. After all, none of the best things in life are ever easy to attain.

On the plus side, big, lucrative long-term opportunities allow more time to build a solid foundation for enduring customer relationships. The risk is bigger, but so is the reward. If you're a people person who's good at building relationships and you have the capital to hang in there over the long haul, you'll have a competitive advantage.

Selling is very much a game of give and take. You give a little; you get a little. Rinse and repeat.

In your first serious meeting with a customer, for example, you might provide just a general outline of your company and product lines and then ask them for the same so you can at least determine if there's a potential fit. Sometimes the order is reversed. It just depends. Once you determine what they're trying to do and understand their needs, you're better equipped to provide a solution. If, on the other hand, you spill your guts all at once and they say "Not interested," you've provided a ton of information, gotten nothing in return, and possibly blown your only chance to get your foot in the door. It's like losing a battle without firing a single shot.

If you want to succeed in the end, you don't want to say too much or push too hard in the beginning. The more you learn about your customer, the better your chances of winning. Think of it as a game of successive approximation.

There are, of course, strategic considerations involving channel development, geographic expansion, and organizational structure, but a book isn't exactly the right forum to teach you how to build a worldwide sales force. That said, you always want to start with the channel and geography that make the most sense and expand in discrete, well-planned, well-funded phases over time.

Selling is a lot like your career. Come to think of it, it's a lot like life. It's a marathon, not a sprint. Take your time and do it right. It'll pay off in the end.

GO BIG OR GO HOME

I'm sure you've heard of the 80/20 rule. It essentially means you should spend the vast majority of your effort on your biggest potential customers because that's where most of your revenue will come from. Amen to that.

When you see an opportunity to get your foot in the door with one of the big guys, even if it's the tiniest crack, do whatever it takes to get something going. Jump through as many hoops as you have to. How you perform on that one opportunity might make all the difference, as it did when I won my first big customer.

Back in the early days of the personal computer, I had an opportunity to pitch the fastest-growing company in the industry, Compaq Computer. All the big semiconductor chip makers wanted a piece of this hot company's business, and mine was no exception.

I'll never forget what my boss said to me in the copy room as I was printing out my pitch before leaving for the airport. He said, "This is important. Don't fuck it up." That put the fear of God into me, but I took it as a challenge. There was no way I was going to screw up that opportunity.

So I flew to Houston and met with their PC development team. It was the first time I had ever visited a big potential customer on my own. I was terrified.

As it turned out, nearly all the custom chips in Compaq's PCs used standard industry technology, so there was no way for me to differentiate our chips vs. our competitors'. Besides, they were happy with their current vendors. At first, I thought we were screwed.

But there was a new manufacturing process Compaq needed for a couple of high-end chips, and mine was one of only a few companies that had it. The problem was the software. Nobody had yet developed the tools to design chips with this new technology.

I immediately knew that was the one and only opportunity to get our foot in the door. So I went out on a limb and promised to deliver it, although I had absolutely no idea how I was going to make that happen and they made no commitment on their part, either. It was a big risk, but my gut told me it had to be done this way or not at all.

When I got back to the office, I made another pitch, this time to my own company, to fast-track the software development for what I hoped would become my first big customer win. They turned me down flat, saying they didn't have the resources to commit on a hope and a prayer.

I was devastated, but I didn't give up. I had made a commitment, and I'd be damned if I wasn't going to find a way to make it happen. So I decided to develop the software tools Compaq needed myself.

In addition to my regular job, I worked long nights for the next few months and ultimately delivered the goods as I said I would.

Compaq was so impressed with the support that they not only awarded us their high-end chip business but ultimately gave us a big share of their standard chips as well. And as Compaq grew to become one of the top PC makers in the world, it became one of my company's biggest customers in the U.S.

I know this sounds a bit chicken and egg-ish, but if you don't take risks and go out on a limb for those big customers, you've got exactly zero chance of winning their business, because one of your competitors will. Figure out what your customer needs, tell them you'll do it, and move heaven and earth to deliver the goods, even if it means working 24/7 for a few months. And don't screw it up.

NEVER TURN DOWN A PAYING CUSTOMER

Speaking of sales fads, the latest feel-good advice making the rounds is that you should be highly selective about the business you are willing to do and the clients you want to engage with. After all, if you have to focus, and you should, then why not focus on the kind of work you want to do and the kind of people you want to work with?

Sounds reasonable, doesn't it? It does . . . if you don't mind living hand-to-mouth for the rest of your life.

In 30-plus years, I've never once seen that strategy work. More important, some of the world's most famous entrepreneurs and companies would never have achieved a fraction of their success if they'd followed that ludicrous advice. You may have already heard a version of the following story before, but this is my take on what happened.

In the summer of 1980, a bunch of suits from IBM flew to Seattle to meet with Bill Gates, a geek who ran a startup called Microsoft. IBM was looking for an operating system for a new product called a personal computer. At the time, Gates was into programming languages, so he referred them to Digital Research Inc. (DRI), where Gary Kildall had developed the popular CP/M operating system.

When the suits showed up at DRI, they met with Kildall's business manager, who also happened to be his wife. She refused to sign IBM's NDA—not a good start. And while they met with Gary eventually, they weren't able to reach an agreement to license CP/M.

So the IBMers went back to Gates, who finally agreed to help them out. He bought QDOS from Seattle programmer Tim Paterson for $50,000, made some changes to it, and licensed it to IBM on a nonexclusive basis for a per-copy royalty fee. That, of course, is how Gates became the richest man in the world and chairman of one of the most powerful companies in history.

The lesson is simple and clear. While IBM wasn't either founder's ideal customer—Gates because he didn't do operating systems and Kildall because he didn't like the suits—Gates was far more flexible than Kildall.

When I say never turn down a paying customer, I don't mean it literally. Of course you need to focus, and there's obviously more than one criterion for doing business with a customer. That said, you should always be open and flexible for a very important reason: Customers typically know their needs and how you can serve them better than you do. They're often aware of new trends, and sometimes they come up with market-making breakthroughs, as was the case with IBM.

That's why the vast majority of successful startups don't make it big with their first idea. They learn from their customers. They learn from the market. And if they're smart, they adapt.

Also, characterizing or judging a potential customer in any way other than in business terms is, to be blunt, idiotic. You never know if someone in a suit or torn jeans is going to become your biggest customer.

YOU'RE ALWAYS SELLING

As I alluded to above, you're really not new to selling. I'd be willing to bet that every single one of you has used persuasive means to get what you want over the years, starting with influencing your parents, siblings, and friends to do your bidding. In all likelihood, you've never really stopped.

Whether you're pitching investors on a new concept, a potential partner on joining you, your board on a risky strategy, or your spouse on supporting your new venture, business owners are always selling something to somebody, more or less.

Motivation and manipulation are two sides of the same coin. You've actually been motivating and manipulating people since you were born. You're probably better at it than you realize. And it's not a bad thing as long as nobody loses . . . except your competitors.

The truth is, salespeople spend at least as much time selling their own company as they do selling their customers. In the corporate world, the sales force is actually the customer advocate within the company. They're sort of on the same team. And that's as it should be.

Think about it. All your stakeholders are customers, in a way. And just as your relationships with stakeholders are not adversarial, your relationships with customers shouldn't be either. That's why it's important to truly believe in your product. You're actually trying to fulfill your customers' needs, to do what's best for both you and them.

The great irony of the sales process is that the customer usually has to do some selling on your behalf as well. One of the most important aspects of your relationship is to find out what whoever you're working with needs from you to get approval from her boss, development head, purchasing head, whoever.

Wherever you are, there's selling going on in all directions, even ways you would never think of. So forget the stigma. There is none. You're just doing the same thing everyone does every day of their lives, even if they don't realize it. And you're probably much better at it than you think.

COLD CALLING DOES NOT MEAN WASTING PEOPLE'S TIME

The very idea of cold calling sends chills up nearly everyone's spine. But there are actually several different kinds of cold calling, so let's break it down. With rare exception, nobody should be cold-calling consumers. That's what Google AdWords, storefronts, and direct marketing are for. So let's talk about business-to-business.

When I first became a sales rep, I was handed a territory with hundreds of potential customers, but the biggest by far were Hughes and Xerox. This was in the heyday of both companies, so they had thousands of employees scattered over dozens of buildings and locations in Southern California. Nevertheless, I made it my mission to crack open those two accounts, and that's exactly what I did.

I spent weeks getting to know the receptionist in the lobby of Xerox's corporate headquarters, and eventually I schmoozed her into giving me a copy of the company phone directory. I started calling on a few leads I got from my manufacturers, bought a few lunches and drinks, and, in time, developed a pretty detailed tree of who was responsible for what products and functions and who the key decision makers were.

I took things as far as I could with all the gatekeepers and eventually got to the point where I needed to get in to see some high-level decision makers. For that, I developed a technique: I simply called their administrative assistants and set up meetings, just like that. You'd be amazed how well that works. Most senior executives don't even know their own calendars. They just go blindly from meeting to meeting. And once you get to know their admins, you can find out all sorts of information.

The bottom line is, there are plenty of tricks to minimize cold calling and make your life easier. You just have to be smart about it and do some research and a little schmoozing. And once you do manage to set up an important meeting, don't screw it up by wasting people's time. There's a good chance you'll never get a second bite at the apple.

There's an old saying in litigation: Never ask a question you don't know the answer to. It's the same with customers. Always know whom you're talking to, what their role is, what motivates them, and how to approach them. That way you can come up with a strategy that makes sense.

If you're pitching, never rehearse. There are several reasons for that, but the most important one is that it's harder to think on your feet and adapt to new information. Instead, know your material cold, walk in with a reasonable plan, ask lots of questions, listen for answers, and adjust as needed. Trust your gut.

If you've ever wondered how some people can think on their feet and come across so smoothly, they're just prepared and confident. And that comes from experience and knowing your stuff. Do your research. Be prepared. In time, you'll gain confidence.

BE YOUR GENUINE SELF

When it comes to selling, most people try too hard. They try too hard to be something they're not. They try too hard to appear smart. They try too hard to relate personally to customers. They try too hard to make things happen and close the deal.

That's the opposite of how you should be selling.

Business is not about you, what you want, or how fast you want it. It's about customers: what they need, and when they need it. And customers are real, genuine people. So if you want to engage, connect, and build long-term relationships with them, the best way to do it is for you to be your genuine self.

If you're too pushy or try to get too personal too quickly, you risk invading their personal space, coming across as slimy, offending them, and turning them off. Instead, pay attention and react to their cues, tone, and body language.

Sometimes, in a transparent attempt to relate, we come off like know-it-alls. Whatever you do, don't show off how smart you are. Customers don't give a crap about how much you know. They just want to know if you have a solution to their problem, if you can fulfill their needs, and whether they can count on you to meet your commitments. That's why it's so important for you to find out what their problems and needs are. And you can only do that by asking questions and listening, not by filling the room with the sound of your own voice.

You know that reality distortion field Steve Jobs was famous for? To this day, nobody knows how he talked the entire music industry into selling out to iTunes for a song and a dance. And while we can learn lots of lessons from the guy, the most important one is to be your genuine self, as he was.

Remember that selling is nothing new; you've been doing it your whole life. It's as natural as waiting until your mom is in the right mood and then getting her to let you stay out late when you were a kid.

Remember that persuasion and motivation are two sides of the same coin. As long as your goal is to sell customers a product they'll be happy with at a reasonable price, you're doing God's work, as far as I'm concerned.

Sure, you'll make lots of mistakes in the beginning, but you'll get better. People seem to think I'm a natural-born salesperson. They say I could sell religion to the Pope. Nothing could be further from the truth: I'm just an observant, motivated, hardworking people person.

I'm sure you too can do what comes naturally: Believe in your product, research and prepare, listen to your customers, learn from experience, and have a little common sense. Don't sweat it. You'll do fine.

CHAPTER 16

UNRAVELING
THE MYSTERIES
OF MARKETING

DURING THE HEADY DAYS OF THE DOTCOM BOOM, I got tired of playing second fiddle to a chief executive I should have had more respect for but didn't and decided it was time to run a company. My ego was about as inflated as the market bubble, but that wasn't entirely on me. Executive recruiters were calling. So the next time the phone rang, I said, "What the hell," and threw my hat into the ring.

I got the job, but not before jumping through the usual hoops, including interviews with the VCs who sat on the company's board. I was feeling pretty confident as I strode into the spacious office of one general partner, exchanged pleasantries, and sat down across from him.

The venture capitalist looked down at my resume for a bit, tossed it on his desk, leaned back in his chair, and said, "So how did a marketing guy end up interviewing for a CEO job?" If that sounds condescending, that's because it was. The guy turned out to be an arrogant asshole, and not very useful or successful as a VC, either. But that's neither here nor there.

The point is, with two technical degrees and a 20-year career that included some pretty impressive accomplishments as a senior executive with several well-known high-tech companies, what popped into this guy's mind when he looked at my resume was that I was a marketing guy. You'd think I flipped burgers at McDonald's—not that there's anything wrong with that.

I'd be lying if I said it wasn't annoying, but I was used to it. It's a relatively common meme among the Silicon Valley elite. There are some notable exceptions we'll get to in a minute, but for the most part, they just don't get marketing. And for many, that's their downfall.

The question is, why? What the hell is the deal with marketing? If you ask ten CEOs and business leaders to define marketing, you'll get ten completely different answers. I know that because I've asked dozens of executives that question over the years and never gotten the same answer twice. Never mind that it's without a doubt among the most critical functions in any company.

Wait, what? I bet you're thinking marketing is just ads, direct email, and lead generation. I can't be talking about the same thing. You're right; I'm not. So let me set the record straight by explaining what the geniuses who literally wrote the book on business and management have to say about marketing.

Peter Drucker, the legendary father of modern management, said, "Because the purpose of business is to create a customer, the business enterprise has two—and only two—basic functions: marketing and innovation. Marketing is the distinguishing, unique function of the business."

Hewlett-Packard cofounder David Packard famously said, "Marketing is too important to be left to the marketing department."

Indeed, in his seminal book *Relationship Marketing*, Silicon Valley icon Regis McKenna wrote, "Marketing is everything and everything is marketing. Marketing today is not a function; it is a way of doing business. Marketing is not a new ad campaign or this month's promotion. Marketing has to be all pervasive, part of everyone's job description, from the receptionists to the board of directors."

McKenna, incidentally, was the marketing wizard who learned much of what he knew about marketing on the job at National Semiconductor and helped Intel launch its first microprocessor. He also helped a young Steve Jobs launch the world's first personal computer. He worked with a who's who of high-tech companies during their formative years and is often credited with putting Silicon Valley on the map.

In *The Marketing Imagination*, world-renowned economist, author, and Harvard professor Theodore Levitt said, "A chief executive who does not himself have a sense of the marketing requisites of his business or who does not have chief lieutenants who do is almost certainly headed for disaster. Marketing is, indeed, everybody's business, and everybody had better know it."

And while Steve Jobs probably had the most brilliant marketing mind in the history of the high-tech industry, the man hated the word "marketing." He didn't like what it represented in people's minds. He wanted to come up with insanely great products and show customers how they could be used and what they could do. That's all marketing. Just don't call it that.

"It's not about pop culture, and it's not about fooling people, and it's not about convincing people that they want something they don't," Jobs said in a *Fortune* interview. "We figure out what we want. And I think we're pretty good at having the right discipline to think through whether a lot of other people are going to want it, too. That's what we get paid to do."

Nobody would argue that Apple's unprecedented success in recent years is in no small part due to its ability to divine the next big thing, to figure out what people want even when they don't know it themselves. In that same interview Jobs quoted Henry Ford, "If I'd have asked my customers what they wanted, they would have told me, 'A faster horse.'"

Well, I'm here to tell you—and I'd tell Jobs, too, if he was still here—that what he was doing all those years was about the best job of marketing the industry has ever seen. And I'm sure the experts would agree.

McKenna also said, "The goal of marketing is to own the market, not just to sell the product." And in *Marketing High Technology*, Davidow, whom we discussed earlier, said, "Marketing must invent complete products and drive them to commanding positions in defensible market segments." That's exactly what Apple and Intel did.

So if all these extraordinary businesspeople are right, that marketing is critical to the success of any business—and believe me, they are—how do we reconcile that with the reality that few business leaders actually understand marketing and give it the focus it deserves?

I pondered that question for a good many years before I finally knew enough about business and psychology to come up with an answer that satisfied me. Clearly, marketing has a perception problem, which is truly ironic if you think about it. But that perception is based in reality, because marketing also has a competency problem.

While left and right brain dominance is a myth—the hemispheres don't actually work that way—people do generally tend toward the analytical or the creative. Marketing requires both—not just a balance between the two spheres of thinking and feeling but aptitude toward both. And few people are comfortable with and capable of straddling that line.

That's why senior-level marketing talent is so hard to find. And that's why marketing has a bad rap. Analytical types think marketers are all fluff. Creative types think they're just cutthroat salespeople. And neither type likes MBAs and all their dumb charts and popular jargon.

Since executives and business leaders tend to be a pretty cynical bunch and few marketing executives have the ability to articulate the importance of the function, marketing has, to a great extent, been marginalized in the business world.

Remember how I said selling is relatively straightforward and intuitive? Well, marketing is not. Marketing is complex and nuanced. That's why it mystifies so many. It's both analytical and creative, both art and science, both logical and emotional, both tangible and amorphous.

And yet, as all the experts say, it's absolutely critical to business success. And that's why this chapter and the seven principles I'm about to put forth are among the most important in the book.

PRINCIPLE 1: IN COMPETITIVE MARKETS, IT'S WINNER TAKES ALL

Markets are elastic. They do tend to grow and shrink over time. But at any point in time, markets are static, and so is market share. Those near the top enjoy higher margins, pricing power, and more money for employees, perks, and future development. Those near the bottom will soon be goners. And it's a tough slog for everyone else.

Contrary to today's popular feel-good wisdom, in business, winning is everything. To win, your products, support, sales, and communications have to be hands down better than your competitors' in the eyes of the customer. And since you have the best products, the customers win, too. The only people who lose are your competitors. That's the goal. If you're not cool with that, you shouldn't be in business. Period.

It's a good rule of thumb to aim to be number one in every market you enter. Your strategies and plans must reflect that goal. If they don't, competitive life will get ugly. That's just the way it is. Sure, you can gain market share, but something has to change for that to happen. It takes planning, strategy, money, and time to gain market share.

For example, Toyota entered the U.S. luxury car market with a well-thought-out plan to take on entrenched leaders BMW and Mercedes. To overcome its image as an economy brand, it created a new one, Lexus. It captured the customer's imagination with new benefits—ergonomics and quality—and reinvented the customer experience with a low-stress showroom. And it undercut competitors' prices to gain entry, customer traction, and market share. Today, Lexus is neck and neck with BMW and Mercedes and enjoys healthy margins, but that took many years.

Another way to gain entry and quickly dominate competitive markets is through technology disruption. Today, companies are using breakthrough concepts to turn age-old industries upside down. There's Google in advertising, Uber in transportation, Airbnb in travel rentals, GrubHub in food services, Zillow in real estate, WhatsApp in messaging, and Alibaba and Amazon in commerce.

It's a competitive world. It takes a lot to win. The equation that determines the success of your products and your company has many variables. Business is all about how effectively you use and control those variables. It's not exactly winner take all, but ask any company what it's like to have single-digit market share and they'll tell you: It sucks.

PRINCIPLE 2: INNOVATORS TURN IDEAS INTO PRODUCTS PEOPLE CAN USE

In the winter of 1976, a cross-country trip with my college roommate and his brother took a fateful turn when we visited their uncle, Jim Bair, a senior scientist at Stanford Research Institute (SRI) in Menlo Park, California. Bair demonstrated a computer mouse and graphical user interface for us, an event that inspired me to change majors and eventually led to a career in the high-tech industry.

Steve Jobs saw a similar demo three years later at Xerox PARC and famously integrated the technology into the Apple Lisa and then the Macintosh. Interestingly, Apple acquired Siri—its intelligent personal assistant—by acquiring the company of the same name. Siri uses Nuance's speech recognition technology. Both Siri and Nuance were spinoffs from SRI.

The point of the story is that neither Jobs nor Apple invented that technology, but, since they're the ones who incorporated it into products millions of people buy and use on a daily basis, that makes *them* innovators. Innovation isn't necessarily coming up with a novel idea, but coming up with a product people can use.

Besides, *first to market* is rarely an advantage. That's just an observation, but if I had to come up with a reason, it's that technology is so complex that it usually takes several iterations for the right combination of functions, features, ease of use, and price to emerge before the market takes off.

Personal music players, smartphones, and tablets had all been around for years when Apple entered those markets with the iPod, iPhone, and iPad. You can search far and wide for the first movers in those markets, but you're not likely to find them.

Some people are great inventors. They come up with wild concepts nobody's ever thought of. But great marketers tend to be innovators who turn ideas into products people want and need. Marketing thrives on reusing ideas in new ways, and companies with great marketing thrive as a result.

When industries are brand-new, if you build it, customers might come. But once markets begin to mature and the competition heats up, product development and marketing need to be joined at the hip. In innovative companies, they usually are.

PRINCIPLE 3: MARKETING IS LIKE SEX: EVERYONE THINKS THEY'RE GOOD AT IT

It's funny how even those who really don't get marketing or think it's just a bunch of BS still think they're experts. The CEO, the engineers, the IT guy—I bet half the people in your company think they know more about what customers want than the customers do. Everybody's a focus group of one.

Maybe it's a function of the competency gap so everyone feels the need to step in. Or maybe they all took Packard's advice to heart. Who knows?

In any case, when it's the boss's or a board director's opinion, it's hard to ignore. And yet, when the marketing guy comes up with a brilliant idea, those same people want it substantiated, analyzed, and researched. Hypocrisy.

It reminds me of the old line: "Those who think they know everything are annoying to those of us who do." The problem is it's not easy to tell the difference between the two. After all, those people—the hypocrites who shouldn't be imposing their *focus group of one* opinions on you but do it anyway—might be right.

I didn't always see it that way, especially when my chief executive was the guy doing the imposing. Then, one day, I realized that I did exactly the same thing. I'd swoop into meetings and trash everyone's carefully thought-out plans in favor of my own focus group of one. And not to sound like I have a fat head, but more often than not, I was right. So again I ask: How can you tell the guy who knows his shit from the guy who's full of it? People don't just walk around with big signs on their foreheads that say *guru* or *blowhard*. It's a dilemma, to be sure.

In my experience, it certainly doesn't correlate to job title or educational background. After all, none of the brainiacs I quoted earlier were schooled in this sort of thing. Levitt was an economist. Davidow's degrees are all technical. So are mine.

The truth is, you only need a focus group of one if it's the right one. As we showed earlier, the wisdom of crowds is a myth. There's no such thing as collective intelligence—certainly when it comes to the nuanced thinking and feeling required for marketing. In reality, most breakthroughs are the result of a simple idea by an individual or small team.

In the *Fortune* interview, Jobs explained why Apple doesn't use or need focus groups: "We did iTunes because we all love music. We made what we thought was the best jukebox in iTunes. Then we all wanted to carry our whole music libraries around with us. The team worked really hard. And the reason that they worked so hard is because we all wanted one. You know? I mean, the first few hundred customers were us."

Still, there are more posers in marketing than in other fields, probably because the demand is strong, the supply is weak, and it's easy to fake. As David Hornik, a VC at August Capital, once blogged, "VCs like to think that they are marketing geniuses. We really do." The reason, he says, is because "we can fake it far more convincingly than in other areas."

They're not the only ones. How can you tell the difference? Experience. And trust your gut. Sometimes you do only need a focus group of one.

PRINCIPLE 4: DIFFERENTIATE OR DIE

We talked about the necessity of having a differentiated value proposition earlier, but here are two stories to drive the point home.

Just the other day I got an email from a reader in her 40s who desperately wants to be successful but has never found her thing in life. She's tried nearly everything but appears to have no real competency in anything.

Meanwhile, on Charlie Rose a few weeks ago, Apple CEO Tim Cook said he could fit all the products Apple makes on the little table that sat between them. Here's a company with thousands of ridiculously talented people and more cash than God, but they work hard to figure out what they can do better than anyone and force themselves to be disciplined about it.

Can you see the extreme contrast between those two scenarios? It's all about focus, or lack thereof. It's a problem many entrepreneurs and companies struggle with. Just ask investors in Yahoo!, HP, and Sony—companies that have seen more than their share of criticism for lack of focus. And I seriously wonder about Google spreading itself too thin under cofounder Larry Page.

But differentiation isn't just about focusing on what you're best at. Often it's more about positioning: how you define and segment the market.

For example, how did WhatsApp, a four-year-old company with an app, 55 employees, and no revenue to speak of garner a half-billion highly engaged users and end up being acquired by Facebook for $19 billion? After all, the market is flooded with thousands of apps, including dozens of messaging apps, some from the likes of Google and Apple.

The answer is part focus group of one, part market segmentation, and part development. Its founders wanted a simple messaging app that didn't store messages, collect user data, or bombard users with ads, games, and gimmicks. They thought others would want that, too. That was their value proposition. When it comes to some markets, less is more. Who knew it could be that simple?

In his book, Davidow said, "Segmentation lets Davids slay Goliaths." That's exactly what happened with WhatsApp. Product positioning and market segmentation are perhaps the most powerful tools for coming up with a differentiated value proposition that can set your business apart from hordes of competitors.

It's not complicated. You simply want to leverage some sort of unique capability, innovative positioning, or both to target a distinct market segment with specific customer attributes. Once you establish a beachhead—a niche you can call your own—you expand from there. Geoffrey Moore does a pretty good job of explaining the transition from niche to mainstream adoption in *Crossing the Chasm*.

That's what Volkswagen did with its "Drivers Wanted" campaign. It sounds selective, but now it's among the largest car companies in the world. That's also what Starbucks did by launching upscale cafes. The same is true of Dell and custom PCs sold direct. Dr Pepper, Snapple, Whole Foods, Harley-Davidson—the list goes on and on.

If you can't distinguish your company and its products against the competition in a way that's meaningful to customers, you're doomed to slim profits and minuscule market share. And just because you say you're different doesn't make it so. If customers don't agree, forget it. That's how marketing connects products to customers: through a differentiated value proposition. Without it, you're doomed.

PRINCIPLE 5: YOU CAN NEVER AFFORD TO LOSE A CUSTOMER

There's a lot of confusion over cause and effect in business. Too many entrepreneurs think it's all about them and their employees. It's not. Not even close.

There are actually three and only three major stakeholders in any company: investors, employees, and customers. Investors give employees money to make and sell products to customers. Without customers, employees lose their jobs, and investors lose their money. No customers, no company.

Winning and keeping customers is the sole purpose of any business. That doesn't mean you need to do anything a customer asks you to do. It just means your primary goal is to bring unique value to customers.

Figuring out how to do that is the hardest thing you'll ever have to do. And doing it in a vacuum is remarkably challenging, to say the least. Sometimes it's damn near impossible.

I'll never forget what it was like starting my own management consulting business after 23 years of working for others. I had a pretty good idea of the customer problem I solved and the competitive niche my business would target. Then it dawned on me that I had no idea how to get the word out beyond my network. After decades of doing just that for big companies, I had no clue how to do it for myself.

Luckily, the opportunity to blog sort of fell in my lap. Still, I wasn't sure how to connect the dots and turn that marketing opportunity into a consulting business. The answer, of course, was that my content had to be differentiated in a way that resonated with an audience and set me apart from the growing hordes of bloggers.

But that was easier said than done. After all, I was writing more or less in a vacuum. The only feedback was the comment section, social media, and page views, and that was only of marginal use since that audience was far broader than the target customers for my consulting services.

Nevertheless, the goal of my consulting practice and my blogging was more or less the same—to advise existing and up-and-coming executives and business leaders—so I made sure my content was consistent with that. Lo and behold, the writing became a business of its own. The only difference is, you are now my customer.

Regardless of whether you're a corporate executive, a small-business owner, or a solopreneur, the goal is the same: to win and keep customers. By all means, have a purpose. Set your sights on achieving professional goals. But if you can't create customer value, you won't succeed in either.

Many of today's would-be entrepreneurs have that backwards. They're focused on themselves, not the customer. It's all about me, me, me. My personal brand. My blog. My social media platform. My friends and followers. My network. What can you do for me? What's in it for me?

What a load of self-serving crap.

In a world where so many are focused only on themselves, it's never been easier to stand apart by focusing on what really matters: serving the customer. That doesn't just lead to success. It leads to fulfillment and good karma, too.

PRINCIPLE 6: YOUR PRODUCT IS YOUR BRAND

Faced with a dilemma of how to gain awareness as "The Computer Inside" when competitors like AMD and Cyrix were marketing lower-priced chips using the same 386 and 486 nomenclature, Intel marketing manager Dennis Carter and microprocessor head Dave House decided it was time to get creative.

They learned about ingredient branding—NutraSweet on Diet Coke cans, Teflon on pots and pans, Gore-Tex on clothing, and Smucker's jam on boxes of Kellogg's Pop-Tarts—and came up with a groundbreaking branding campaign and co-op advertising program that paid PC makers to use the now-familiar Intel Inside swirl in ads and on computers.

When the campaign launched in 1991, Intel was the world's third-biggest semiconductor company. The following year it climbed to number one, a position it has retained ever since. The company further differentiated by trademarking Pentium, its first named processor. Today, Intel is one of the most recognized and powerful brands in the world.

While that's a great story about the power of branding as a strategic marketing tool, Intel would not enjoy the reputation and market share it has today if not for the fact that it designs and manufactures great products.

Contrary to popular belief, branding is not about names, logos, or advertising. It's about reputation. It's the sum total of customer perception through experience with your company, its products, and its services. But make no mistake: It's mostly about their experience with your products.

Many predicted the internet age would kill branding—that ecommerce, Amazon, Google, and social media would level the playing field. Not only did that not happen, I can make a pretty good argument for the opposite being true. More information and increased competition make a company's reputation even more important, since nobody has the time or the patience to deal with crappy products and lousy customer service anymore.

Bob Pittman, now CEO of iHeartMedia, has run everything from MTV and Nickelodeon to Century 21 and Six Flags. When he was president and COO of AOL back in the heyday of the internet pioneer, he said, "Coca-Cola does not win the taste test. Microsoft does not have the best operating system. Brands win." And today, big brands like Apple, Google, Coca-Cola, IBM, and Microsoft have never been more powerful.

That said, it would be a very big mistake to assume that companies with powerful brands are all about branding strategy. That's an important component of a company's reputation, but if the product doesn't deliver, it's all for naught.

Look at it this way. Your word is your promise. So is your brand. It's a promise you make to every customer that, when they use your products and engage with your company, they can expect a certain level of performance, a certain type of experience, a certain customer service attitude, a certain level of quality. It's your job to make sure you—not your competitors or the media—define and control that promise. And it's even more important to ensure that your brand promise is consistent with an expectation of customer experience with your products.

Communication strategy can create a groundswell of customer excitement and viral demand for a product nobody's ever heard of, even on a shoestring budget. It can make or break a product launch or an entire company, yet most executives consider it an afterthought. That's not just a missed opportunity; it's a risk no business can afford to take.

Especially now—in this era of communication overload where the emphasis is on frequency and volume—it's more important than ever to control the message and the delivery. If you can boil complex concepts down to simple messages, sound bites, and stories people can connect with, that makes all the difference.

Your product is your brand, and its value to customers should be at the very core of how, when, and what you communicate to the world.

PRINCIPLE 7: COMPETITIVE BARRIERS WORK BOTH WAYS

Naval Ravikant is an entrepreneur who founded or cofounded several companies, most notably Epinions and AngelList. He also invested in Twitter, Uber, and Yammer, among others. He's obviously a very smart guy.

In 2014 he tweeted this: "1999—$5M to launch a product, 30M serious computer users. 2014—$5K to launch, 3B serious phone users. Leverage / $ is up 100,000x."

Regardless of whether his assumptions are entirely correct—after all, what's a few billion phones between friends—his point is a good one. The internet has dramatically lowered barriers to entry for startups.

There's just one problem with his analysis: It cuts both ways. The web leveled the playing field for *everyone*. Sure, it's relatively easy to launch a blog, an app, or a product and reach out to a few billion people, but that's true for every one of those few billion people.

In other words, while it's never been cheaper and easier to start a company and reach a broad audience, that audience has never been more overloaded with information, communication, products, and services. The noise level has never been higher and the competition has never been tougher.

While I'm tempted to call it a wash, I'm afraid it's not. It's a fairly nuanced equation that depends on how differentiated your products are in the customer's eyes, among other things. If you're going up against a gazillion competitors with a relatively undifferentiated product or service, I don't care how many people you can reach—customers will be hard to come by and easy to lose, and you'll have no pricing power, so profits will also be scarce.

To make matters worse, social media increases the pressure to conform to cultural norms, as we've discussed at length, so if you buy into all the popular groupthink being blogged, tweeted, and posted all over the internet, that just makes you less differentiated.

There's no better example of this phenomenon than the feel-good mantra that everybody's a winner, nobody has to lose, and competition is just a figment of your imagination. Not only is that utopian nonsense patently false, you've got to marvel at the irony.

Think about it. Everyone and his brother is encouraging you to enter the most crowded and competitive markets in history while at the same time telling you not to worry about competition. All you need is a website, a personal brand, and some social media followers, and everything will work out great.

But that's not the way it works, not in the real world or the virtual one. Here's the way it really works:

Low Barriers to Entry = High Competition

High Competition + Cultural Conformity = No Differentiation

No Differentiation = No Pricing Power

No Pricing Power = Dog-Eat-Dog Business

Dog-Eat-Dog Business = Poverty

Besides coming up with a differentiated customer value proposition, you can avoid that unfortunate outcome by understanding competitive barriers and switching cost. What you want is low barriers and costs for customers to come to you and high barriers and costs for competitors to take them away.

One way to do that is by creating and protecting your intellectual property, including patents, trade secrets, and trademarks. If you come up with an innovative product or solution, you want to protect it and put up barriers so competitors can't easily follow. Otherwise, bigger companies with greater resources will come in and eat away at your market share and profit margins. Of course, you can try to outrun them by staying ahead of the innovation curve, but that's very hard to do against bigger companies with more resources than you have.

The other big way to lock in customers is to create a proprietary ecosystem of infrastructure partners and software tools around your products and services. Examples include Apple iOS, Apple Store, and iTunes; Google Android and AdWords; Amazon Web Services; Microsoft Windows; Cisco network routers; and LinkedIn's Pulse blogging platform.

Remember, open source software and tools are cheap and easy to use, but that cuts both ways. If you have no real differentiation (and no, a personal brand with a cool website and a logo doesn't count) and no real competitive barriers, there's no reason for your customers to stick around—or even come to you in the first place.

Clearly, marketing will always have a perception problem. I was just on a small-business website that listed its management team in descending order of importance, from the president all the way down to the guy who installs graphic signage. Way down the list, just beneath the office manager, was the marketing director. Sadly, that's the way it is in most companies.

I was watching a business news program about continuing sales declines at McDonald's when a pundit said, and I'm paraphrasing here, "They don't need marketing. McDonald's has great ads. The problem is they have hundreds of products on their menu while hot fast-casual chains like Shake Shack and Five Guys are far more focused . . . like McDonald's used to be."

Note the perception that marketing is all about ads. Never mind that marketing's primary function is to determine which products to develop and sell. Go figure.

Make no mistake, business is all about marketing. The two are more or less synonymous. That's why business leaders and CEOs who leave marketing to the marketing department are not doing themselves, their investors, their customers, or their employees any favors.

Marketing may be more art than science, but great marketing shouldn't be as rare as a Picasso. It certainly doesn't have to be that way.

CHAPTER 17

WHICH
WAY
IS UP?

S O YOU CAME UP WITH AN IDEA, GOT YOURSELF SOME funding, developed a product, gained customer traction, found a market niche, and generated some revenue. Maybe even a lot of revenue. That's great. You've gone farther than the vast majority of your peers. Pat yourself on the back and have a margarita.

The problem is you can't just keep putting one foot in front of the other forever. Sooner or later you'll reach a point where that no longer works. It happens from time to time.

Maybe things are going right and you want to capitalize on it. Perhaps business is slowing and you need to find a way to reinvigorate it. Or maybe things have gone terribly wrong and you're wondering if it's time to pivot or change direction entirely. Whatever the reason, every company big and small reaches plateaus and inflection points.

Sometimes those inflection points are hard to see until you're right on top of them. By then, it's often too late. The problem is inertia: getting lost in day-to-day operations and blindly following the status quo. It brings lots of companies to their knees. That's because things change. Markets change. Competitive landscapes change. So you always have to keep an eye on the big picture and adapt as needed.

Life may be about living in the moment, but you still need to pop your head up above the tops of the trees and get a look at the whole forest. You've got to have some sort of direction and make sure you're always on course. Businesses are the same way. That's what this chapter is about. It's about always knowing what's going on and where you're heading so you can make quicker and better decisions that help you get there.

Yes, I know you want to be *successful*. Everyone throws that word around like it has some sort of concrete meaning. The problem is it doesn't. Success is amorphous. It's a moving target. There are simply too many variables for it to be otherwise. So success is not a goal. It's not a mission. And it's certainly not a strategy.

Success has to be the most overused word in the entrepreneurial lexicon. I'm guilty of it myself. I count 135 occurrences in the book so far. It's also often misused. We use it to describe an event that doesn't really exist. Success is not an event. It doesn't happen all at once, and it certainly isn't permanent. Once-successful companies unravel all the time. Sun, Nortel, Yahoo!, Kodak, RadioShack, J.C. Penney—it's a long, long list.

The life of a company is a lot like that of a person. It never goes straight up like a rocket ship. There are always hurdles, plateaus, pitfalls, and segues. There are pathetic retreats when our decisions don't pan out and crazy viral growth when our plans work far better than anyone could have dreamed. Great companies flop. Lousy companies come back.

The point is you have to have an overarching vision or strategy for your company. If you don't, you simply can't make smart decisions to help you get there. You won't be able to answer the questions that come up from time to time, such as: *Where do we go from here? How do we grow? What's the most effective way to scale? Will processes make us more effective or more bureaucratic? Should we focus or diversify? How do we know whether to stick with the plan or pivot?*

Questions, questions, questions. Whenever executives ask me questions like those, I tell them I have no answers. They always look perplexed.

When it comes to figuring out where to go from here, the first thing you need to know is you're the only one with the answers. Granted, you have to ask yourself and your team a bunch of questions and maybe do a little research, but I assure you the answers are there. But here's the catch: There are way more wrong answers than right answers. So I'm going to show you how to find the right ones.

In Chapter 4 we talked about taking a road trip from point A to point B. Until now, we used that metaphor to describe your career journey. This is the business version.

A very smart VC named Fred Wilson from Union Square Ventures says a CEO should just focus on doing three things: "Set and communicate the overall vision and strategy of the company; recruit, hire, and retain the best talent; and make sure there's always enough cash in the bank." He's absolutely right. And for lack of a better term, we'll use his nomenclature, *overall vision and strategy*, to describe where you want to go and how you plan to get there. Once you know that, answering all those other questions is a lot less problematic.

When I take leadership teams through the process of figuring out their overall vision and strategy, it can take anywhere from a few days to a few months. Sometimes it takes forever to tease out what's going on or decide between two competing strategies, while other times a light bulb goes off and everybody's magically on the same page. It really depends. It's specific to your company, culture, and situation. But there are some key ingredients that matter a lot, so let me take you through it and, if you run into trouble, you can always give me a shout.

First, let's talk about timing. It's fine to do this periodically, say, annually, with one big exception. Once you realize you need it—that you're at or approaching a plateau or inflection point—forget the calendar. Don't wait; just do it. Here's why.

Back in 2000, Cisco was one of the world's most valuable companies. But as the dotcom bubble began to deflate, CEO John Chambers realized the company was more or less out of control. It had grown too fast, acquiring companies left and right with little focus and oversight. He knew that needed to change fast. So he got his leadership team together for a couple of days and mapped out a complete overhaul, including the company's first significant layoff. It was gut-wrenching, but it had to be done. Some thought he cut too deep too quickly, but that decisive move allowed him to stabilize Cisco during the tumultuous years to come and weather the downturn better than its peers.

On the flip side, Sun Microsystems suffered an agonizingly prolonged demise that saw its sales, margins, market share, and stock price plummet over a period of years. The reason? Its strategy was no longer effective. After at least seven or eight different restructurings and layoffs—a sort of death by a thousand cuts—it was finally acquired by Oracle for a tiny fraction of what it was once worth. For whatever reason, Sun never came up with an effective new strategy.

Likewise, I've seen loads of small businesses fail to capitalize on huge opportunities because their owners had no overarching vision or strategy. As a result, they weren't sure how to proceed and ended up making enormous mistakes or doing nothing at all, which is just as bad.

One story that sticks in my mind is that of a mom-and-pop gluten-free bakery. It had some great recipes and fabulous-tasting products and succeeded in getting shelf space in all the local markets. Finally, that attracted the attention of a large nationwide retailer. Unfortunately, the bakery had outgrown its facilities and was having trouble keeping up with demand. The big deal was on the table, but the company needed capital to move to a larger facility and buy equipment. Several investors were clamoring to fund this hot up-and-comer in a fast-growing market, but, for whatever reason, the owners never pulled the trigger. I guess they just weren't sure where they wanted to go with the business, and that uncertainty paralyzed them. They ended up losing the opportunity, losing their lease, and just fading away.

I've actually seen public companies suffer the same kind of paralysis. It's inexcusable. Every company, no matter how big or small, has to have an overall vision and strategy. Otherwise, there's no context for any kind of important business decision. How can you possibly decide on product, diversification, channel, acquisition, capitalization, or any other kind of strategy without first figuring out the big picture?

That's right, you can't. So don't.

Now, I bet I know what some of you are thinking. How in the world can a public company not have an overall vision and strategy? Oddly, there are lots of reasons. Some are led by control freaks who want to be the only ones that know the big picture. Some CEOs have enormous egos and don't think they need what mere mortals need to succeed. Some leadership teams are so dysfunctional they get stuck between alternatives and can't decide. Others, I'm almost embarrassed to say, can't agree on how to define it, so they never do.

It doesn't matter what you call it. What matters is that you come up with a vision and strategy, that it's the right vision and strategy, and that everyone who matters knows and agrees on it.

STRATEGIC PLANNING 101

I've taken a lot of leadership teams through this process since I first went through it myself more than 20 years ago and, in my experience, these are the seven steps to doing it right:

Step 1: Define Your Team

If you have a leadership team, that's the core team throughout the entire process. The CEO is still the boss, but you might want to have an impartial facilitator to keep things moving and keep folks from killing each other (this stuff can get pretty heated). Everyone stays focused at every meeting. Everyone commits to being *all in*.

Step 2: Be Transparent

Everyone is completely open and brutally honest. Everything is on the table. There are no preconceived notions, sacred cows, pet projects, or personal agendas. You're not there to play politics. You're there for one reason only: to come up with the right overall vision and strategy for the company.

Step 3: Take Stock

Someone should present an objective snapshot of how the company and its products stack up next to the competition within their respective markets. A SWOT (Strengths, Weaknesses, Opportunities, Threats) analysis is a very good idea. Consider interviewing or surveying key stakeholders (board directors, employees, customers) and present notable findings.

Step 4: Hash It Out

Within that context, first a) brainstorm, then b) debate, and finally c) come to consensus on the overall vision and strategy until you can't stand to be in the same room anymore. That may take several sessions depending on the specific process you choose to employ. You may need time in between meetings to explore various market opportunities and report back.

Step 5: Call BS If Necessary

Whatever you come up with has to comply with the laws of physics and economics. It can't be like that "Then a miracle occurs" cartoon from Chapter 13. You don't live in Utopia, and nothing happens in the real world simply because you want it that way. That's the reason for brutal honesty: so at least one person is there to call bullshit when he hears it.

Step 6: Get Feedback

Once you have a proposed vision and strategy, it's a good idea to try it out on those who will ultimately have to embrace and execute it to see if it makes sense for your situation. Bounce it off some key employees, outside consultants, or even trusted customers and partners to see what they think.

Step 7: Finalize and Communicate

Consider the feedback, iterate if necessary, finalize, and communicate. Restructure to align current products, organization, and plans to the new vision and strategy. Everything must align. You can also put together an externalized and sanitized version, formulate it into a brand platform, and incorporate as needed into external marketing, communication, sales, and investor material.

You can scale this process up for a big company and down for a small one. But whatever you do, make sure you do it. If you don't have an overall vision and strategy, it's hard to make effective decisions and answer critical questions like *how do we grow*, *should we diversify*, and *how do we know whether to stick with the plan or pivot?*

Here is a very public example. Twitter filed its S-1 prospectus to the SEC on October 3, 2013, and went public about a month later. At that time, the company wrote, "We aim to become an indispensable daily companion to live human experiences." It went on to provide a number of strategies for accomplishing that goal and growing its business, all of which hinged on substantially growing the number and engagement of its users.

Unfortunately, the growth rate and engagement of the company's users has slowed dramatically and seems to be flattening out way short of its goals. And while its revenues are growing, expenses are growing almost proportionately. Meanwhile, its advertising market share continues to be very small relative to market leaders Google and Facebook. To make a long story short, at present, Twitter doesn't appear to be on the right track. And since it's a public company and a highly visible one, CEO Dick Costolo has come under fire by analysts, pundits, and the media.

As a result, Costolo has been on a bit of a roller-coaster ride, turning over the majority of his leadership team and coming up with various strategies du jour and new forms of metrics that might present the company in a more positive light, seemingly on the fly. Meanwhile, the stock has plummeted by roughly 50 percent since its post-IPO peak about a year ago. Finally, the embattled CEO was forced to step down.

The point is, trying to come up with a company's business strategy in real time under the excruciatingly bright lights of the public markets is brutal, to say the least. Moreover, that sort of flip-flopping around on top-line strategy can be tumultuous for a company. It can be distracting for the leadership team, demotivating for employees, and particularly hard on decision making.

Not that any of this is easy. As I said, there are a lot more wrong answers than there are right ones. But no matter how big or small your company is, having a reasonably coherent overall vision and strategy is the best way to find the right answers and make good decisions.

IF YOU'RE NOT GROWING, YOU'RE DYING

These days it's popular for entrepreneurs to question whether they should even be chasing revenues, profits, market share, and shareholder value. Why not instead focus on being better employers, custodians of the environment, and all-around corporate citizens? Let's put that silly argument to bed once and for all.

Lists of the best companies to work for are inevitably stacked with growing, profitable, financially solid companies with great products like Google, Procter & Gamble, Apple, Southwest Airlines, Qualcomm, and Genentech. There's a good reason for that. Great products create lots of satisfied customers. That leads to healthy growth and profits. And that leads to happy shareholders and motivated employees that make more great products.

You see, markets grow. And if you're not at least growing with the market, then you're effectively on the decline. So when a company is stagnant, that's a sign for employees, shareholders, and customers to start looking elsewhere.

Something else inevitably happens to companies that aren't growing. Their products lose their differentiation and become commodities. Their profit margins erode. Their profits decline. They generate less cash. And over time that produces a slow, steady decline.

Just look at RadioShack, Kodak, Sony, and BlackBerry. Those are just the big names we're talking about these days, but there are literally hundreds, even thousands of companies big and small that lost their edge.

And it isn't any fun working for a company in that situation. There's less security, fewer perks, and fewer exciting projects for your employees to work on that'll allow them to achieve any kind of personal or professional growth.

Besides, it's risky for customers to buy from a company in decline. They might get a better deal, but you know what they say: *You get what you pay for.* And who knows if the company will be around to provide support if anything goes wrong?

Likewise, investors are anything but forgiving. They've abandoned those declining businesses without one hint of regret.

Ultimately, companies need great products to attract customers. They need to grow revenues and gain market share to thrive. They need profits to fuel growth. They need empowered employees to develop great products that attract customers. And the wheel goes round and round.

THE MYTH OF THE ONE-TRICK PONY

Determining how best to grow your business is not rocket science. After going through it once or twice, you'll find it's more or less common sense. People just have a funny habit of making easy things way harder than they have to be by getting creative when they shouldn't. Your products should be differentiated, but that's not necessarily true of your growth strategy.

Startups should have a laser focus on doing one thing better than anyone else. There's nothing wrong with being a one-trick pony— that's a myth. If you're number one in a big and growing market, that's a damn good trick. Facebook is more or less a one-trick pony. Google's one trick is search advertising. Intel's is processors. Microsoft has Windows. Cisco makes routers. Apple's iPhone business alone is bigger and more profitable than nearly every company in the S&P 500.

Generally speaking, the easiest and least costly way to grow is not by diversifying but by expanding an existing business: enhancing your products and services, improving the customer experience, and staying ahead of the competition. Likewise, the best way to grow your customer base is through repeat business from existing customers. The next best way is by gaining market share from competitors. That's followed by attracting new customers by growing the overall market geographically, demographically, or in some other way.

Keep in mind, you must have the capital, organizational structure, sales channels, infrastructure, and operating resources to scale. If not, any one of those factors can limit your growth.

Take Uber, for example. It didn't just show up with thousands of drivers and three tiers of service in 200 cities and 50 countries overnight. It started as a mobile app that summoned a town car in San Francisco. Then it grew geographically, added the UberX service, and raised venture capital to fund its expansion.

Still, what appears to be a seamless and reliable user experience required a complete top-down reimagining of a car service. The software development, logistics deployment, and rapid recruiting and operations ramp-up in dozens of cities around the world represented an enormous scalability challenge. But it's still essentially a single-product company.

Airbnb began when founders Brian Chesky and Joe Gebbia turned their living room into a bed-and-breakfast to help pay their exorbitant rent in San Francisco. The pair then added a technical guy, Nathan Blecharczyk, launched a website, and initially focused on lodging for high-profile events. Today it has more than 1 million listings in 34,000 cities and 190 countries.

Founded in Chicago, GrubHub expanded geographically and by acquisition via venture funding, eventually merging with New York City-based Seamless and then going public. The company has continuously added restaurants and improved its service and user experience. The OrderHub in-restaurant tablet and DeliveryHub driver app together provide real-time updates so users can track their orders.

These examples show us that there are all sorts of ways to explore expansion of an existing business before even considering significant diversification. It's usually a good idea to minimize risk by first grabbing low-hanging fruit—offering complementary or synergistic products to an existing customer base or increasing marketing reach, for example—before venturing into uncharted waters with costly expansion plans.

Nevertheless, if you've got an idea that screams expansion in a big way and you have the wherewithal to scale it and investors willing to fund it, by all means, go for it. If your trusted lieutenants and advisors think you have to move fast and your gut agrees, don't wait around for bigger competitors to come after you and steal your market share.

One way to evaluate risk is to consider all the different factors that add risk to the equation. Anything materially new and different—sales channel, customer base, geographic location, manufacturing process, acquisition, technology, moving up or down the food chain—adds risk. It's best to take on one risk at a time and make it count. If it works, then replicate that process over and over. Avoid compound risk.

Whatever you do, learn to say no. If it falls outside your overall vision and strategy, don't do it. If it's not what you do best, don't do it. You've got to be disciplined, and that means turning down dozens of opportunities that just aren't right for you and your company. Doing too many things is one of the biggest problems with today's entrepreneurs. It's like an epidemic. Don't fall into that trap. Stay focused.

If it's time to change your overarching strategy, that's a different story, but don't take on more risk than you can reasonably handle or overtax your resources. All that does is increase the number of things that can go wrong—and rest assured, they will.

All that said, there are times when you should consider diversifying or pivoting—going in a somewhat different direction. When you're emotionally invested in a business or venture, however, it's often hard to be objective and make that call. God knows, I've seen dozens if not hundreds of experienced founders and executives screw it up. It's certainly not the sort of thing you want to take lightly.

I SEE PRODUCTS IN YOUR FUTURE

Here's an example that might resonate with you. If you've ever run a service business, you know that model comes with a unique challenge: The only way to scale it is to keep adding people, and that takes time and capital. No people, no growth. That's why companies like IBM, FedEx, and Wells Fargo have hundreds of thousands of employees.

While it's certainly not impossible to make it big with a service business, you've got to have broad demand, a unique value proposition, and capital to invest in growth. If not, you're in for a rough ride.

If your service business is not working out, you'd be wise to consider selling or licensing a complementary product line. You'd be surprised how many big, successful corporations started life as tiny service businesses that eventually grew into enormous product companies. Take a look:

- James L. Kraft sold cheese wholesale door-to-door in 1903 Chicago. Today you know his company as Kraft Foods.
- Michael Dell assembled computers for friends out of his Austin dorm room before founding Dell Computer.
- Sony began life as a radio-repair shop in postwar Tokyo. Its first product was a tape recorder, but its real breakthrough was a transistor radio.
- In the early days, Microsoft was a contract developer of programming languages.

Had those companies not pivoted to a product model, you'd have never heard of them.

Likewise, if your current business is still profitable but running out of steam—it's not growing and you've tried every reasonable way to ignite or reignite it—then you should probably hang on to it as a cash cow and look into diversifying. Just keep a few things in mind as you do that:

Always try to stick to your DNA. You're most likely to be successful at what you're good at and love to do. When PepsiCo saw the need to diversify, for example, it moved into noncarbonated beverages and snack food. Coca-Cola, on the other hand, wasn't aggressive enough and is now paying the price as global consumer demand for carbonated soft drinks is on the decline.

It's also a very good idea to listen to what customers are telling you, especially in terms of finding complementary opportunities within the same market. Your customers probably know a lot more about their markets than you do. More often than not, new product opportunities—problems in need of solutions—will come from them. Listen.

Sometimes it helps to expand your team by adding an equity partner with a complementary skill set, as Airbnb did. Remember, a smaller piece of the pie is worth a lot more than 100 percent of nothing. Just be sure you organize and capitalize your different businesses or products appropriately. Don't let an old business that isn't growing subsume your resources and management attention.

Remember that most successful companies don't make it big with their first product idea. Whatever you do, don't become unnecessarily risk averse or tuck in your wings. You still want to think big. Just make sure you stay focused on whatever strategy you come up with. Pivoting is good, but having a dozen irons in the fire never works out.

The hands-down most important thing to keep in mind as you grow your business is this: You want to add just enough structure and process to facilitate business operations, scalability, and growth without adding bureaucracy, limiting flexibility and adaptability, and dampening the entrepreneurial spirit that got you there in the first place. That's a tough balancing act for a lot of founders. Don't overdo it.

CHAPTER 18

FAILURE
HAPPENS

WHEN YOU TAKE RISKS, FAILURE IS A FACT OF LIFE. It comes with the territory. Nevertheless, it's a mistake to take failure lightly, to simply write it off as a rite of passage, something everyone goes through: "C'est la vie, and better luck next time." If your attitude is, "I'm an entrepreneur, a risk-taker, and failure is part of the game. No worries," you'll likely repeat the same mistakes over and over.

That sort of thinking is imprudent. This is the real world, and if you do the same thing over and over and expect a different result, you're either nuts, foolish, or both.

I bring this up because I hear a lot of casual references to failure these days. The entrepreneurial crowd in particular seems to have a cavalier attitude toward it. You might even say that popular literature has romanticized the notion of failure. But there is nothing romantic about it. And if you brush it off like it's no big deal, it will consume you, leaving nothing but a trail of sweat, unrealized dreams, and red ink.

I'm not saying that when it happens, and it will, that you should let it take you down, wipe out your drive, and destroy your confidence. And you certainly shouldn't let it stop you from taking risks. But you shouldn't take it lightly, either. There's simply too much to learn from it.

It's hard to overstate how much you can learn by observing how companies fail. Not only will it help you avoid making those same mistakes, it will teach you critical best practices. In my experience, these are the most common business pitfalls.

PITFALL 1: RUNNING OUT OF CASH

I've said it before, and I'll keep saying it until you're so sick of hearing it that you run out and start raising a round of funding: Most companies run out of money. I've probably heard a million reasons why, but way too often they're just excuses for poor business planning, hubris, or greed.

Either they try to bootstrap when they shouldn't, their burn rate is too high, they underestimate the cost of scaling, or they don't realize that you simply can't raise capital overnight. They understand product development and manufacturing timelines, but not that raising capital works exactly the same way; you have to pipeline and synchronize both.

I can't begin to tell you how common this is. I remember one Web development firm that was founded by two former managers from a large enterprise software company. They actually left excellent careers to try to self-fund an undifferentiated and therefore low-margin service business in a ridiculously competitive market. By the time they contacted me, they were already running on fumes with no hope of survival. Suffice to say these experienced executives should have known better. Maybe next time.

I can tell you a hundred stories just like that one. As for why so many otherwise intelligent people become stupendously dumb when cash is involved, I think it generally comes down to two fundamental flaws: magical thinking, as in "we're special, so the rules don't apply here," and greed, as in "we don't want to give up too much of the pie."

When asked why he only owned 4.1 percent of Box, the cloud computing company he founded, CEO Aaron Levie said, and I'm paraphrasing here, "I'd rather have 4 percent of something than 100 percent of nothing." Now he's worth about $100 million. Smart guy.

There's one thing nearly every successful entrepreneur has in common: a solid grasp of business and financial fundamentals. You'll need to understand this stuff sooner or later; you're better off learning it sooner and simply avoiding the whole "Shit, we're about to run out of cash, now what?" thing.

PITFALL 2: A LITTLE SUCCESS CAN BE A DANGEROUS THING

Ever wonder why high-tech companies never stop innovating? Why they continuously produce improved versions and entirely new generations of products? It's ridiculously expensive to keep that technology flywheel going. They don't spend billions out of the goodness of their hearts, and they certainly don't do it just because they can. They do it because, if they don't make their own products obsolete, their competitors will. And then they'll lose customers, market share, and ultimately their business in the process.

While many of us learned that lesson so long ago it seems like ancient history, it's amazing how often it bites successful founders and executives in the ass, even in the technology industry. There's a simple reason for that: A little success can be a dangerous thing. It's human nature to at some point decide you've worked your tail off for long enough, and now it's time to rest on your laurels and enjoy the good life.

That's fine, as long as you step down and turn the company's reins over to someone else first. The problem is that a lot of founders and CEOs don't do that. Instead, they just tell themselves that everything will be fine, that they've been successful and will continue to be successful. But that's not how it works. Market success is almost always met with increased competition. Others want to get in on the action. So you have to keep innovating just to maintain market share. And if you want to keep growing, you *really* can't afford just to sit still. You've got to maintain that competitive edge. You've got to keep reinventing yourself.

This is a competitive world. The biggest threat to a successful company is its own inertia, the status quo, the notion that past success is an indication of future results. It's not. Not even a little. That's why a killer instinct, a relentless drive to win 100 percent market share, is so important in business. It's an *all or none* proposition for one simple reason: If you don't continuously advance, if you fail to put up barriers, your competitors will take a beachhead and use it to penetrate farther and farther. I know that because I've used that same tactic countless times. And it's worked every time.

Remember when I explained how we repositioned Cyrix to develop processors for low-cost computing? It was a smart strategy, but that didn't stop Intel from coming after us. They knew what we knew: that price elasticity would create a large new segment of customers. And they knew that if they gave that up, they would eventually lose even more ground. So they dumbed down their Pentium II processor by turning off some features, rebranded it as Celeron, and sold it for less to compete with us.

Low-cost computers did end up becoming the bulk of the PC market. So had Intel not used the market segmentation strategy we discussed in Chapter 16, it would probably have lost control of the market. But neither Andy Grove nor his disciples would ever let that happen, and, as a result, Intel still dominates that market to this day. Smart guy, that Grove. He knew that a little success was never enough. Once you start to let go, it's a slippery slope. Look out below.

A business is a lot like a shark. If it doesn't keep moving forward, it dies.

PITFALL 3: SOLUTIONS IN SEARCH OF PROBLEMS

It's generally a good idea to do what you love for a living, but if you love eating good food or driving fast cars, that may or may not work out so well.

Let's face it, most of our ideas for products or companies are what we want to have or do without giving much thought to the far more important side of the equation: that customers have to buy whatever it is we're selling. In other words, we tend to put customers in our shoes instead of putting ourselves in theirs.

The business world is full of solutions in search of problems, products in search of markets, ideas in search of needs, inventions in search of uses. That's why there are always so many companies in search of customers they'll never find.

Look, there's definitely a place for mad scientists with their garish gadgets, idealistic inventors and their crazy concepts, and people who have a thing for Styrofoam furniture or wine made from avocados. But the business world is definitely not it.

There's a very good reason VCs will rarely fund a solution without a problem—a customer *pain point*, as they like to call it—or a product that isn't ten times better than everything else out there. It's because the odds of getting a decent return on investment are slim.

Granted, customers don't always know what they want until you show them. As Henry Ford famously said, "If I asked people what they wanted, they would have said faster horses." But that doesn't mean the car was a solution searching for a problem. The need to get from point A to point B, and faster, was clear. The demand was already there.

Take wearable computing, for example. Once it became clear that people couldn't live a day without their smartphones, it wasn't much of a leap to assume a lot of consumers might go for having that sort of thing on their wrist, Dick Tracy style. That's what Pebble set out to do. It raised a record $10 million on Kickstarter, no less, and now it's sold a million smartwatches. Go figure.

First figure out the problem, then come up with a solution. That's the right order. It's hard enough to do it the right way. Don't make it that much harder on yourself by trying it the other way.

PITFALL 4: LOUSY VISION

What's the difference between a visionary and a lunatic? The visionary turned out to be right.

If only we all had crystal balls, we could all be visionaries. The way most founders and CEOs pitch their ideas, you'd swear that's exactly what they have sitting on their desks. But they don't. Which is why most of them turn out to be completely wrong, if not completely crazy.

Vision is a funny thing. And the analogy between business ideas and visual perception is so accurate it's terrifying. Nearsighted or myopic people can't see the forest for the trees. If you're farsighted, you can't see what's staring you in the face. Tunnel vision means you lack perspective. There are founders with utopian views or grandiose visions, neither of which fares well in the real world.

And don't think for a minute that famous entrepreneurs or chief executives of large public companies have better or saner vision than you do. For years we watched Sony CEO Howard Stringer try to explain the nonexistent synergy between the company's consumer electronics and movie businesses—he claimed that a Sony movie is somehow better when it's streamed through a Sony PlayStation or watched on a Sony TV. It's not. Not even a little.

I once coached an internet TV startup founded by a brash Hollywood Millennial. He had developed a platform and an app that were pretty cool, and he couldn't understand why VCs weren't lining up to fund his venture. It turned out that if you looked under the hood of his vision for an independent internet channel, there was little more than smoke and mirrors. He thought coming up with compelling content 24/7 was the easy part—just hire a bunch of guys off Craigslist to do it. Yup, he'd had a bit too much Kool-Aid to drink.

The thing is, you can improve your vision. If you ask yourself and maybe a few smart people some tough questions and force yourself to assess the answers objectively, you can actually tip the scales quite a bit in favor of your turning out to be a wealthy visionary instead of a broke lunatic.

PITFALL 5: LACK OF FOCUS

Everyone has three or four careers going at once these days. The problem is nobody can keep that many balls in the air at the same time.

If you don't focus on holding on to one, sooner or later you're going to drop them all.

That's fine if you don't mind living hand to mouth on slim profits, if any. But if you actually want to succeed in business, you've got to have a laser-like focus on doing one thing better than anyone else.

I was recently counseling a young software developer. He had several business ideas, but they had all been done before. He could tell me what he wanted to do and name similar sites, but he couldn't tell me how his ideas were different, how he was going to come out on top. No wonder he couldn't decide which one to focus on.

In a 2014 *Wall Street Journal* essay, venture capitalist Peter Thiel wrote, "If you want to create and capture lasting value, look to build a monopoly." He said entrepreneurs should ask themselves, "What valuable company is nobody building?" and added, "This question is harder than it looks." He's right. Most startup founders and CEOs never come up with the right answer.

The only way to be successful is by figuring out what you're best at and focusing on doing just that. It's true for every entrepreneur and every company, big and small.

In the aforementioned Charlie Rose interview with Tim Cook, the Apple boss said striving to stay focused on being the best was a core principle Steve Jobs instilled in the company. "It's easy to add. It's hard to edit. It's hard to stay focused. And yet we know we'll only do our best work if we stay focused," he said, "and so the hardest decisions we make are all the things *not* to work on."

On the flip side, our good friends at Sony have been trying to turn the floundering company around for so long I can't remember a time they weren't. They fail over and over for one simple reason: Sony has a split personality. It can't excel at being a global entertainment company and a consumer electronics giant at the same time, not without there being some material synergies between the two, which there aren't.

Nearly a decade ago, then Yahoo! senior veep Brad Garlinghouse tried to convince his fellow Yahoo! employees that the company lacked cohesive vision and focus, that it was trying to be too many things to too many people. His internal memo, which ended up in the *Wall*

Street Journal, came to be known as the Peanut Butter Manifesto. All these years and I don't know how many CEOs later, the internet company is still struggling with the same problem.

Focus. Period.

PITFALL 6: THE DINOSAUR EFFECT

Focusing on doing what you do best is not the same thing as staying the course when it's clear that your strategy has failed and it's time to make some changes. And yet we often see founders and CEOs stick to their plans like deer caught in the headlights of an oncoming vehicle.

That's more or less how BlackBerry (then Research in Motion) cofounders Mike Lazaridis and Jim Balsillie handled the explosion of Apple and Google onto the smartphone scene they once dominated. They weren't just caught completely flatfooted. They responded with disbelief, then mockery, and finally with agonizingly slow, grudging, and futile efforts to catch up. They never admitted they were in trouble, even as iPhone and Android decimated their market share.

The hapless pair was again caught by surprise when Apple's iPad hit the market three years later. After losing $70 billion in market value, they finally stepped down and appointed a Kool-Aid-drinking crony, then co-COO Thorsten Heins, as their successor. In his first Wall Street conference call, Heins actually said, "I don't think that there is some drastic change needed." You know how that turned out. Nobody owns a BlackBerry today.

That sort of thing happens all the time.

Sun Microsystems cofounder and chief executive Scott McNealy and his handpicked successor Jonathan Schwartz did more or less the same thing. The company was sold to Oracle for a fraction of what it was worth in its heyday.

I'm not going to put Coca-Cola CEO Muhtar Kent in that same class just yet, but as Coke and Diet Coke continue to fizzle amid declining global demand for carbonated drinks, Kent recently doubled down on his Coke marketing strategy instead of diversifying more aggressively like rival PepsiCo.

The sad thing is it doesn't have to be that way. When Microsoft used its operating system leverage and pricing power to dominate key PC applications and utilities, not every company went the way of the dinosaur like WordPerfect, Borland, and Ashton-Tate. Adobe, Intuit, and Lotus all managed to adapt and thrive, the last as a subsidiary of IBM. And while just about every other big iron computer company is gone, IBM survived the fallout of the PC era by reinventing itself as an IT services company.

Markets change. Competitors change. Everything changes. For your business to survive and thrive over the long haul, you have to be flexible and adapt or end up like the dinosaurs.

PITFALL 7: FEAR OF FLYING

Everyone knows the story of Icarus, the mythical character who ignored his father's warnings about flying too close to the sun on wings made of feathers and wax. In case you forgot the ending, his wings melted. Bye-bye Icarus. The moral of the story is that hubris is bad, and indeed it is.

But given a better wing design, you'd have the Wright Brothers instead of a Greek tragedy.

We've already discussed how real entrepreneurs don't do things in half measures. They go all in. But they're not all adrenaline freaks. Some do it for practical reasons. While none of us are truly fearless, if you don't at least *act* that way when it comes to taking risks, you'll never face your first failure and survive to do it again until you finally take off like a rocket.

I've seen way too many companies fail to capitalize on opportunities and pay the ultimate price. The problem is that markets tend to be pretty unforgiving. If you don't have the guts to go big, somebody else will, and that'll be the end of your sweet gig, as the founders of the gluten-free bakery we talked about earlier discovered.

The most famous example of companies that failed to capitalize on their efforts is Xerox's PARC—the research center whose inventions led to all sorts of cool things like personal computers and networks. Unfortunately, PARC never commercialized any of it.

Another great example is Kodak. I bet you didn't know that Kodak invented digital photography and just sat on it. The once-great company eventually filed for Chapter 11 bankruptcy protection, a dead relic of a foregone era before digital photography took over the market.

After being diagnosed with pancreatic cancer and facing imminent mortality, Steve Jobs learned the folly of being afraid to fail and lose what you have. He expressed that lesson in a way that only he could during that Stanford University commencement speech: "Remembering that you are going to die is the best way I know to avoid the trap of thinking you have something to lose."

PITFALL 8: THE DYSFUNCTIONAL FOUNDER PROBLEM

I've had the distinct pleasure of working with more than my fair share of talented and innovative entrepreneurs. While some of them could use some executive coaching, others would be better off with a good shrink. Sadly, some of their behavior was just dysfunctional enough to royally screw things up for themselves and their companies.

That's not meant to be as irreverent as it sounds. Believe me, I have empathy for founders and their stakeholders. After all, I wasn't exactly a paragon of virtuous behavior when I was an executive, either. Nobody's perfect.

Nevertheless, the most common preventable failure mode by far is when CEOs and business leaders are simply not willing to put their own narrow beliefs, myopic views, utopian ideals, selfish greed, hubris, or fragile egos aside; face reality; and do what's right for the company.

I say "not willing" because it is a choice. Denial is a choice. Failing to challenge your comfort zone and deal with your limitations is a choice. Complacency is a choice. Listening to groupthink is a choice. Lacking the courage to face your fears is a choice. Letting your oversized ego write checks that reality can't cash is a choice. And putting your own self-interest ahead of those of your stakeholders and your business is a choice.

Any decent psychiatrist will tell you that on some level people always know what's really going on. They know what they're doing, and they hear what others tell them. So when they suppress it, bury it in their subconscious, and hear only what they want to hear—that, my friends, is a choice.

There are lots of failure modes for startups and small businesses, but if you do a little digging, the root cause is often leaders or owners living in denial of what's staring them right in the face. And the results are often devastating.

Whenever we hear about a company in trouble, our initial reaction is to say that their leaders are stupid. Well, I've got news for you: Their minds are usually pretty damn smart; it's their actions that are dumb. We call them incompetent and blame failure on the Peter Principle. They're probably competent enough to know they're screwing up, but they choose not to deal with it.

Why do they do it? I'm no shrink. All I can do is observe how their dysfunctions manifest, and that's usually in the form of bad decision making:

▶ They hire the wrong people, who don't have what it takes to do the job.

▶ They take crazy risks by acquiring companies and executing megamergers without appropriate due diligence.

▶ They opt for quick fixes when they should know there are no shortcuts to long-term success.

▶ They somehow think they don't need a differentiated value proposition, when that's clearly fundamental.

▶ They have holes in their strategies that miracles couldn't fill.

▶ They listen to sugarcoating yes-men who tell them what they think they want to hear.

▶ They act as if they have all the answers, all evidence to the contrary.

▶ And they engage in petty internal battles with their cofounders instead of parking their egos and working together as a team.

I see this stuff every day. And none of it is rocket science, folks. It's Startup 101. I don't care how inspired or passionate you are. Like it or not, there are laws of physics, finance, management, and human nature your ego simply cannot overcome. You should all know better. In all likelihood, you probably do.

By all means, reach for the stars, but keep your feet planted firmly on the ground. We all have limitations. We all have issues. We're all human. So act like it. Have the guts to take a good, hard look at yourself and deal with what you see. If that doesn't work, try a coach . . . or, better yet, a good shrink.

PART IV

THE
REAL
LEADER

CHAPTER 19

THE
NO BS
LEADER

WHEN DID LEADERSHIP BECOME A THING? Maybe that's the wrong question to ask. Maybe the right question is: When did leadership fall into the hands of amateurs? When did it become the domain of self-help writers, silver-tongued motivational speakers, and coaches armed with certificates?

It's no coincidence that leadership became trendy soon after Web 2.0 became a thing. That's when it became easy for anyone with a Mac and an IP address to come up with a gimmick and feed the hungry masses what they so desperately wanted to hear. You know the drill by now. Once there's a market, everyone rushes in to capitalize on all the clicks and consulting fees.

And now, to grow their audience, these self-serving posers are telling everyone you don't have to be a manager, be an executive, or even run a business to be a leader. You can be a leader by getting people to subscribe to your blog or follow you on social media. So anyone can be a leader; all you have to do is subscribe to their brand of Kool-Aid to become the next Tony Robbins.

What a complete load of BS. Leadership is about running a company or an organization. Period. And all that nonsense won't help you do that one bit.

Sadly, much of what passes for leadership content these days is more likely to inspire and engage *you* than help you inspire and engage others. It's more likely to motivate you to cough up a few bucks and waste your time than provide genuine insights into motivating your stakeholders.

The remainder of the book is devoted to dispelling some of the more popular and corrosive leadership notions of the day and providing a solid framework for today's and tomorrow's executives and business leaders. Let's get started by introducing you to a novel concept: that leadership is nothing special. The path to becoming a real leader doesn't start with you at all. It starts with whatever it is that so captured your imagination that it's become your life's work. The hard part is figuring out how to turn that into a successful enterprise. The rest is just experience and fine-tuning, more or less.

Think about it. Everyone wants to work on what they're interested in. Everyone wants to contribute to something that has a real chance of making a difference. Everyone wants to work with like-minded people who work well together. And everyone wants to be successful and fulfilled.

If you're inspired by your work, if you're engaged and motivated to do great things, and if you have certain basics covered, you'll have no trouble inspiring, engaging, and motivating others. And you won't need any fads or gimmicks.

Skeptical? Perfect. Let's get started by looking at the leadership styles of some of our most successful CEOs.

THE BILL GATES SCHOOL OF LEADERSHIP

What do Steve Jobs, Bill Gates, Andy Grove, Larry Page, and Mark Zuckerberg all have in common? Besides being some of the most famous entrepreneurs and successful CEOs of our time, they're all well-known for being among the most difficult people to work with, and that's putting it kindly.

If you look at all the popular dogma about what a great leader is supposed to be like, those guys wouldn't even be in the conversation. We're talking egotistical, low-EQ, hyper-competitive jerks. And yet they didn't just build some of the most valuable corporations on earth; they created what are undoubtedly some of the best companies to work for.

How exactly did that happen?

Simple. They built great companies with unique cultures where employees were inspired to make killer products that changed the world. Granted, you probably don't have to be an asshole to make that happen. At the opposite extreme are far more likable characters, such as Richard Branson, Herb Kelleher, John Mackey, and Tony Hsieh, who also built great companies.

And between those two extremes are an enormous spectrum of styles, behaviors, and personalities. So what does that prove? It proves without a doubt that all the common wisdom about leadership is crap. Nothing the self-proclaimed gurus say matters. I'll tell you what does matter in a minute, but first let me tell you something about Gates.

I don't know him personally, but I have worked with Microsoft and I do know people who know him well. It goes without saying that Gates is a brilliant technologist and businessman. But during his more than two decades at the helm of Microsoft, he was a ruthless and predatory competitor and often confrontational, petulant, and verbally abusive.

While I was at Stac, we sued Microsoft for patent infringement, and a federal jury later agreed, ordering the software giant to stop shipping the offending code—its then-flagship operating system, MS-DOS 6—and awarding us $120 million in damages.

Both Gates and Stac's Clow testified during the four-week jury trial. But it was probably Gates' own testimony that sank Microsoft's case. Observers said he came off as defensive and disingenuous on the stand and Stac's attorneys caught him in numerous direct contradictions between his testimony and internal company emails and public statements.

Wendy Goldman Rohm's *The Microsoft File: The Secret Case Against Bill Gates* describes how Gates blew up at CBS News' Connie Chung after the trial. He apparently threw a massive temper tantrum and abruptly ended the interview after she referred to something Clow said: "A lot of people make the analogy that competing with Bill Gates is like playing hardball. I'd say it's more like a knife fight."

Gates would have saved himself a lot of personal agony if he'd developed a little humility and a thicker skin earlier in his career. The Stac case was the first of many legal entanglements Microsoft would find itself wrapped up in over the coming years. The Department of Justice's antitrust case against Microsoft would bring out all sorts of ugly comments, including Novell CEO Ray Noorda's comparison of Gates and his executives to Nazi generals.

Why bring all this up about a man who built a company that boasts 1.5 billion users, created more than 10,000 millionaires, and always ranks among the top companies to work for? A man who has since dedicated his life and much of his fortune to enhance health care, reduce poverty, and improve education around the world by creating the largest private foundation in history?

I have no interest in raking Gates over the coals. I think that's been done to death, and at this point the guy has clearly grown up and made us proud. While I certainly had issues with Gates back in the early 1990s, I couldn't have more respect or admiration for the man today. Besides, I've seen a lot of similar behavior from dozens of executives and business leaders I've known over the years. And since we're the same age, I can admit to being no less immature and rough around the edges as Gates was back in the day.

I simply wanted to demonstrate that leadership is not what it's cracked up to be. That it comes in all shapes and sizes. That your particular style, strengths, weaknesses, emotional intelligence, and personality traits don't necessarily factor into the picture exactly as you'd expect.

To that extent, leadership is a lot like physical appearance. People may look beautiful or striking, but upon closer examination, they don't usually have perfect noses, eyes, mouths, or bodies. It's how it all goes together that matters. And that's just looks. Once you get beneath the skin, the analogy becomes even more compelling.

Beauty isn't skin deep. Neither is leadership.

THE WARREN BUFFETT SCHOOL OF LEADERSHIP

Ironically, around the time of the Stac trial, Gates met a guy who would become a real mentor, Berkshire Hathaway chairman Warren Buffett. According to his 2014 *Wall Street Journal* op-ed, when Gates asked the Oracle of Omaha to recommend his favorite business book, Buffett named a book that had been written 20 years before, *Business Adventures* by John Brooks. Since it was out of print, Buffett sent Gates his copy, which Gates apparently still has.

Brooks was a great storyteller whose chronicles of the executives of Xerox, General Electric, Ford, Piggly Wiggly, and many others are about as close to experiencing them in real life as you can get. As a result, they provide powerful insights into what it really takes to lead a successful business.

As Gates said in the article, "Unlike a lot of today's business writers, Brooks didn't boil his work down into pat how-to lessons or simplistic explanations for success. You won't find any listicles in his work. Brooks wrote long articles that frame an issue, explore it in depth, introduce a few compelling characters and show how things went for them. . . .

"Brooks's work is a great reminder that the rules for running a strong business and creating value haven't changed. For one thing, there's an essential human factor in every business endeavor." He says the book has stood the test of time because it's as much about human nature—how leaders react to challenging circumstances—as it is about specific businesses.

Indeed, had Gates and Buffett concerned themselves with amorphous concepts like leadership abilities when they were young instead of building and growing their companies, they would not be among the richest and most successful entrepreneurs the world has ever known. They became great leaders over decades through the experience of building their companies one day at a time.

Leaders are not born, proclaimed, or entitled. CEOs don't just fall out of the sky into cushy corner office chairs. They are the product of an extraordinarily complex combination of internal and external factors, chains of events, circumstances, and experience. The business world has so many moving parts it makes a modern sports car seem like a Lego toy.

If you want to become a great leader, the best way to accomplish that is by following your passion, being true to yourself, creating great products, hiring the best talent, and building a successful business that values its employees and customers. If you want to learn how to be a great leader, start by learning how to build a great business. The rest will follow as you mature and gain experience.

THE ANDY GROVE SCHOOL OF LEADERSHIP

I never worked for Intel's Grove, but I've often felt as if I did. As a partner and then a head-to-head competitor in the cutthroat microprocessor business, I came to know many of Intel's top executives quite well. Besides, Silicon Valley is overrun with former Intel employees. You can't walk down the street without running into one or two.

In any case, Grove's unique management style, at least as I came to understand it, has greatly informed my own methods and thinking on the subject.

For one thing, I don't think it was possible to BS Grove. If Steve Jobs had a reality distortion field, Grove had a BS shield. I used to work with a top executive who began his career at Intel. The guy was one hell of a BSer. I heard from several former Intel employees that he and Grove didn't get along very well. I'm not the least bit surprised.

Grove was a big fan of constructive conflict. In his book *High Output Management*, Grove provides a diagram of the ideal decision-making process. It starts with "free discussion," then "clear decision," and finally "full support." If the decision turns out to be wrong, the process repeats. I'm embarrassed to say I never got around to reading the entire book, but that description alone provides brilliant insight into what's probably the most critical management process in any company.

Here's how I've come to view that decision-making process. Everything is on the table—and I mean everything. Everyone tells it like it is. It's not enough to simply encourage everyone to be completely open and honest; it's a requirement to achieve optimum outcomes.

Participants leave their personal agendas at the door. To be successful at Intel, that actually means leaving your personal agenda at the entrance to the company.

There's no place for those who sugarcoat the truth or cover their asses. Phrases like *how it's done* and *how we do it* have little meaning. Sugarcoating, political correctness, and the status quo are all enemies of an effective decision-making process.

If you want to determine the best course of action, figure out how best to achieve the goals of the company.

Once a clear decision is reached—either by consensus or, if necessary, by the responsible executive—then it's documented and everyone commits full support to the decision. If your side loses the debate, you still have to *disagree and commit*, meaning everyone's on the same page from that point forth until the plan succeeds or fails.

The process is beautiful in its simplicity and effectiveness. It generates outcomes with the best chance of success given the information and expertise at hand. It also creates an aligned high-performance management team that works together to execute agreed-upon strategies and achieve common goals.

Nevertheless, the process can still be corrupted and potentially derailed after the fact, primarily by passive-aggressive behavior or publicly agreeing with a decision while undermining it behind the scenes. You might call that *disagree and betray*. Passive-aggressive behavior is dysfunctional and corrosive in terms of management effectiveness.

Grove's management (I doubt he's fond of the term *leadership*—too amorphous) style—which is still evident in the way Intel operates today—created a highly flexible culture that adapts rapidly to changing market conditions. It's also surprisingly resilient to scale. At times I've seen Intel move and pivot as rapidly as a startup.

Encouraging constructive conflict during decision making goes a long way toward eliminating the *de*structive effects of conflict, not to mention the insidious results of groupthink and corporate inertia.

THE KNIGHTS OF THE ROUND TABLE SCHOOL OF LEADERSHIP

One of the trickier concepts for any CEO or business leader involves delegation and authority. When a business transitions to more than one level of management, decision making can get much more complicated.

The issue generally comes down to this. It's always best to have clear lines of responsibility, so you want your lieutenants to have authority over their functional areas. But you also want to encourage their peers to voice opinions that carry some weight. After all, functions overlap, and you want your leadership team to be aligned. Besides, they're diverse executives with broad experience. You want them to bring it all to the table.

Take marketing, sales, and product development, for example. Marketing has to define products that engineers can design and sales can sell. Clearly, they each have a vested interest in how the others do their jobs. In other words, they're all mutual stakeholders in each other's operations. So how do you ensure they meet each other's needs without compromising their individual authority?

Consider the Knights of the Round Table as a leadership team model. Everyone has an equal voice and is encouraged to express her opinion on all matters, whether it's in her area of functional responsibility or not. The only difference is that the functional executive always gets to make the final call.

The process works because of peer pressure. If marketing comes up with product features that engineering can't design or sales can't sell, they should openly call him on it. It's hard for a marketing head to override his peers without a pretty compelling argument. And since they're all encouraged to get everything on the table and hash it out, marketing will usually end up making the right call—or pay the price for failing.

As for chief executives overriding lieutenants on decisions that are clearly within their functional domain, I'm not a fan. One former CEO of mine said it best. I had just joined the company as senior veep of worldwide marketing, and during our initial one-on-one, he said, "Look, I'm a very opinionated guy, so I'm always going to tell you what I think and sometimes pretty forcefully, but marketing is still your domain and you get to make the call." He paused for a moment, then added, "Just so we're clear, if you do decide to follow my advice and it turns out to be wrong, that's on you." That's how it should be, but there are exceptions.

When a company is in trouble, that's when the boss needs to get hands-on wherever the trouble lies. While the processes I've defined should still be the same, a chief executive should never hesitate to apply as much pressure as necessary to bring critical issues into focus and get the company back on track. And if certain issues become chronic, that's when it might be time for a personnel change.

In other words, as long as you have the right managers in place and you've organized your leadership team so they're aligned with the company's goals, you should get out of the way and let them do their jobs. When that's not working, it's time to get hands-on and look at your processes and people.

Of course, in matters of corporate strategy and other decisions of that nature, the CEO always makes the call. By all means, listen to what everyone has to say, but trust your own instincts when making the final decision.

One last thing. You can do everything right to build an effective team, but that will all be for naught if their goals and metrics are not aligned. The best way to ensure that is to make the process of goal setting, alignment, and measurement reasonably open and transparent among the management team. And that needs to affect a significant component of executive compensation for it to have teeth.

THE *YOU* SCHOOL OF LEADERSHIP

When it comes to running a business, it's one thing to consider various methods that have worked for others and resonate with you, but you don't want to go overboard for two simple reasons.

First, the number of variables is enormous. Every situation is unique. Not only is every industry, competitive market, company, customer base, leadership team, and senior executive distinct, but the number of factors that impact each of those entities is also practically limitless and always in flux. To say one size does not fit all is a ludicrous understatement.

Second, don't underestimate the "you" factor. Whichever business leader you happen to admire—Branson, Jobs, Grove, Hsieh, Kelleher, Mackey—remember that, if they hadn't done things their own way, you wouldn't be admiring them. They achieved success by being themselves, thinking for themselves, and running their companies the way only they saw fit. Granted, they all had mentors who informed their thinking—we all do—but they had the courage and the drive to create their own path instead of following someone else's.

The world doesn't need another Richard Branson or Andy Grove. The world needs *you*. The most important factor in leadership is the *you* factor. Whatever it is that inspired you to start a business and motivated you to build a company will inspire and motivate others to join you. Let it speak for itself.

CHAPTER 20

THE MYTH
OF THE
ROCK STAR LEADER

WE'RE ALL DRAWN TO ICONIC LEADERS WITH CAPTIVATING visions and rock star presence. If that were a prerequisite for top executives, we'd be deprived of some of the greatest entrepreneurs and CEOs of our time. The most obvious examples are Gates and Buffett. If you've ever seen them onstage, you would never confuse either with Mick Jagger or Paul McCartney.

Some of the most commonly held beliefs about leaders are complete myths. But their remarkable popularity and persistence have a decidedly toxic effect on many of our careers and companies. It's long past time we shred those misconceptions.

THE MYTH OF THE EXTROVERTED LEADER

Charismatic leaders clearly possess a powerful ability to attract followers. But if that were a requirement for running a successful company, not only would Gates and Buffett be out of luck, so would Cook, Page, Charles Schwab, Colgate-Palmolive's Ian Cook, Campbell Soup's Doug Conant, and countless other current and former chief executives. The trait they share: they're all introverts.

According to the *The Wall Street Journal*, a 2011 survey of more than 1,500 senior managers by TheLadders.com drew a fascinating conclusion: Nearly two-thirds saw themselves as introverts and felt that characteristic would hurt their chances of climbing the corporate ladder and becoming successful senior executives. While that barrier may indeed exist in terms of perception, reality is another story entirely.

Having worked with thousands of senior executives, not only have I not seen any evidence of a correlation between job performance and introversion or extroversion, I'm not even sure business leaders tend one way or the other. If you tested a large sample of senior executives for that trait, you'd probably see a relatively normal Gaussian distribution. I'm not saying there's no cultural bias, but that doesn't seem to stop introverts from getting the job and doing it well.

Now that I think about it, many of the most effective executives and business leaders I've worked with over the years were introverts. One well-known high-tech CEO once told me he was so painfully shy as a youth that he lived in terror on a daily basis at the very thought of speaking in class. How did he succeed? By having the courage to face his fear, challenge himself, and venture out of his comfort zone every day. He's still doing it, even though he could have retired a wealthy man long ago.

Another chief executive I've worked with for many years was such a poor verbal communicator that when we first spoke on the phone I nearly fell asleep in the middle of the conversation. The guy is brilliant—he has a Ph.D. in physics—but he was so slow and methodical that I wanted to pull the words out of his mouth. He couldn't present for beans. But that didn't stop him from raising tons of money and leading one company to a successful acquisition and another to an IPO and a multibillion-dollar valuation.

While common descriptive terms such as extroverted, visionary, inspiring, empathetic, and likable are in no way predictive of business success, cultural conformity around certain attributes actually limits diversity, innovative thinking, and unique behavior.

It's a good thing the tech industry pays no attention to those stereotypes.

If you take a step back and look at what's going on, you'll notice a remarkable transformation occurring in nearly every industry. Entertainment, banking, retail, food, transportation, pharmaceuticals, energy, real estate, media—wherever you look, tech executives are completely altering the competitive landscape. And these disruptors of age-old industries bear little resemblance to stereotypical CEOs. They come in all varieties, but mostly, they're high-tech geeks.

I sometimes think Jesus misspoke when he said, "The *meek* shall inherit the earth." I think he meant to say "geek."

Former One Kings Lane chief executive Doug Mack now runs online sports retailer Fanatics, but he's a veteran of the software industry who cut his teeth at Adobe, Scene7, and Broderbund. PayPal cofounder Elon Musk is attempting to revolutionize the auto industry and space travel. And another serial entrepreneur from the tech industry, Uber's uber-competitive Kalanick, has turned the public transportation industry on its ear.

GrubHub and a host of food-tech companies are raising enormous amounts of venture capital. Zillow and Trulia are changing the real estate market, Google and Facebook are new forces in advertising, and a slew of online companies including BuzzFeed, Vox, Medium, and VICE have a whole new take on the media business. Biotech giants Genentech and Amgen have forever changed how drugs are developed. And Amazon and Netflix are making hit TV shows and just getting started on making original movies.

While there are definitely a few extroverts and visionaries at the helm of some of those companies, mostly they're just passionate, driven, and talented entrepreneurs bringing new ways of doing things to starchy old industries that could use some shaking up. One thing's for sure: They don't fit the mold of what leaders are supposed to be like. They do things their own way.

THE MYTH OF THE VISIONARY LEADER

Microsoft cofounder Paul Allen sees himself as a visionary. You can infer as much from the title and hoopla surrounding his book, *Idea Man: A Memoir by the Cofounder of Microsoft.* And while he was at one time Gates's closest friend, he left the company in the early 1980s, leaving his younger partner to continue running the show for nearly two decades.

Allen's stake in Microsoft at one time made him the third richest man in the world, but he's since diversified his fortune by investing in all sorts of other business ventures. And while he does own a great football team in the Seattle Seahawks, his other endeavors have not fared so well. Today, Allen is No. 47 on the *Forbes* billionaire list. That's a big drop.

We shouldn't cry for Allen, but he has lost at least $10 billion over a period when Gates, Buffett, Ballmer, and others have only increased their wealth. Moreover, while Gates and Ballmer led Microsoft for more than three decades, Allen seems to be more comfortable as the man behind the scenes of his many interests.

While every chief executive should have some sort of vision for his company, that doesn't necessarily mean he must be a visionary. The two are not the same. And I would argue the term *visionary* has not only become overused but also overrated, especially as a quality of leadership or entrepreneurship.

The problem comes down to this. A visionary has original ideas about the future. The term implies revolutionary concepts. And while I might be off by a point or two, I'm pretty sure that such ideas turn out to be wrong at least 99 percent of the time.

As I've said before, the only difference between a visionary and a lunatic is the visionary turned out to be right. And far too often we've seen self-proclaimed visionaries with overblown egos take their companies and their stakeholders on wild rides that never made a bit of sense to begin with.

That dynamic was behind pretty much every doomed megamerger, including AOL-Time Warner, Sprint-Nextel, and Alcatel-Lucent, to name a few. It was probably behind HP's choice of Carly Fiorina as its rock star CEO and her ill-fated acquisition of Compaq Computer.

A grandiose vision was certainly behind former Sony chairman Nobuyuki Idei's expansion into motion pictures to create a global entertainment giant. The once-dominant consumer electronics company has been slowly unraveling ever since.

When Yahoo! was desperately searching for a way to reignite its growth, it promoted one of its cofounders, Jerry Yang, to chief executive. The thought was that Yahoo! needed a new vision, and Yang was just the guy to come up with one. He didn't. Not only was his short-lived tenure as CEO a disaster, the company has continued its slide into obscurity ever since.

One of the biggest problems with visionaries is that they can become blinded by their own ideas and ideals. They often become myopic, lose their objectivity and common sense, and make unnecessarily high-risk bets. In other words, their egos write checks that reality can't cash.

More practical leaders don't put their visions up on pedestals. Perhaps they do have a unique take on an existing product, an innovative solution to an old problem, or a new way for employees to view their role in a company. Regardless, they stay grounded in reality, and that allows them to be flexible and adapt to the challenges ahead.

Besides, vision is but one component of what it takes to run a successful business. At least as important is coming up with innovative strategies to grow market share, beat the competition, and achieve that vision. So are developing differentiated products customers love, motivating employees to excel, and making smart decisions.

While the most underrated leadership qualities are probably perseverance, execution, and intelligence (real, not emotional), the most overrated is, without a doubt, communication.

WHEN IT COMES TO COMMUNICATION, LESS IS MORE

I recently watched a video of Google founders Larry Page and Sergey Brin speaking to a group back in 2004. Brin wasn't bad, but Page was so stiff and uncomfortable it was almost like watching a robot. Not that I hadn't seen that sort of thing before. It's not uncommon among tech founders, and it certainly hasn't stopped Page from founding, growing, and now running one of the world's most valuable companies.

More recently, Page was diagnosed with a rare and chronic nerve problem that makes it difficult for him to talk. One of his vocal cords is permanently paralyzed, and the other has limited movement. As a result, he can only talk softly and hoarsely and must limit his public speaking. In a rare Google+ post, Page discussed the condition but added, "Sergey says I'm probably a better CEO because I choose my words more carefully."

While Brin was probably only half serious, there's something to be said for his comment. The popular trend that has executives and business leaders thinking they should communicate more and more—to employees, to the media, on social media, in all sorts of public forums—is way overblown, counterproductive, and in many cases actually destructive for their companies and their careers.

Case in point: serial entrepreneur Gurbaksh Chahal, who I mentioned briefly in Chapter 6. At the age of 16, Chahal dropped out of high school to found an advertising network company and sold it less than two years later at the height of the dotcom bubble for $22.2 million. Four years later, he leveraged that windfall to form another advertising company, BlueLithium, and sold *that* to Yahoo! in 2007 for $300 million.

At that point, Chahal began what can only be described as one of the most blatantly garish and flamboyant self-promotion campaigns in business history. There were professional photo shoots of himself and his lavish San Francisco penthouse, a photo op with President Obama, and appearances on TV, including *The Oprah Winfrey Show*, which billed him as one of the world's youngest and wealthiest entrepreneurs. Not to mention that his personal blog and social media posts seemed to be those of an unabashed narcissist.

That would prove to be his downfall.

In 2014, nearly five years after founding a third advertising tech company, RadiumOne, Chahal found himself at the center of a social media firestorm after he pleaded guilty to one count of misdemeanor battery and one of domestic violence battery against his then-girlfriend. Actually, that was the good news. The DA was forced to drop a 45-felony-count indictment when a judge ruled a 30-minute security camera video from Chahal's apartment—allegedly showing him hitting and kicking his girlfriend 117 times in 30 minutes—was inadmissible because it was seized without a warrant.

Instead of managing this self-inflicted crisis as he should—admitting he screwed up, apologizing, and letting things settle down—the 31-year-old made a bad situation much worse by writing long, rambling blog posts and promoting them to his many followers on social media.

In one 18-paragraph rant dramatically titled "Can You Handle the Truth?" Chahal tried to defend himself by unwisely replaying every detail of the night in question. He said he did not hit his girlfriend 117 times (yes, he did repeat the allegation) and remarkably painted himself as the victim, blaming everyone but himself for the incident, including the police, the DA, the media, and even his girlfriend.

The media of course had a field day, and since Chahal continued to fuel the fire instead of letting it drop, the board eventually had no choice but to fire him. That of course prompted another online tirade, this one called "An Open Letter to the Board of RadiumOne: Greed, Betrayal, Dishonesty," in which he whined about how the board abandoned him when he needed their support and threatened them with "severe legal consequences" for terminating him.

The board's terse response was, "Gurbaksh Chahal's own actions impaired his ability to lead RadiumOne as CEO and gave the board no choice but to terminate his employment and name a new CEO."

Meanwhile, had Chahal handled the mess he created like a mature adult instead of indulging his overinflated ego and delusions of grandeur and acting out like a whiny child, there's a chance he might still be running the company.

Granted, that story's a bit extreme, but we are seeing this sort of thing more and more since the advent of Web 2.0 and the coming of age of Generation Me.

Now contrast Chahal's actions with those of Evan Spiegel, the CEO of ephemeral messaging company Snapchat. When news broke that the 23-year-old founder had turned down a $3 billion all-cash buyout offer from Facebook, the tech pundits thought he was crazy, but the young entrepreneur kept his head down.

And when a string of embarrassing emails—full of vulgar references to sex, drugs, and underage drinking—from his frat days at Stanford surfaced in 2014, he handled it like a pro. Spiegel told *Business Insider* he was "mortified and embarrassed" about the "idiotic emails," adding, "I have no excuse. I'm sorry I wrote them at the time and I was [a] jerk to have written them. They in no way reflect who I am today or my views toward women."

That was of course the right thing to do, and, unlike Chahal, he kept his job. It bears mentioning that Spiegel has since raised more than a billion dollars from a who's who of top VCs, valuing the startup at $16 billion. And Snapchat has quietly become the hottest social media platform since Twitter. Nearly a decade Chahal's junior, Spiegel could probably teach a course in communication for business leaders.

The overcommunication trend isn't just true for Millennials or external communications, either, as AOL CEO Tim Armstrong came to learn.

Back in 2013 there had been an unfortunate media leak about a coming layoff at the company's underperforming Patch unit, so Armstrong held an all-hands conference call with more than 1,000 employees to shed some light on the subject and hopefully improve morale. Unfortunately, things got a bit out of hand a few minutes into the call:

"There's a couple of things I want you guys to realize and really think about and sink in, and if it doesn't sink in and you don't believe what I'm about to say, I'm going to ask you to leave Patch. And I don't mean that in a harsh way . . ." said Armstrong.

"If you don't use Patch as a product and you're not invested in Patch, you owe it to everyone else at Patch to leave. If you think what's going on right now is a joke, and you want to joke around about it, you should pick your stuff up and leave Patch today and the reason is, and I'm going to be very specific about this, is Patch from an experience—Abel, put that camera down right now! Abel, you're fired. Out!"

That was it. The 41-year-old chief executive of a large public company really did publicly fire Patch's creative director and go on with the call without missing a beat. To be fair, he later issued an apology, but I seriously doubt that would have happened had the audio not been leaked to the media, which, as you might expect, stoked more than a little controversy.

On another call a few months later, Armstrong explained to employees how the company's rising health-care costs were in part due to million-dollar insurance payments made for two AOL employees with distressed babies. This was somehow meant to explain why the company had to change its 401(k) plan.

Here's a tip for the communication genius who thought blaming a hike in health-care premiums on mothers with sick newborns was a good idea: Someday you'll find your ideal profession. Keep looking. And if it was Armstrong's bright idea, he should know by now that these all-hands meetings are not benefitting AOL in any way. They're certainly not helping his reputation.

Unfortunately, this sort of thing happens a lot more often than you'd think, and certainly not just at AOL.

You might recall from Chapter 6 how former PayPal president David Marcus may have emailed himself out of a job after sending a shockingly demeaning, demotivating, and scathing message to all employees.

Whenever that sort of thing happens, every self-proclaimed leadership and communication guru comes out of the woodwork with 20/20 hindsight lessons on how executives should be more effective communicators and crisis managers in an era in which anything juicy gets recorded, leaked, posted, and tweeted.

But these are the same *experts* that sold corporate America on the idea that communication is not only the most critical leadership skill but the best thing since Homo sapiens evolved lips. And of course there's no such thing as too much communication.

Therein lies the rub.

This isn't about executives needing to communicate more often, more effectively, or more sensitively. This is about top executives communicating too much because they're being misled by their communications people and the agencies and consultants they hire. The now ubiquitous all-hands meetings, town-hall meetings, and all-employee emails are not the best way to communicate with and motivate employees.

I'll let you in on a little secret: CEOs have been saying caustic things that do more harm than good since the beginning of time. That's because they have a lot going on, and, for the most part, they're far better at running the show than they are at putting on a show.

Sure, top executives may give lip service to the idea that they need to communicate effectively, but it's simply not their highest priority. So things don't come out the way they should, feet end up in mouths, and the next thing you know, it's crisis management and apology time.

Granted, we now have smartphones, social media, a 24/7 news cycle, and an insatiable appetite for executive train wrecks. But all that means is the public now gets to witness all the dumb things executives say when they desperately try to explain every little decision they make.

We'll be learning a lot more about Lao Tzu's *Tao Te Ching* in a couple of chapters, but here's what it has to say about leadership communication, according to an adaptation called *The Tao of Leadership* by John Heider:

"The wise leader speaks rarely and briefly. After all, no other natural outpouring goes on and on. It rains and then it stops. It thunders and then it stops. The leader teaches more through being than through doing. The quality of one's silence conveys more than long speeches. Few things under heaven are as instructive as the lessons of silence."

The point is simple. Communication is but one aspect of running and growing a business. Don't make it into more than it is. Instead of all-hands meetings and companywide memos, create a culture where communication occurs in more natural and organic ways. Walk around. Communicate openly and frequently with your staff. Encourage them to do the same. Sure, there are times when you have to speak to everyone, but those should be rare. The same goes for social media, blogging, or any other one-to-many communication channel.

When it comes to communication, as with so many things in business, less is usually more.

THE PROBLEM WITH "FAKE IT 'TIL YOU MAKE IT"

There once was a big technology company with a long and storied history that, through no fault of its own, found itself in need of a CEO in relatively short order. Nevertheless, the board conducted a search process and, after a few months, announced the choice of a relatively inexperienced executive from a much smaller company.

My reaction at the time was one of surprise. But when I later met this first-time CEO, I understood what had happened. Whether it was in his office or onstage in front of thousands of people, the man dominated the room. He had a powerful vision for the company and an enormous ego that was bigger than life. On the outside, he was a rock star. But his performance turned out to be far more sizzle than substance.

I'm reminded of that every time I see another company's logo where the former company's distinctive mark used to be.

That sort of thing happens far more often than boards, employees, and investors would like. It brings to mind a phrase that's become quite popular in entrepreneurial circles: *Fake it 'til you make it.*

It's one thing to promote your potential to reach for new heights, but your self-image should always be grounded in reality. When Browning said, "A man's reach should exceed his grasp," he wasn't implying that competence plays no role in the outcome. Completely ignoring your limitations and weaknesses is a very bad idea, especially for those in leadership positions.

If you really are faking it to try to boost your confidence when, in reality, you don't have the talent, capability, and experience to back it up, it probably won't end well. On some level you know the truth. We always do. Try as you might to bury it, your subconscious knows it, and that creates anxiety that will hurt your performance. You may come across as deceitful or disingenuous. In all likelihood, you'll make mistakes that will erode your confidence, and that's not the outcome you're looking for.

On the other hand, if you have what it takes but still feel insecure about it—a not uncommon phenomenon that goes by the name of *impostor syndrome*—then you're not really faking it, are you? If experience tells you that you know what you're doing, that's what you should be focused on. You're not faking anything because you don't have to.

The only way to boost confidence and create positive outcomes is to be well prepared, take reasonable risks, make smart decisions, and learn through experience what works and what doesn't. If you're completely honest with yourself about how things turn out, you'll gain confidence from your successes and wisdom from your failures. Self-awareness through experience is the key to confidence. Nothing else works.

To be clear, leadership presence, communication, and vision represent potential, not actual management or leadership ability. In my experience, one is in no way predictive of the other. It takes a lot more to effectively run a company than looking and acting the part.

In any case, business leaders serve their stakeholders best by sticking to phones, not microphones. And stages are better suited to rock stars than rock star CEOs.

CHAPTER 21

UNDERSTANDING COMPANY CULTURE

Ask ten CEOs about company culture—what it is and why it matters—and you'll get ten different answers. The funny thing is, that's exactly as it should be. This is one of those rare instances when a vague definition may actually be a good thing.

For the purposes of this chapter, however, I see company culture as just like any other type of culture: It's how people behave. When a company is successful, we try to define what made that happen—to capture what worked, preserve it, and replicate it as the company grows.

But plenty of successful companies don't give a moment's thought to their culture, and a cool culture won't count for beans when you file for bankruptcy.

Nevertheless, company culture matters, and I'll tell you why. Business success may be all about making killer products that capture markets and keep customers coming back for more, but culture plays a big role in *how* a company does that. It also helps determine how well your company scales and adapts to an ever-changing competitive landscape. And, in a very real sense, it embodies how vision becomes reality.

Until recently, that generally happened on a more or less adhoc basis. Founders created culture without making a big deal over it or, in many cases, even realizing they were doing it. Today, as with leadership, the concept has become way overblown. So let me be very clear about this: You can't copy and paste company culture. They're unique to specific leaders, companies, industries, and even points in time.

That said, there are certain principles that do seem to travel well between companies and situations. Here's my take on what works, what doesn't work, and why. The *how* will be left to you. It's that unique thumbprint that often creates new corporate cultures that manage to outperform all the others.

EMPOWERMENT, NOT ENGAGEMENT

The good folks at Gallup and other consulting firms have turned employee engagement into an enormous moneymaking fad. But for decades, innovative entrepreneurs and business leaders have been creating company cultures that go far beyond engaging employees by empowering them to make a real difference.

Let's not mince words. Employee engagement is just employee satisfaction 2.0. Sure, Gallup added the words *involvement* and *commitment* to the definition, but that's nothing new. More important, I don't believe that what Gallup or anyone else is selling necessarily leads to greater productivity, higher customer engagement, or improved operating results.

But then, that should come as no surprise. If you think about it, the term *engagement*—meaning emotional involvement, in this context—implies manipulation, since emotions are the limbic system's autonomic reaction to environmental stimuli.

Don't you think it might be more effective to motivate employees to do great work by giving them good reasons to do so, rather than trying to control them by playing on their involuntary survival instincts?

Ever since Peter Drucker identified the importance of human capital in a successful company, senior executives in the best-run corporations have been working to do just that by relating business drivers to human drivers. Align those two things, and you've unlocked the secret of business management.

The way to do that isn't by engaging or manipulating employees. What you do is empower them to make a real difference by investing in them, trusting them with responsibility, and truly making them part of the company. Instead of trying to control them, empowerment transfers control to the employees.

Give employees what they value most:

▶ A chance to have a real impact

▶ As much responsibility as they can handle

▶ An environment that challenges them to reach new heights and mentors to help them do it

▶ Exceptionally competent and driven managers who work as hard as they do, if not harder

▶ A successful, growing company that makes great products that customers love

▶ A piece of the action

In other words, employees want leadership that doesn't just say they believe in them but put their money and their faith where their mouths are. Good leadership fosters meritocracy—in which employees are promoted and rewarded based on achievement and talent—so they know that success at the company is based solely on their abilities. Indeed, most technology companies I've worked with over the decades are primarily meritocracies, in which employees are empowered to take their careers as far as they will go.

I'm not sure if it was Intel or HP that first granted stock options to most employees, but whichever company came up with that idea, it was brilliant, and much of the tech sector followed suit.

It's really not that hard to build a culture that empowers employees to achieve great things and be part of something that makes a real difference. Just make sure you align their goals with their peers and those of the company and hold them accountable. That's the part that trips up a lot of leaders.

CULT-LIKE CULTURES

How do some leaders inspire such fanatical devotion from employees you'd swear they're running a religious cult? And how do they manage to retain that loyalty and dedication as the company grows? The answer may surprise you.

If you recall, back in Chapter 12 we talked about how real entrepreneurs were driven by passion, let nothing stand in their way, follow no one, and create cult-like cultures. If you think about it, that's sort of the definition of leadership, is it not? Now hold that thought for a second.

While many have observed that great companies often seem to have cult-like cultures, that's simply what entrepreneurs who become real leaders do. They do things their own way. If it works, they document and attempt to scale it. And if *that* works, the result is a highly successful company with a culture they've built around their own unique beliefs and behaviors.

Would it surprise you to know that the word *cult* is derived from the root of the word *culture*, meaning a core system of beliefs and behaviors? And there you have it. The observation that lots of great companies have cult-like cultures is simply the result of successful entrepreneurs doing what they do. And while we like to think they're all iconic, god-like figures with reality distortion fields like Steve Jobs, that's simply not the case.

Take Trader Joe's founder Joe Coulombe, for example. You would imagine the guy who came up with those tropical-themed markets with all that great booze would be a Jimmy Buffett party-animal type. In fact, Coulombe was a Stanford MBA who, after running a handful of Los Angeles-based convenience stores, came up with an idea that upwardly mobile college grads might want something better than 7-Eleven. That simple idea led to everything else that made the company successful and its culture unique.

Since 747s were just beginning to make travel to tropical locations a whole lot easier, Coulombe used that for the theme of his first market in Pasadena, which opened in 1967. He stocked it with good wine and booze simply because he'd read that educated people drank more. Then he hired good people, paid them a living wage, and voila, the formula worked. So he added more locations, primarily near universities, then began selling health foods, and the company took off.

But trust me when I tell you the guy is about as charismatic as a bar of soap. I don't mean that in a bad way, it's just that everything he did had a purpose. And it worked. The company has virtually no turnover to this day.

Speaking of charisma, to me, Cyrix's Rogers looked something like Lurch from *The Addams Family*. No, I'm not kidding. I wish I were. He was really tall, gray (not just his hair; his skin had a grayish tinge, too), and somewhat scary-looking. And on the rare occasion that he smiled, it was terrifying, because you knew something bad was about to happen. And yet he built a company of some of the best microprocessor designers on earth, who built a processor that could compete with Intel's best with a fraction of their resources. The company absolutely had a culture all its own.

These days, every entrepreneur wants to change the world, dress like Steve Jobs or Mark Zuckerberg, and let employees bring their dogs to work or some other such nonsense. None of that has anything to do with company culture. Cult-like culture comes from the beliefs and behaviors of entrepreneurs who are driven by passion, let nothing stand in their way, and follow no one. True entrepreneurs create company cultures in their own image.

DAVID VS. GOLIATH

As a veteran of many David vs. Goliath battles—from being the shortest guy in the class growing up in Brooklyn through many of the corporate adventures detailed herein—I've long known the power of the underdog.

We all love to see a person, a team, or a company come out of nowhere, face enormous obstacles, and win. It's even more exciting to watch the little guy take down a powerful giant. There's a good reason for that: Our memories of childhood run deep.

You may not be aware of it, but somewhere in your subconscious, buried beneath the layers of experience, are memories of how helpless and scared you were as a baby. So are the memories of all the terrifying firsts of youth. And who hasn't been bullied or bossed around? There's an emotional part of all of us that still sees ourselves as weak underdogs.

Perhaps it also comes down to the universal desire to defy our parents. To be in charge. To make the rules. For that to happen, the little guy has to triumph over the big guy. The underdog has to win.

The idea that a common enemy unites people has been around for a long time. It brings us together, focuses our efforts, and places a crystal-clear target on the goal. It's powerful in its simplicity, clarity, and the way it resonates with our deepest feelings.

It also brings to mind our earlier discussion of how adversity, friction, stress, and competition are responsible for natural selection, survival of the fittest, and evolution. That's how all species survive and thrive. It also explains why so many successful entrepreneurs always seem to have a chip on their shoulders, something to prove.

It's by no means a requirement, but it's a remarkably effective motivational tool, especially in the early days of a startup. When everyone has to find a superhuman ability to work ungodly hours for months on end, to focus like a laser on getting that first product done right, nothing galvanizes our efforts and steels our resolve better than a bull's-eye on an enemy's head, so to speak.

Apple has had several enemies. First it was Big Blue, IBM. When Microsoft became the force behind the PC, the Redmond software giant became Apple's next target. And when Steve Jobs felt that Google's leadership triad of Eric Schmidt, Larry Page, and Sergey Brin had betrayed him by copying the iPhone when they were supposed to be partners and Schmidt sat on Apple's board, he made the search giant his third and final enemy.

At Cyrix, we didn't need a tombstone with the Intel Inside, RIP epitaph in our lobby to know what we were after. Every employee knew our goal was to beat the semiconductor giant. But it was a calculated marketing strategy that got the pundits, the media, and many others rooting for us at a grass-roots level. It was a David vs. Goliath strategy. I should know. I sold it to our board and executed it.

There's a long list of David vs. Goliath battles that enabled far weaker competitors to challenge and topple their larger opponents. Some were purposeful strategies, while others grew organically. Regardless, these conflicts, real or perceived, have been fought for centuries, perhaps even millennia.

THINK (AND ACT) DIFFERENT

The status quo is without a doubt the most insidious source of business bureaucracy. It erodes effectiveness, productivity, and competitiveness and destroys morale in the process. Behind most great company cultures is a CEO who doesn't just see things differently but has the confidence and courage to fight the status quo and do things differently.

Apple may have the most unusual culture of any large company, but that's mostly a function of putting the product and the customer experience first. It's no accident that the Cupertino giant's culture is as distinct as its products are groundbreaking. One leads to the other. It's evident in every interaction with every employee, from executive management to the salespeople in its renowned Apple stores.

From the beginning, employees learn to Think Different. It's not written anywhere and there are few processes to follow, but they learn it just the same. Think Different isn't just a tagline from an ad campaign; it's a mindset that captures and reinforces the company's unique culture, the way it operates from top to bottom. And it works, big time.

Concepts like conventional wisdom and status quo don't exist at Apple. It does everything its own way and on its own schedule. In an era when everyone craves information, no company controls the message and content better. Transparency is for everyone else. Apple is famously secretive.

If Silicon Valley's entrepreneurial spirit, employee ownership, and casual style changed corporate America, Apple took that one giant step further. Apple's culture is like a genetic mutation of the corporate America genome. And by putting the emphasis on the product and the customer experience, Apple frees its employees from all the usual corporate bullshit so they can actually do their best work.

When German software giant SAP began to suffer from slowing revenue growth, customer defections, and plummeting employee morale, the board determined it had too many irons in too many fires, a growing bureaucracy, and a lack of vision of how to grow the company. Meanwhile archrival Oracle was growing in leaps and bounds.

Ironically, they determined that the company was too internally focused to the point of "being obsessed with [its] own internal nonsense," said then co-CEO Bill McDermott in a 2010 *Bloomberg Business* interview.

McDermott and Jim Hagemann Snabe were named to lead the company after the board ousted former chief Leo Apotheker. The pair wasted no time eliminating bureaucracy, streamlining operations, getting products to market faster, and acquiring California-based Sybase, a critical move to keep pace in the fast-growing big data and mobile spaces.

It's interesting how customer experience and company culture go hand in hand. And it doesn't seem to matter which comes first.

Southwest Airlines is known for light-hearted flight crews that sing goofy songs and tell funny stories, but that's simply part of a culture that encourages employees to be themselves, have a good time, and use their brains and creativity instead of just following the rules. And that has a real impact on the bottom line.

In a dog-eat-dog industry known for horrendous customer service, Southwest isn't just a standout in terms of customer loyalty and employee morale; its market valuation is nearly on par with far larger competitors American, Delta, and United. That's the benefit for leaders with the vision to see things differently and the courage to challenge the status quo.

HIRE THE BEST, ORGANIZE THE LEAST

Every top executive will tell you that employees are their company's most important assets, but when it comes time to hire, train, and motivate that talent, they're nowhere to be found. That's somebody else's job. Actually, it's not. It's your job.

If human capital is your primary asset and your culture defines what they're supposed to believe and how they're supposed to behave, how do you expect that to work unless you hire the right people? And how do you expect to retain them unless you give them the attention they need and deserve?

Look, I know this is one of the trickiest aspects of running a company. I've known dozens of corporate CEOs who couldn't hire the right people or keep them motivated to save their lives. It's a remarkably common pitfall of small businesses and startups as well.

But the reason is that they simply don't make it a priority. Take any company we've talked about so far—Apple, Trader Joe's, Southwest Airlines. The one thing they all have in common is that their founders made hiring and retention a priority. And whatever process they used to do that effectively became part of the company culture.

Think about it. If you take any society and begin diluting it with people who simply don't fit, in time you'll lose whatever it is that distinguished that society. That's why recruiting and retention are so critical to the success of any company. Not only are bad hires and losing good people extremely costly in the short term, but they weaken the culture over the long term as well.

Organizational structure is similarly critical because it plays an enormous role in your employees' ability to act the way you want them to, excel at their jobs, and contribute to the overall success of the company.

While everyone makes a pretty big deal of specific interview and organizational practices these days, let me tell you why they don't matter as much as you'd think.

What's important is that you clearly define your company's goals and accurately describe its culture. What's important is that you realize the necessity of hiring and retaining the best talent and make that a priority. What's important is that you organize in a way that empowers your people to do their best work and aligns their efforts to most effectively achieve the company's goals.

Exactly *how* you do all that is part of the secret sauce that makes every company unique. You're smart. You'll figure it out the same way all great entrepreneurs and business leaders do—in their own way.

My only caveat: This is one of the few things a CEO should be hands-on with. That doesn't mean you have to be involved in every single interview and organizational decision—although many CEOs are—but since these are the people you need to do great work and they have to be organized in the most effective way, you can't afford to delegate how that takes place or the responsibility for the outcome.

My only specific advice: Implement the flattest and simplest structure and the fewest processes that will facilitate desired behavior and outcomes. Keep in mind that the most valuable corporation on earth, Apple, has just ten senior executives and eight board directors, and that's counting Cook twice. With the right people in the right roles, you don't need many.

ONLY THE ADAPTABLE SURVIVE

When it comes to company culture, leaders generally make two mistakes. They think the culture comes first. And they think it's a one-step process. Neither is true.

Culture is simply the embodiment of how you think and what you do. Think of it as a sort of behavioral blueprint, the DNA for how a company operates. It requires daily execution to stay on track. And like genetic codes, it changes and evolves. After all, what good is questioning the status quo if you don't question your own?

The truth is every company runs into trouble from time to time. The more open and self-aware your culture is, the better your chances of seeing threats coming well in advance. The more adaptable your culture is, the faster and more effectively you'll deal with them and get back on track or pivot to a new course.

Of all the companies I've known and worked with over the decades, I remain most impressed with Intel's ability to anticipate competitive threats and adapt to changing market conditions. In spite of its size, Intel retains the agility of a startup. In spite of its success, Intel remains as paranoid as ever. That's a tribute to the culture Grove built. It should come as no surprise that Grove was a key mentor to Steve Jobs.

That leads us to two key takeaways about company culture. One is the cause and effect of how breakout business leaders build companies that are successful over the long haul: *First* they come up with innovative products and services that customers love in a way that seems right in the moment. It's a process that develops organically over time. If they're successful, *then* they attempt to capture what worked as a means to retain that culture as the company grows.

The other is that *replicating* is just another word for *following*. We're all influenced by others. And while it's fine to consider certain fundamental elements that worked for those who came before us, you should have confidence in your own ability to take their methods and concepts to a new level. That's what real leaders do.

CHAPTER 22

THE POLITICALLY
INCORRECT
LEADER

ONE OF THE GREATEST CHALLENGES FOR MODERN business leaders is determining how to navigate the treacherous waters surrounding an ever-increasing number of controversial workplace issues.

There's diversity and inclusion, political correctness, racial and gender bias, sexual harassment, executive pay, corporate governance, income inequality, generational differences, health care, and corporate responsibility, to name a few of the stickier ones.

While most of us would just as soon steer clear of many of these issues and focus purely on business, that is not optional. If you try to ignore them, they will not reciprocate. Likewise, if you take a position based solely on your personal or political beliefs, that strategy is sure to backfire. These are heavily nuanced issues that call for practical and objective decision making, not inflexible ideals. The best way to minimize unnecessary disruptions, distractions, and risk that can do great harm to your brand and your business is to learn what you need to know, set clear direction based on what feels right to you and seems best for your company, and stick to it.

Before we get into all that, let me make a suggestion. There's a good chance you have some pretty strong beliefs that might not exactly jibe with my approach to these issues. Nevertheless, you'll be saving yourself a lot of grief down the road by leaving those beliefs on a back burner and being open-minded.

Don't worry; it's not forever. And rest assured that, as with everything else in this book, I have no skin in this game. As always, my only goal is to provide at least somewhat objective and practical insight that helps you make smart decisions when it comes to admittedly hairy issues like diversity, meritocracy, and political correctness.

DIVERSITY AND DISCRIMINATION

As a young engineer, I volunteered to be the college recruiting liaison for my department. We were ramping up for some big programs and needed to hire a boatload of engineers, and I thought it would be great experience to have under my belt.

This was no minor side job, mind you. It involved poring over hundreds of resumes and interview notes from recruiters we sent to college campuses across America, choosing the best candidates to bring in, coordinating on-site interviews and feedback, and helping hiring managers determine the best fit. The experience did turn out to be invaluable, if not eye-opening.

One day the department head stopped by, took me aside, and threw me an unexpected curveball. He said the human resources people were coming down on him and we had to hire two black engineers, or something to that effect.

Wait, what? Could he really ask me to do that?

Having grown up in a liberal inner-city environment and being somewhat idealistic and perhaps more than a little naive, I pushed back. I knew enough about equal opportunity employment to know you could not discriminate one way or the other. What I was being asked to do was discriminatory, at least in my mind.

When I asked if we shouldn't hire the best-qualified candidates regardless of their race, the manager said this was not negotiable. His message was clear. Just do it.

That was that. I'd pushed back, been rebuffed, and now it was time to do what I was told. And it was quite a challenge. For one thing, race wasn't listed on the interview forms and, even when I did somehow manage to make that determination, there were few candidates to choose from. Nevertheless, I got the job done.

Indeed, that experience was a real eye-opener. It was my first glimpse into the many shades of gray involving human capital management. While that was 30 years ago, it seems to me that, with all the best intentions, we continue to slide down a slippery slope that is, at best, barely ethical and legal.

It reminds me of the heady days of *stock option backdating* during the late 1990s and early 2000s. In case you're not familiar with it, it was a once-common practice of granting employee stock options on dates with more favorable—meaning lower—share prices so employees would instantly be in the money on their hire date.

For example, if the stock closed at $10 on your hire date of October 1 but it was $9 on September 1, your options might be granted on the earlier date, giving you a built-in $1 per share gain on your hire date. For executives with hundreds of thousands of shares, that could amount to a huge windfall, especially during a stock market bubble, when shares can rise very rapidly. And yes, the practice was legal as long as companies accounted for it properly.

Lower option prices mean bigger gains for employees and higher expenses for companies. But a lot of companies forgot about the expense part and didn't account for the backdating properly. By the time the dust settled around 2007, more than a hundred companies became enmeshed in the scandal, causing the resignations of top executives, civil suits, and in some cases criminal indictments at high-profile companies, including Apple, Altera, Broadcom, Brocade, Cirrus Logic, KLA-Tencor, Maxim, UnitedHealth Group, Verisign, and Vitesse.

Today, we have what could in some ways be viewed as a similar situation brewing under the nicely branded heading of *diversity recruiting.* To solve the problem I'd had decades before, a San Francisco-based startup named Entelo, for example, has a software tool that helps employers filter candidates based on gender and ethnicity, among other criteria. It's interesting to note how that practice skirts the Civil Rights Act of 1964, which clearly prohibits making hiring decisions based upon race, gender, or age.

In a 2014 interview, founding CEO Jon Bischke said Entelo's product is designed "to allow employers to develop a more diverse candidate pool," but it's not intended to be used in making hiring decisions based on race or gender. That left me wondering what reason a company could possibly have for altering the candidate pool with respect to race or gender if not to influence hiring decisions? That looks very much like a slippery slope to me.

Now let's take a step back and look at the big picture for a moment. Discrimination based on race, gender, and age is illegal for a very good reason. It should be. We can all agree that diversity is good and homogeneity is not so good. Diversity, after all, facilitates new ideas and viewpoints. It creates constructive conflict and debate that leads to better decisions. It improves team dynamics that fight the status quo, the spiral of silence, and the treachery of groupthink.

But I would argue that the most qualified person should always get the job or the promotion. When you undermine the tenets of meritocracy and personal accountability by giving unfair advantage to a chosen group or individual—for whatever reason—it breeds resentment and diminishes organizational performance. It always comes back to haunt you, one way or another.

Consider the high-profile gender discrimination and retaliation lawsuit brought by Ellen Pao in 2012 against her former employer— one of Silicon Valley's biggest and most respected venture capital firms, Kleiner Perkins Caufield & Byers.

According to reported trial testimony and performance reviews, it seems that Pao—a partner in the firm—was not exactly a model employee. She was often involved in workplace dramas that included repeated clashes with colleagues and an affair with a married coworker. Meanwhile, it appears that general partner John Doerr was her sole champion from the day he hired her right down to the day she filed the suit. For quite a few years, that reportedly put Doerr at odds with the rest of the firm's partnership.

Doerr actually had a golden opportunity to let Pao go when Google Ventures attempted to recruit her in 2009, but he didn't. He fought to keep her. The question is, why would one of the most brilliant and accomplished VCs on earth—a billionaire who makes critical business and hiring decisions for a living—put himself in that position?

This is purely conjecture on my part, but there only seems to be one plausible explanation. Up-and-coming women with VC potential are hard to come by. The candidate pool is very small. And Silicon Valley firms have long been under fire as good-old-boys clubs. So female partners are coveted. Doerr apparently bent over backwards to help Pao minimize her shortcomings. He mentored and defended her in the hope that her performance would improve and she would reach her potential at the firm. It was a noble pursuit that backfired.

That's probably why such a private company with nothing to gain risked having its reputation dragged through the mud in open court. I believe Doerr et al. were confident that they did everything they could to keep Pao and help her succeed at the firm. And while Kleiner ended up winning on all counts, it was skewered by much of the media and convicted in the court of public opinion.

For the venture capital firm, the end result was a tarnished brand, years of internal strife, and one less coveted female partner. Personally, I think Pao, Doerr, and Kleiner all lost long before anyone entered the courtroom.

True, the firm *is* male-dominated, as are nearly all venture capital and technology companies in Silicon Valley. And I doubt it's escaped anyone's notice how male-dominated all the examples in this book are. Clearly, we need more women and minorities in STEM-related (science, technology, engineering, and math) fields. But until we do a better job of addressing the supply problem, I don't believe favoring individuals on the basis of race, gender, or age helps those individuals or their employers.

There's an old saying, "No good deed goes unpunished." Another is, "The road to hell is paved with good intentions." There's a lot of truth to both proverbs. In business there are no good intentions, only good decisions. Don't do a *good* thing. Do the *right* thing. And remember, following the crowd is never a good idea, especially when it skirts legal and ethical boundaries. That's a slippery slope indeed.

THE MERITS OF MERITOCRACY

People are defined by their deeds, not their words. And yet the way we communicate reflects, reinforces, and has the power to change our behavior. The Declaration of Independence and the U.S. Constitution are just words. But those words created a nation. They defined the behavior of a culture that would change the world.

Words were just about all Martin Luther King Jr. had. And those words played a key role in driving the American civil rights movement. Words incite action. When words and the ideals they represent gain traction, they can change the trajectory of an entire culture, for better or worse.

Since words and actions influence each other, our words are both indicators of where we are as a society and powerful influences on where we're heading. And there is probably no more visible sign of the times and trajectory of our culture than the growing pervasiveness of political correctness.

On the surface, the idea of filtering our communication so as not to exclude or offend anyone seems entirely well-intentioned, and I've no doubt that it is. But its resultant impact on our behavior and our organizational performance has been anything but benign. Its effects are far-reaching and the reasons are relatively straightforward . . . if you understand what motivates people.

The success of our culture is based on meritocracy and personal responsibility. All things being equal, people will generally do what they perceive to be best for them. If they believe they can accomplish great things and obtain great rewards on their own merits, that's what they'll strive for. If you show them that the sky's the limit and how far they go in life rests more or less on their own shoulders, abilities, and behavior, they'll be incentivized to perform at their best. And they will reach the highest levels of achievement their capabilities and circumstances permit.

Those are, in fact, the principles that built America. Everyone gets life, liberty, and the pursuit of happiness. The rest is up to the individual. And make no mistake: Personal accountability and the incentive of being recognized and rewarded for superior performance plays an enormous role in creating the entrepreneurs, innovators, and leaders of the world.

If, on the other hand, you take that incentive away by telling folks that it makes no difference how they perform because everyone is the same, you give them nothing to strive for. If you tell them that competition is bad, everyone's a winner, and exceptional qualities will not be rewarded, you essentially strip them of the will to achieve, and they'll settle into a life of dependency and mediocrity. After all, if you remove the incentive to reach for the stars, there's no reason to shine.

Filtering communication to avoid offending employees waters down information, strips out critical data, dilutes meaning, and slows down information processing. It undermines genuine understanding and effective decision making. When managers are unwilling to give employees genuine feedback for fear of being sued or accused of harassment, discrimination, or being a bully, that also diminishes organizational effectiveness. We all want workplace civility and freedom from discrimination, but that must not come at the expense of meritocracy, personal accountability, and organizational performance. Executives and business leaders are responsible for doing what's right for their companies. They should answer to their stakeholders, not cultural trends or those who represent special interests.

If you want to lead a high-performance team, run a pure meritocracy. Here are some guidelines I try to follow:

▶ Hire the best people for the job and incentivize them to do their best work.

▶ Promote only on merit and pay people what they deserve; that includes you and your leadership team.

▶ Document your policies and be consistent.

- ▸ Make people decisions with a blindfold. Business leaders should not see people as black, white, male, female, straight, or gay. They should see people as individuals.

- ▸ Always do the right thing, and that includes staying on the right side of the law and not compromising your moral compass. You'll sleep better at night, have less stress, and make smarter decisions that have better outcomes. And you'll never have to kowtow to bullying threats from employees, activists, agitators, or their lawyers.

- ▸ Finally, never give in to the status quo, the fads of the day, popular wisdom, or the most obnoxious voices just to get them to go away and make your life easier. They won't, and it won't.

Your stakeholders depend on you to be a wise leader who makes smart decisions and does the right thing on their behalf. That's exactly what you should do.

CHAPTER 23

THE TAO
OF
LEADERSHIP

MY FIRST DAY AS A VICE PRESIDENT OF A PUBLIC company was all about signing forms, meeting my employees, and getting indoctrinated into the culture of Cyrix, that crazy Texas company out to kick Intel's ass. That's about as long as the honeymoon lasted.

The very next day felt like I'd been dropped out of an airplane into a pool of water so cold and deep my *cojones* disappeared for weeks.

Cyrix was getting ready to launch its first microprocessor to compete head-on with Intel's vaunted Pentium chip, and they'd hired me to lead the way. The challenge was enormous, and time was short. We were ridiculously outgunned by the incumbent in every way that mattered. My reach had surely exceeded my grasp, and, while Browning would be proud, it was time to see if I really had what it takes to make it in the big leagues. It was time to sink or swim.

I barely treaded water that first week. I had some good ideas for the launch, but they were 180 degrees from the company's current plans, and that put me at odds with some very smart and opinionated executives. I knew I somehow had to persuade the rest of the leadership team to change direction but wasn't sure I had the courage, salesmanship, or political wherewithal to pull it off.

Since I was commuting weekly back and forth between Dallas and my home in Silicon Valley, I reluctantly boarded a plane Friday night feeling a bit lost and more than a little overwhelmed. The following morning after breakfast in Santa Cruz, my wife and I walked over to Logos, a popular used music and bookstore we frequented.

On any other day, you would have found me flipping through CDs or browsing the sci-fi and classic literature sections, but not that day. I'm not much of a business book guy, but I needed help, and it wasn't going to come from the likes of Mark Helprin or Neal Stephenson, that much I knew.

Rapidly scanning the business book titles looking for who-knows-what, a tiny little paperback caught my eye. I guess I'll never know how things would have turned out if I hadn't come across Heider's masterful *The Tao of Leadership: Lao Tzu's* Tao Te Ching *Adapted for a New Age* that day. Those 81 ancient lessons would come to change my entire perspective on leadership . . . all for the price of $2.40.

I read the book that afternoon and again on the flight back to DFW. Somewhere along the way, the path became clear. I knew what I had to do and how to do it. And it worked perfectly. That marked the beginning of what would become the most rewarding and exciting years of my career. The book helped me find it in myself to play the exact role I needed to play to help this remarkable company accomplish some pretty astounding things. And, you know, it was one hell of a team to work with.

Cyrix's engineers were the best and brightest I'd ever known. What I did was position and launch the breakthrough products they built. I'm proud to have brought that remarkable team the limelight they so richly deserved. And there's a good chance that wouldn't have happened if I hadn't found that little book.

This isn't about becoming a monk or getting all Zen on everyone. It's about understanding yourself and others. It's about understanding how everything works. Yes, everything. And it's about gaining perspective so you can come up with innovative solutions to tough problems.

Perhaps some people are so grounded and self-aware that they have no need of Lao Tzu's insights. Likewise, some entrepreneurs are so talented it doesn't matter that they're their own worst enemy. But I'm not one of them. Few leaders are.

If you track the development of many of the high-tech industry's most famous entrepreneurs, you'll find an interesting trend. They start out with an overpowering sense of urgency, a desperate need to prove themselves. Full of hubris, they truly believe they're special, they can do no wrong, and the rules don't apply to them. And their instincts are to dominate and control to achieve their lofty goals.

But experience has a way of tempering those powerful drives. In time, they learn to talk and push a little less and listen and persuade a lot more. Unbridled passion gives rise to calm self-confidence. Bright flashes of brilliance are joined by wise decision making. They're still people of action, but they act with greater purpose and foresight.

Those who stand the test of time and lead their companies to great heights do so by achieving a certain level of balance. They never lose the edge that made them exceptional, but they gain maturity from experience. Years of victory and defeat, love and loss, and painful lessons learned the hard way reshape them into well-rounded business leaders. It was definitely true of Gates and Dell. Perhaps Jobs and Ellison did not evolve quite as much, but their talents tipped the scales in their favor. As for the likes of Mayer, Musk, and Zuckerberg, only time will tell if their yin catches up with their yang. Mine certainly did.

The question is, will you achieve that level of maturity, or will you someday look back in regret because you never really grew up or attained that balance?

The Tao of Leadership teaches that "all behaviors contain their opposites." "A show of strength suggests insecurity" and weakness. "To prosper, be generous." To understand how things work, you should not ask why, but simply observe. When you feel anxious and compelled to act, that's a time for "silent reflection."

If you're a driven person who pushes the envelope and wants great things out of life, you will inevitably face obstacles that will challenge your comfort zone and worldview. Events will threaten to shatter your self-image or long-held beliefs. When that happens, and it will, your instinct will be to fight for control. To act aggressively. To consolidate power.

Don't.

The only way to achieve balance is to be open to whatever threatens you. It's not that everything you think you know when you're young is wrong. It's that your viewpoint is inherently narrow. And the only way to gain wisdom and maturity is to be willing to let go of the notion that you understand how things work and embrace the possibility that you really don't.

That's called knowing what you don't know. The longer you live and the more you come to understand, the more you'll realize how little you know. How little we all know. And I know this is counterintuitive, but that realization will provide just enough audacity to think that maybe somewhere inside you are answers nobody has ever come up with.

It's one of the great paradoxes of life, that the more in awe you are of all the great unknowns the universe has hidden away, the more empowered you feel to become the one to figure them out. If not you, then who?

Those great entrepreneurs didn't make it big by looking at things the same way everyone else does. They didn't succeed by following the path of least resistance—or by following anything or anyone else, for that matter. They did it by challenging the status quo, ignoring conventional wisdom, looking at things differently, and taking big risks.

If you hope to achieve lasting success and balance in your career and your life, you have to apply the same logic—not just to your business and your products, but also to yourself. When things don't go as planned, when you face enormous obstacles, it's important to resist the urge to act brashly, look for quick fixes, or blame others.

Instead, be calm and look inward. The answers are always there. And sometimes, you'll be surprised to learn that the problem was you all along. But you'll never achieve that if you lack the courage to take a hard look in the mirror and face the truth about what you see.

EMBRACE THE CHAOS

I was standing behind the bar of my Laguna Niguel condo making drinks for a few friends when the phone rang. Another day, I might not have picked up the phone, but this time I did. It was someone my roommate had dated, although we'd never met. Her name was Kim. She wanted to return some of her ex's stuff without running into him. She said some unflattering things about him. I didn't disagree. After all, the guy was sort of a jerk.

Anyway, Kim was feisty on the phone. I like her.

A few days later, I was home watching *Monday Night Football* with a buddy from work when there was a knock at the door. Full of pizza and beer, I was feeling pretty comfy on the sofa, so my friend answered the door. But when I heard her voice the lightbulb went on. It was Kim. I glanced up at the doorway, and there stood the woman of my dreams. She was beautiful. I practically leapt over the couch and fast-talked her into staying.

At this point I'm supposed to say "it was meant to be" or "the rest is history" like some silly fairy tale, but that's not how it happened. We were married a year later, but we really didn't think it through. One day we just boogied down to the county courthouse and tied the knot. We were so *not* compatible. The first few years were pretty rocky and I don't know how we got through it, but we did.

We just celebrated our 25th anniversary.

It may sound clichéd, but the best thing that ever happened to me was the result of a completely random string of low-probability events that never should have happened. Meeting in my doorway is far-fetched enough. And had one of us given the slightest thought to what we were doing at any point along the way, things never would have turned out the way they did.

Speaking of which, I was an engineering manager when Kim and I met. Everything that happened from then on—transitioning to sales and marketing, the move to Silicon Valley, the jump to senior executive, and the crazy notion of giving it all up to start a consulting firm—might never have happened without Kim's support every step of the way. It's exactly what I needed for my career to unfold the way it did.

The funny thing is, every pivotal event in my life—every big career move, every inspiration, every product innovation—occurred just like that. As I discussed back in Chapter 8, the universe tends toward ever-increasing entropy, while our role as organisms is to control our environment and create organization out of chaos. That said, inflection points that change our lives, disrupt industries, and move society forward are unpredictable events. They're like beneficial mutations in the ecosystem of life.

The message is clear. In business as in life, embrace the chaos. Put yourself out there and take risks. Big ones. I'm not saying that's all there is to success and happiness. There's a lot more to it than that. You have to work hard, make things happen, compete to win, and take responsibility for your actions. You also have to face your fears and learn from your mistakes.

Granted, a lot of things are within your control, but the major make-or-break events always involve letting go, giving up the illusion of control, and embracing the chaos. Any successful entrepreneur knows that's true.

Runaway product successes are impossible to foresee. You can't predict which websites, apps, or TV shows will go viral. And dozens of VCs will tell you you're crazy before one sees the real potential of your disruptive idea and writes you a check.

The same is true of events that change entire industries and create consumer trends. In 1995 the average price of a personal computer was well over $2,000, cost-prohibitive for most people. Then one man with a vision started a chain of events that would change that forever. When *San Jose Mercury News* reporter Dean Takahashi interviewed Cyrix cofounder Tom Brightman for a prophetic article called, "Cyrix faces skeptics: Technology plan for a $500 personal computer encounters technical doubts," I was sitting right there.

At first I wondered if the guy was crazy. But it got me thinking about price elasticity—the enormous untapped opportunity if we could just get the price down in the $1,000 range—and again, that lightbulb went on.

The price of PCs didn't magically come down on its own. We drove it down to gain a market niche against Intel, who then followed suit. A new killer app called the internet created consumer demand, and the rest, as they say, is history.

Likewise, when Mark Zuckerberg created Facemash to rate the looks of his Harvard classmates, there was simply no way to know that it had the potential to become a social network of more than a billion users.

How do you know which risks to take, which chaotic rides to jump on, which random events to see through? If it feels right, do it. Trust your gut. If it works out, if you accomplish something good, it'll boost your self-confidence. If it doesn't work out and you learn from it, that'll give you strength. And through it all you'll gain experience, insight, and perspective. And maybe someday the planets will align and fate will shine down upon you.

These days, it seems that everyone who wants to get ahead is some sort of information junkie. Everyone wants to be more productive, effective, optimized. That's OK for a little fine-tuning, but don't lose sight of the big picture. In this world, control is an illusion. How you respond to random events is far more important. There's a lot to be said for making good choices and smart decisions. You do have to connect the dots in your life. Just remember that a lot of those dots come out of nowhere. Pay attention, or you'll miss them.

THINK LESS, FEEL MORE

Modern man has a fundamental problem: He thinks too much and feels too little.

We spend way too much time keeping our thinking brains engaged and not enough time accessing feelings buried in our subconscious. A perfect example is the sheer volume and popularity of online tips and tricks for motivating, inspiring, and improving productivity. Just when you think you've seen it all, another article promising the secret to health, wealth, and happiness goes viral. Inevitably, it's some sort of daily ritual, diet, or exercise routine that supposedly changed someone's life.

This focus on productivity has everyone looking in the wrong direction. Productivity is about efficiency and output, which only counts if you make cars or semiconductor chips, for example. Even if work productivity had anything to do with daily rituals or habits— which it doesn't—for the overwhelming majority of us, it doesn't mean a damn thing.

Our creative juices flow better when we're not productive—or particularly alert, for that matter. We're actually more innovative when we're tired, half-asleep, or doing something simple and mundane. In any case, everyone's unique. If we listened to our own instincts, we'd be far better off. Unfortunately, most of us are much too busy binging on all sorts of online distraction to pay attention to what our gut is telling us.

The great irony is that the caveman had that down pat. He awoke with the sun, ate when he was hungry and could find or hunt for food, and slept when he was tired. Not only that, he was far more keenly aware of environmental threats than we are. He did all that with a brain about a third of the size of ours. And therein lies the rub.

What distinguishes the brain of modern man from the dominant limbic system of our archaic ancestors is our highly evolved neocortex. At their best, the two systems mesh pretty well. But these days we're allowing mindless nonsense to occupy our thoughts, and that makes it far more difficult to be aware of our instincts and feelings.

The thing is, we didn't develop the capacity for complex reasoning to sit on our butts and ponder stuff a caveman could do without even thinking. Our frontal lobes developed to enable us to compete and thrive in an ever-more-complex ecosystem.

But today, man has conquered the earth. For most of us, food is plentiful and threats are minimal. So those enormously sophisticated brains of ours are becoming neurotic. We're overthinking everything because our brains have nothing better to do. In many ways, the caveman had an advantage because he reacted naturally to his instincts and wasn't burdened by all that pesky gray matter.

Wouldn't it be great to have the best of both worlds—to use complex reasoning to solve problems while paying quiet attention to our instincts and emotions? Of course it would. But that's far easier said than done. The problem is we now live very long, complex, busy lives. Our true feelings and instincts are buried beneath layers of mechanisms and years of experience.

By way of analogy, if your brain were a simple computer disk drive, your emotions would be hidden files buried deep under terabytes of data. That's why it's so much more challenging to look deep within ourselves than it was for our ancestors.

I don't know about you, but half the time someone asks me, "What's wrong?" my answer is, "It's complicated." And then, after spending an hour pouring out my guts, I realize what was really bothering me was something I wasn't even aware of. Sound familiar?

Human behavior is generally buried in the limbic system. That part of your brain doesn't understand conscious logical thought any more than a newborn baby would. It doesn't have the ability to reason, so understanding what's going on doesn't change your behavior. Your limbic system is just doing what it's programmed to do, dispensing neurotransmitters that reinforce survival instincts. And it'll keep doing it until you actually deal with your issues on an emotional level. But since those coping mechanisms are designed to bury emotions—which they do quite effectively, I might add—it takes a long time, a lot of reinforcement, and plenty of hard work for things to sink in so your behavior can change.

There are layers and layers to peel away, just to get you to feel what you have blocked since childhood. Then you have to learn to change habits, rituals, mechanisms, and sometimes addictions you've been hard-wiring into your brain for years and years. That's no easy task, and it's not always successful.

Why the psychology lesson? Because your head is the only one you have access to. And while each of us is unique, our minds work more or less the same. So if you can get down deep and understand yourself—what makes you tick and what makes you behave the way you do—that goes a long way toward understanding everyone else. And if you can somehow master your own issues and limitations, the possibilities are endless.

This simple lesson is expressed in one of the *Tao Te Ching*'s most powerful proverbs:

He who knows men is clever;

He who knows himself has insight.

He who conquers men has force;

He who conquers himself is truly strong.

The point is, business is about people. Leadership is about people. To be most effective at either, you have to understand others. And to do that, you have to understand yourself at an emotional level. All your insight and strength come from within. And when you learn to be at peace with yourself, that enables you to see answers to elusive problems.

Endlessly engaging your conscious mind with nonsense and searching for answers externally are not just futile—they're complete folly. Ironically, the information age that gives us unlimited access to everyone and everything 24/7 makes it that much harder to know what's really going on.

A QUESTION OF BALANCE

This may come as a shock, but I'm not actually a Buddhist monk. I have the same problems and limitations as everyone else—maybe more.

Sometimes I sit and stare at a blank screen for hours without a single creative thought in that cavernous mass of gray matter I call a brain. It's very frustrating, especially when I'm supposed to come up with a column or a chapter that's actually worth reading.

But approach me with a problem, and watch me instantly spring into action. No wonder I loved being an executive. Every day was a new set of problems to solve. And problems require action, interaction, and engagement. For me, that always felt comfortable. Problem solving is very *yang*. Writing insightful commentary, on the other hand, requires creativity and patience. It's solitary and somewhat passive, which for me is challenging and uncomfortable. (And sometimes, so difficult it drives me nuts.) Writing is very *yin*.

I used to think I was such a good executive. Maybe even a good leader. Strong, decisive, results-oriented. I was all about making things happen, taking action, solving problems, accomplishing goals, and getting the job done. But there are times when a leader is better off doing absolutely nothing. Far better off, actually. The *Tao Te Ching* is very big on the limitations and pitfalls of action and aggression, not to mention the wisdom and insight that come from being patient and passive.

Young up-and-comers are inevitably heavy on the yang, as I was. But as we mature, we tend to develop more of a sense of balance. We become more adept at knowing when to speak up and act decisively and when to sit quietly, listen, and wait.

I remember hearing the term *equilibrium* a lot in college. In more than two decades in the corporate world, I'm not sure I heard it once. It's rare to find leaders who have achieved that sort of stability and balance—where their team or company operates so effectively that you can say their organization is in a state of equilibrium.

I actually *have* worked with a handful of CEOs on one or two management teams that fit that description. And what we managed to achieve was as remarkable as it was rewarding for everyone involved. The whole was truly greater than the sum of its parts.

That's probably why I find it so amusing—in a twisted and cynical sort of way—to hear all the chatter about leadership qualities like emotional intelligence and soft skills. Our sound-bite culture inevitably misinterprets that to mean leaders should be more sensitive and empathetic and communicate more effectively.

To me, that's like boiling down the *Tao Te Ching* to "Be passive" or the *Art of War* to "Appear weak when you are strong." It trivializes some deep and powerful concepts that you can spend a lifetime studying and practicing and still come nowhere near mastering.

If you've ever wondered what a management consultant does—that's what I do when I'm not writing—look no further than Peter Drucker. Drucker helped executives understand new concepts and see things in different ways, but he rarely told them what they should do. The guy was like a modern-day Lao Tzu.

Too bad Drucker never ran a corporation. He might have been the best CEO of all time. Then again, maybe he achieved his balance by writing 39 books. Maybe executives and business leaders can tone down their yang and improve their yin by writing. Maybe the key to equilibrium is literally at your fingertips. Maybe that's how Lao Tzu did it.

Writing may be hard, but it's a hell of a lot more practical for a busy executive than becoming a monk. Speaking of which, this lesson from Heider's adaptation has always resonated with me. Whenever I feel the urge to overindulge my yang, it provides some much-needed balance:

> When you cannot see what is happening in a group, do not stare harder. Relax and look gently with your inner eye.
>
> When you do not understand what a person is saying, do not grasp for every word. Give up your efforts. Become silent inside and listen with your deepest self.
>
> When you are puzzled by what you see or hear, do not strive to figure things out. Stand back for a moment and become calm. When a person is calm, complex events appear simple.
>
> To know what is happening, push less, open out and be aware. See without staring. Listen quietly rather than listening hard. Use intuition and reflection rather than trying to figure things out.
>
> The more you can let go of trying, and the more open and receptive you become, the more easily you will know what is happening.
>
> Stay in the present. The present is more available than either memories of the past or fantasies of the future.

We may live in an era of unprecedented access to content and communication, but that's not where genuine understanding, wisdom, and leadership capability come from. The two greatest sources of learning and insight are your experience in the real world and exploration of your inner one.

CHAPTER 24

THE
EVOLVED
LEADER

WE LEARN FROM EXPERIENCE AND TEACH BY EXAMPLE. It's a powerful combination, especially when using our experience to turn examples into lessons. Of all the lessons I've learned along the way, perhaps the most important relates to two uniquely human characteristics: humility and empathy.

Our culture is highly judgmental, and no group bears the brunt of our opinions more than leaders. After all, they signed up for it. They make the big bucks. Fair enough. But there's an old saying that comes to mind about not judging people until you've walked a mile in their shoes. If you have the good fortune to run a company, you will no doubt come to realize that, as with so many things in life, it looks a lot easier from a distance than it does when you're in the thick of it.

As jobs go, being an executive or a business leader is about as hard as it gets. And while I can't instill in you the humility and empathy that can only come from experience and contemplation, I'm hoping this story comes to mind when you're facing the sort of no-win situations that are all too common in the business world and stressing over making the wrong call. We've all been there. Perhaps no single company in memory has been there more than HP.

LOSING THE HP WAY

For half a century, Hewlett-Packard was a Silicon Valley icon with a proud culture that valued employees, achievement, and innovation above all else. That management philosophy came to be known as the HP Way. During all that time, HP had just two CEOs aside from cofounders Bill Hewlett and David Packard: John Young and Lew Platt.

Of course there were the usual ups and downs that every growing company faces, but, on the whole, HP had a fabulous reputation as it grew to be a Fortune 20 company. It was viewed as a shining model of how an enterprise should be run—until the late 1990s.

Why the sudden change is anyone's guess. Maybe it was the headiness of the tech bubble that had otherwise savvy executives behaving in ways we now know to be surprisingly naive and foolish. Whatever the reason, HP's board became disenchanted with the company's sluggish growth and wanted it to become more agile and competitive.

Platt, the CEO at the time, was a real man of the people. He was fond of managing by walking around and lunching with the troops in the cafeteria. Although he was a model custodian of the HP Way, the board decided it was time for a change. It wanted HP to return to the heyday of its youth. It wanted the kind of revenue growth that the internet kids in the Valley had.

In 1999 HP spun off its test and measurement group as Agilent and hired Carly Fiorina, a rock star CEO from AT&T spinoff Lucent, to reinvigorate the aging company. That's when everything started to slide downhill.

Personally, I don't think Fiorina was anywhere near as bad a chief executive as she was made out to be. The board wanted change, it wanted to reignite the company, it wanted a rock star, and that's exactly what it got. In hindsight, Fiorina's strategy of ramping up for growth and executing a megamerger with Compaq while the tech bubble was bursting and Silicon Valley was falling apart at the seams certainly appears to be poorly timed. But she was doing what she was hired to do. And the board backed her every step of the way.

It bears mentioning that, before the ill-fated Compaq acquisition, Fiorina proposed acquiring the consulting practice of PricewaterhouseCoopers. But when Wall Street gave it a cool reception, she quashed the deal. Fiorina later had another shot at PwC at a fire-sale price but again declined.

That series of missed opportunities cleared the way for IBM to acquire the unit for just $3.5 billion, locking in the final piece of the puzzle in its long-term strategy of becoming the world's top IT services company. In other words, Fiorina had the right idea, and, had she followed through on her instincts instead of second-guessing herself, the outcome might have been much different.

Since she was brought in to shake things up, it's not surprising that Fiorina was viewed as a polarizing figure. Following the controversial Compaq merger, she reorganized the company to a centralized management model to streamline decision making. That was a good move but it also ruffled a lot of feathers and created some internal confusion in an age-old company that was resistant to change.

Unfortunately, market conditions were not in her favor, and Fiorina chronically missed her own growth targets. It certainly didn't help that HP suffered increasing competitive and margin pressures from Dell in PCs and IBM in services. And it did her rapidly tarnishing reputation no good that HP's stock dropped 50 percent and 30,000 employees were laid off during her tenure.

After five tumultuous years, the board of directors came to the conclusion that it had made a mistake and asked Fiorina to step down. Shares of the company surged on the news and once again on the announcement that former NCR chief executive Mark Hurd would replace her as the company's new CEO.

Hiring Hurd was an inspired move. What happened next was nothing short of a miracle as Hurd executed one of the greatest turnarounds in corporate history. He led HP to market share gains across all its core business units, five years of revenue growth, 22 quarters of increasing profits, and a stock price that more than doubled to all-time highs, discounting the dotcom bubble.

Granted, Hurd did have his detractors. He was a ruthless cost cutter who ran the company with an iron fist. His relentless pursuit of operating performance deprived executives of much of the freedom they had grown accustomed to at a company that had always put employees first. And acquisitions of EDS and 3Com failed to live up to their potential.

Hurd's tenure was also marred by scandals. Not your average everyday run-of-the-mill scandals, either. These could have made juicy TV miniseries.

The first actually had nothing to do with him.

After the company's top executives and directors held their annual strategy retreat in California's Palm Desert, the resultant plans were leaked to CNET, which ran a two-page story detailing the company's long-term strategy.

HP board chairman Patricia Dunn sprang into action, instructing general counsel Ann Baskins to hire security experts who used private investigators to conduct some pretty shady sleuthing in order to identify the source of the leak. Using a technique known as *pretexting*, the hired guns posed as board members and journalists in an attempt to obtain their records from the phone company.

Unfortunately, much of this activity was illegal, and the scandal blew up into a media firestorm. There was a congressional investigation that featured numerous invocations of the Fifth Amendment, not to mention criminal charges brought against Dunn, HP's former chief ethics officer, and three outside investigators. Baskins, Dunn, and two other directors ultimately resigned over the fallout. And life went on.

Hurd's tenure continued for four blissful more years without incident until what appeared to be at least an R-rated scandal rocked PG-rated Silicon Valley.

It all started in 2007 when HP hired Jodie Fisher—an attractive fortysomething adult film and reality TV actress—as a contractor to host about a dozen executive summits between Hurd and IT customers around the world. These high-level meetings were run out of Hurd's office, so naturally he was part of the interview process.

For two years, Hurd and Fisher had what appears to have been a relatively close relationship that included private dinners and spending time alone in each other's hotel rooms at these events. While there may have been some infatuation on somebody's part, by all accounts the two never had a sexual relationship.

About seven months after the summits ended, Hurd received a letter from infamous celebrity lawyer Gloria Allred that accused him of sexually harassing Fisher. That started a chain of events that made whatever may or may not have happened between Hurd and Fisher entirely irrelevant.

According to *Fortune*, Hurd turned the letter over to HP's general counsel, Michael Holston. Holston alerted the board's counsel; brought in an outside legal firm, Covington & Burling, to investigate; and hired crisis management PR firm Apco Worldwide. After the whole pretexting mess, it seems Holston wanted to make sure he had his bases covered.

What Covington uncovered would be a huge letdown to soap opera fans. They found no basis for the harassment allegations. But they did turn up a few inconsistencies in Hurd's expense reports, specifically those related to dinners with Fisher.

Regardless, even after the independent investigation cleared Hurd of the sexual harassment claim, the board concluded it needed to publicly disclose the charge. I guess there was concern about another media firestorm should Allred decide to go public with the allegations in order to force a monetary settlement.

Hurd, not surprisingly, was dead set against making the sordid mess public. That created a deadlock, and the board was split on how to proceed.

In the end, the board seems to have favored covering its collective butt over standing behind the guy who single-handedly brought

HP back from the dead. Hurd was forced to resign amid charges of sexual harassment and "violating the company's standards of business conduct." In other words, the board ousted a brilliant CEO who rescued their company, allegedly over some fudged expense reports.

Ironically, the abrupt termination sparked the very media firestorm the board had hoped to avoid. Once again, HP's board was raked over the coals for what Oracle chief Larry Ellison called "the worst personnel decision since the idiots on the Apple board fired Steve Jobs many years ago" in an email to *The New York Times*.

Ellison went on to accuse the board of failing to act in the best interest of HP's stakeholders, and he was probably right. This was a corporate governance train wreck that did far more harm to HP than anything Hurd may have done. And it gets worse. The board had no succession plan, so with Hurd gone, they were faced with a much bigger problem: who to replace him with.

There were several good internal candidates, but, for some reason I've never understood, they were not considered. And there apparently were not many outside executives willing to risk their reputations on HP—not surprising, considering the board essentially stabbed its last two CEOs in the back.

The board ultimately—and reluctantly, it would seem—settled on Leo Apotheker as HP's next CEO. It bears mentioning that Apotheker had recently been fired after a disastrous ten months as CEO of SAP—a detail that some HP directors were apparently not even aware of—and that two-thirds of the board had not even interviewed him in person. Maybe that explains what happened next.

In November 2010 Apotheker began a corporate reign of terror the likes of which I'd never seen in all the decades I've been involved with the high-tech industry. Apotheker and chairman Ray Lane, who was brought in at the same time, first shook up the board, replacing four board members I can only assume were Hurd supporters with their own choices.

Despite a sluggish economy, Apotheker raised HP's dividend, bought back stock, and blew through cash like a drunken sailor. He lowered revenue estimates three times and missed earnings twice while blaming it all on the earthquake and tsunami in Japan, the success of Apple's iPad, and, of course, his predecessor. Meanwhile, the company lost several key executives.

HP bought Palm and announced plans to use its WebOS operating system in everything from smartphones and tablets to PCs and printers. But just months after launching a new smartphone and tablet to take on Apple's iPhone and iPad, the company inexplicably pulled the plug on those products and the entire WebOS program.

The company then acquired Autonomy, a relatively small European software maker, for $11 billion as the centerpiece of a grand plan to transform HP into an enterprise software and services company. As part of that strategy, Apotheker also telegraphed plans to divest HP's $41 billion personal system group within the next year and a half.

Besides wildly overpaying for Autonomy, that last move essentially made HP PCs lame ducks in the market. After all, what IT executive in his right mind would risk investing in HP products with that kind of uncertainty in the wind? Never mind that the company had spent the past ten years becoming the world's top PC maker.

Wall Street panned the crazy restructuring plan. One analyst said it was "like McDonald's getting out of the hamburger business." So Apotheker and Lane went on the road to explain to investors why they just didn't get the new strategy of turning the world's largest technology company into a second-tier software player. That didn't go over so well either.

After the stock had plunged 40 percent, the board, to its credit, realized it had royally screwed up and fired Apotheker less than 11 months after hiring him. But instead of realizing its original mistake and conducting a proper search, the board turned around and immediately appointed one of its own directors, former eBay boss Meg Whitman, as the company's new CEO, with Lane continuing as chairman.

Whitman was an interesting choice. She'd had an outstanding ten-year run at the helm of eBay—taking it from a tiny startup to 15,000 employees and $8 billion in annual revenue—but had recently lost her bid to become governor of California after spending a record $140 million of her own money on the campaign. She had no enterprise, IT, hardware, software, complex supply chain, or turnaround experience. And HP was definitely in need of a turnaround.

At the time, Lane said in a conference call with analysts that Whitman was "the obvious choice from the beginning of the process," but I couldn't imagine what *process* he was referring to. A typical CEO search process takes months. This board made its choice within a matter of days.

What followed was more than three years of layoffs, revenue declines, cost cutting, cleaning up the balance sheet, and writing down almost $20 billion in losses that Whitman attributed to Hurd's acquisition of EDS and Apotheker's purchase of Autonomy. Never mind that, as directors, both she and Lane had approved the latter at the time.

In 2014 Whitman finally announced that HP would split into two companies: one focused on the enterprise and the other on personal computers and printers. She will be the top executive of the former and chairman of the latter. The question is, is that the best solution for the company and its shareholders?

We've seen this scenario play out many times before. In the early 1990s, the wizards on Wall Street called for a breakup of IBM to unlock shareholder value and avoid bankruptcy. Instead, the board hired Lou Gerstner, who came up with a brilliant plan to reposition IBM as an IT services company.

And we recently heard the same old breakup rumblings about Microsoft, just before Satya Nadella was named to replace Steve Ballmer as CEO. Granted, Nadella has a long way to go, but he's shaking up the software giant in what appears to be a very good way.

Splitting HP in two does not provide a solution to either company's competitive or growth problems. There certainly doesn't appear to be any creative vision or insightful strategy behind the move. Whitman herself called it "the right tactic." She's right about one thing. It is a tactic.

I should mention that I once believed HP should be split up as well. That was just before Hurd showed up and proved me wrong. And while his solution may have also been a tactic, it had the virtue of being highly effective. It worked for five years. I don't think a split would have been necessary if Hurd were still running the show.

As a columnist, I've been critical of HP's board since the Hurd debacle. But the truth is, these are all very smart, highly accomplished people. Yes, even Apotheker. Could I have done better? I'd like to think so, but in reality, I have no idea. I wasn't in their shoes.

We're always hearing people complain about corporate America: how executives and directors make megabucks and employees get the shaft. How the big banks and institutional investors have all the clout and retail investors get the short end of the stick. While I've written my fair share about the dysfunctions of our system of corporate governance, including how executive pay and exit packages are in many cases out of control, I've mostly been a staunch supporter of corporate America and free-market capitalism. After all, no system is perfect.

That said, the most important function of a board of directors is to hire and fire CEOs and compensate them accordingly. That's the essence of corporate governance. While I've used HP as a cautionary tale, there are lots of boards that could do a far better job. If they did, the naysayers would have a lot less to say.

In a scathing 2011 *Wall Street Journal* piece, Dow Jones columnist Al Lewis called this sort of dysfunction the new "HP Way." Even if Lewis is right, it's just one corporation of many. I can think of no better reason for you to become an executive or business leader than to show the world you can do better. That's my challenge to you.

Should you take it? I did. And while I started out as most young up-and-comers do—more arrogant and confident than I had any right to be—I came away with copious amounts of humility and empathy for those who choose to lead. Running anything—a business, a division, a corporation, a nonprofit—is a great job. Nothing is more challenging or more fulfilling. Nothing makes you feel more alive. Many of us live for that. If that describes you, then maybe someday it'll be your turn. If and when that happens, Godspeed.

WILL YOU LEAD OR FOLLOW?

When Walter Isaacson's biography of Steve Jobs first came out, executives and business leaders all over the world tried to emulate the man and his management style. They tried to imitate everything from the way he presented to his relentless attention to detail. They even bought copies of the book for their management teams to study.

While I believe some of Jobs's philosophies are fundamental, especially for innovative companies, you simply can't copy and paste talent and wisdom. Talent comes from inside you. Wisdom comes from experience. Both are unique to the individual.

It's one thing to learn from others, but you can't replicate them.

Lei Jun, CEO of Chinese smartphone startup Xiaomi, is such a fan of Jobs he emulates the iconic leader right down to the black shirt and jeans and "one last thing" tease during product announcements. In 2013 *The New York Times* called him a Steve Jobs knockoff. I might say the same about Xiaomi's products.

While imitation may be the sincerest form of flattery, it's not the best way to build a career or run a company. As Apple's former head of marketing Allison Johnson told an audience of entrepreneurs, "The thing that Steve did better than anyone else is, he was his authentic self. We don't need more Apples. We need more you."

If nothing else, successful entrepreneurs are themselves. And the cultures they create reflect their own principles, their own methods, their own unique DNA. That's where their breakthrough innovations come from.

Had Jobs, Mackey, and Schultz decided to be like someone else instead of carving their own distinct paths to create Apple, Whole Foods, and Starbucks, we'd all still be using BlackBerry phones, shopping at Safeway, and drinking Folgers coffee. Then again, fast-forward 20 years and who knows what we'll find.

It's striking how much the business world parallels the biological one. Both are brutally competitive environments in which organisms strive to create order out of chaos. They may even succeed for a time, until a new and better paradigm emerges and changes everything.

In business, as in life, there are no absolutes. There are no givens. Nothing is static. Everything is up for grabs. But first you have to try.

I can still remember walking into Texas Instruments my very first day of work. That was 35 years ago, but to me it feels like it just happened. Everything was so new and exciting, especially the technology. *Thousands* of transistors on a single silicon chip. Mainframe computers that took up entire rooms. Fax machines that transmitted documents anywhere in the world. Extraordinary. That was state-of-the-art then. Today it's nostalgia.

The novelty of being a hot new design engineer at the world's top semiconductor firm didn't last long. Perhaps I failed to mention one of my great achievements in life: somehow managing to graduate from the New York City public school system and obtain two college degrees without ever learning how to write. The first time I tried my hand at a chip specification, my boss called me into his office. He looked angry. "You're illiterate!" he shouted, completely red-faced. "How the hell did you ever graduate college?" I'll never forget the sound that made. It was the sound of a bubble bursting. My bubble.

With that kind of start, it's hard to imagine how I ended up here, as a marketing executive, CEO, management consultant, columnist, and author. Looking back, it's surprising how far a person can come in life. The human capacity for learning, adapting, and problem solving is extraordinary under the right conditions. Competition and adversity can certainly be powerful motivators.

I so wanted to be a success, to have a better life than my parents had, to make them proud. That's what drove me all those years. That's why I fought so hard every step of the way and confronted every obstacle in my path. That's why I've never given up. That imperative to overcome adversity and win is now in my blood. And it's driven every decision and every choice I've made in life.

But then, that's nothing new. From the dawn of life on earth, one simple mechanism has been responsible for every advance that has brought us to where our civilization stands today. Just as genetic mutations alter our DNA and advance the species, only exceptional individuals who think and act differently can shatter the status quo and lead us into the future.

Will you be one of them? The choice is yours.

HUMANITY
VS.
INDIVIDUALITY

RECENTLY RECONNECTED WITH AN OLD FRIEND from the distant past. It turned out we're both knee-deep in our *second-half* careers. It's becoming remarkably commonplace among our generation: After long years of doing what pays the bills, we're pivoting and doing what we love to do.

Although my work schedule allowed for few disruptions while writing the manuscript, I found that regular chats with my new old friend were both inspirational and cathartic, perhaps for her as well. And they provided a surprisingly unique perspective on the book.

You see, my friend is an artist. If you've ever seen an exhibit showing the evolution of an artist's work over the years, then you know that, in a very real sense, it tells their life story. Now imagine your career in that context, as a collection of paintings.

Of course you're still a work in progress, but if you could see your life's work in its entirety, it would likewise tell a story. It would describe a remarkable journey full of hopes and dreams, disappointments and failures, accomplishments and triumphs.

Now imagine yourself at the very end looking back at your entire body of work and the story it tells. If you're anything like me, it would be instantly recognizable as your own—your life's work, your story, your journey—and no one else's.

You would want to feel that it was a journey well taken. A journey in which you were true to yourself, gave your all, and held nothing back. And you would know that the journey was rewarding and fulfilling for that very reason—because it was uniquely and genuinely yours.

After all, an artist may be inspired by another's work. An artist may use the same medium or similar techniques as others. But an artist who represents her own unique perception in a way that resonates with her audience has served herself and her craft well. That is the true measure of an artist's success.

That analogy represents an overarching message of the book. A life lived on its own terms is a precious thing. Your career should represent your own life's work, your own unique path, your own personal journey, and no one else's. That is what matters most. While there are lots of ways to describe success, that's how I see it.

Now that it's over—the book, not the journey—there's one last point I'd like to make about collectivism and individuality. You may have noticed that I'm a highly opinionated and decisive guy. That's no coincidence; telling people what I think and making tough calls have always been part of my job description. While I like to think I'm analytical about it, all viewpoints are by definition subjective.

I bring this up because, just after submitting the manuscript, the daughter of my new old friend came to stay with my wife and me. This was an impressive young woman: smart, independent, focused, and intense. She and many others I've known represent the very best of a generation that has taken some pretty hard knocks both here and elsewhere. But they are in no way part of any collective. They are individuals.

Anyway, this *individual* asked what the book was about, so I told her, and she proceeded to challenge some of its tenets in light of her own personal experience. We had a spirited debate. Now she can't wait to read it, and I can't wait to hear what she has to say about it. And that's exactly as it should be.

After all, the goal of the book is to get you to formulate your own views and make smart decisions based on real-world experience. Implicit in that concept is that you follow no one's doctrines— including mine.

I didn't get to where I am today by accepting anything verbatim but by challenging the status quo, thinking critically, and trusting my gut. That's a given for any successful executive or business leader. The same goes for you. And yes, I'm aware that presenting that as doctrine is paradoxical. It can't be helped.

Likewise, the book's heavy-handed treatment of a laundry list of cultural norms and fads was intentional. But while it's one thing to describe macro trends with bold, sweeping brushstrokes, it's another matter entirely to paint individuals with the same broad brush. Clearly, that's not my intention.

As Margaret Thatcher once said, "There is no such thing as society: There are individual men and women, and there are families." That means cultural trends develop one person at a time, and they can only be changed in the hearts and minds of each individual. There is no such thing as a collective of humans unless each person chooses to give up his or her own individuality.

Which leads us to a great irony: that collectivism is an individual choice. Humanity is defined by individuality, and giving it up to join a collective means giving up what it means to be human. Indeed, we are all the same, and yet we are different. While we share the same DNA and environment, beyond that, nothing is fixed or fated. We each have the potential to paint any picture or, should the stars align, change the entire landscape for all mankind.

ABOUT THE AUTHOR

STEVE TOBAK IS MANAGING PARTNER OF INVISOR CONSULTING, a Silicon Valley-based management consulting firm he cofounded in 2003. Previously, he was a senior executive who led global marketing and sales organizations for several public technology companies and startups that achieved successful IPOs. He started out as a chip design engineer with Texas Instruments more than 30 years ago.

Tobak is a featured columnist for Fox Business, a featured contributor to Entrepreneur Media, and the author of a personal blog at stevetobak.com. Millions of readers have enjoyed his insightful commentary on business, leadership, and technology. Tobak holds a B.S. in physics and an M.S. in electrical engineering from the State University of New York at Stony Brook and lives in the San Francisco Bay area.

INDEX

A

accountability, 30, 99, 254, 256–257.
See also responsibility
Acton, Brian, 125
adaptability, 87, 167, 210–211,
248–249
adversity, 67–72, 75, 283
AdWords, 5
Airbnb, 198, 201
Alibaba, 138
Allen, Paul, 230
Amelio, Gil, 6
Anthem (Rand), 30
Apotheker, Leo, 278–279
Apple, 6–7, 138, 178–179, 181,
245–246

Armstrong, Tim, 234–235
Atlas Shrugged (Rand), 30
authenticity, 130–131, 170, 237–
238. See also transparency; trust
authority, 224–225

B

baby boomers, 16
balance, 268–271
barriers, competitive, 185–188
behaviorism, 25–26
BlackBerry, 210
Blankfein, Lloyd, 70
blogging, 6, 8–10, 89
brand promises, 56, 185
brand reputation, 56

branding, 54–59, 184–185
breakthrough innovation, 35, 78,
    282. *See also* innovation
Brin, Sergey, 5
Buffett, Warren, 221–222
Business Adventures (Brooks), 221
business plans, 142–144

C

career paths, 32–37, 105–111,
    116–117, 286
caring for yourself, 87–88
Chahal, Gurbaksh, 232–233
change, 51–52
chaos, embracing, 263–265
charismatic leaders, 227–230. *See
    also* leadership
choosing your path, 32–37. *See also*
    career paths
Cisco, 192
Coca-Cola, 200–201, 210
cold calling, 168–170
collectivism, 29–32, 287. *See also*
    Web 2.0
communication, 185, 232–237,
    256–257
company culture, 239–249. *See also*
    leadership
    adaptability of, 248–249
    creating, 130
    cult-like cultures, 242–243
    David vs. Goliath culture,
        243–245
    defining, 239–240
    employee engagement in,
        240–241
    empowering employees in,
        241–242

human capital and, 247–248
    role of, 239–240
    self-awareness in, 248–249
    thinking differently and, 245–246
Compaq Computer, 165–166
competencies for success, 93–103
    being human, 97–98
    competitive spirit, 101–103
    critical thinking, 94–96
    differing viewpoints on, 93–94
    discipline, 96–97
    focus, 96–97
    getting things done, 99–101
competition, 71–72, 75, 138–141,
    177–178, 185–188, 283
competitive analysis, 194
competitive barriers, 185–188
competitive edge, 205–206
competitive markets, 138–141
competitive spirit, 101–103
concepts, 138
conformity, 26–28, 72
Coulombe, Joe, 242–243
creativity, 27, 87, 246, 269. *See also*
    innovation
credibility, 66, 148, 149, 157–159.
    See also reputation
critical market needs, 137–138
critical thinking, 94–96
Crossing the Chasm (Moore), 182
cult-like company cultures, 242–
    243. *See also* company culture
cultural conformity, 26–28, 72
culture, company. *See* company
    culture
customer needs, 137–138, 162–163
customer pain points, 137–138,
    206–207

customer relationships, 162–164
customer retention, 182–183
Cyrix, 7, 102

D
Davidow, Bill, 153–155
decision-making process, 222–225
defeat. *See* failure
delegation, 224–225
DeliveryHub, 198
Dell Computers, 200
devolution, behavioral and
    organizational, 21–26
differentiation, 139–140, 165–166,
    180–182, 185–188
discipline, 88–91, 96–97
discrimination and diversity,
    254–255
disruptive innovation, 35, 78, 282.
    See also innovation
distractions, 96–97
diversification, 199
diversity and discrimination,
    252–256
diversity of thought, 27, 229
Doerr, John, 254–255
dotcom bust, 4–5
dysfunction, 212–213

E
eBay, 6
Einstein, Albert, 128
Ellison, Larry, 71, 128
emotional intelligence, 72–73
empathy, 273, 281
employee empowerment, 241–242
employee engagement, 240–241
employees as assets, 247–248
engagement, 152–157, 240–241

entrepreneurial generation, 15–16
entrepreneurs, 30, 99, 121–124,
    127–131, 282
entrepreneurship
    decline in, 15–16
    defining, 35–37
    fads and, 16–19
    Millennials and, 19
    myths about, xvii–xviii, 111–115
    risk and, 42–50, 80–81, 122
    social, 95
    user-generated content and,
        xvii, 5, 16, 59, 94
equity partners, 201
Evans, Mike, 125
evolution, 35–36
evolved leadership, 273–284. *See
    also* leadership
experience, 124
extroverted leaders, 227–230. *See
    also* leadership

F
Facebook, 6, 59, 61, 62, 138–139,
    229. *See also* social media
Facemash, 265
fads, 16–19
failure, 203–213. *See also* success
    adaptability and, 208–210
    bad advice and, 136
    customer needs and, 206–207
    fear of, 211–212
    focus and, 208–210
    innovation and, 204–205
    learning from, 80–81, 203–204
    odds of failing, 134–135
    running out of money, 133–134,
        136, 204–205

startups and, 134–136
vision and, 207–208
faking it, 237–238
fear, 129
feedback, 194
feeling vs. thinking, 265–268
Fiorina, Carly, 274–275
fired, getting, 52–54
first to market, 178
Fisher, Jodie, 277
flexibility, 87
focus, 88–91, 96–97, 208–210
focusing on what matters, 47–50,
    54–55, 79, 84–88
following, xviii–xix
founders, 126
friction, 71–72, 75
Fujita, Den, 68–69
funding startups, 121–122, 133–
    145, 207, 255

G
Gates, Bill, 90, 95, 106, 122, 166–
    167, 218–221
Generation Y, 11–16, 19, 31
generational profiling, 11–14
genuineness, 130–131, 170, 237–
    238. See also transparency
getting things done, 86, 99–101
goals, 86, 91
Google, 5
Grove, Andy, 71, 128, 222–224
growing your business, 196–201
GrubHub, 198

H
happiness, 72–75
Hewlett-Packard, 274–281

High Output Management (Grove),
    222–223
high-tech industry, 31–32
hiring and retention, 247–248,
    252–256
How to Change the World
    (Bornstein), 95
HP Way, 274–281
Hughes, Howard, 127
human capital, 247–248
humanity, 287
humility, 273, 281
Hurd, Mark, 275–278

I
Idiocracy (film), 21–23
Idiocracy effect, 21–28
imposter syndrome, 238
individuality, 30, 35–37, 287
inflection points, 78–79, 189–190,
    264
innovation. *See also* creativity
    breakthrough, 35, 78, 81, 282
    collectivism and, 30–32
    failure and, 204–205
    fanaticism and, 129
    inflection points and, 264
    marketing and, 178–179
    virtual interactions and, 27
inspiration, 74
Intel, 184
internet bust, 4–5
introversion, 159–160
introverted leaders, 228–230. *See
    also* leadership
investors, venture capital, 121–122,
    133–145, 207, 255
iPhone, 7, 9–10

iPod, 7
iTunes, 7

J
jobs, losing, 52–54
Jobs, Steve, 6–7, 53, 71, 125, 127–128, 175, 209

K
Kalanick, Travis, 79, 229
Kemp, Jack, 156–157
Kerner Optical, 133–134
Kleiner Perkins Caufield & Byers, 254–255
knowing yourself, 86, 116–117, 130–131
Kodak, 212
Koum, Jan, 125
Kraft Foods, 200

L
labels, 122–125, 131
Lane, Ray, 278–280
leadership. *See also* company culture
    embracing chaos and, 263–265
    evolved style of, 273–284
    feeling vs. thinking and, 265–268
    no BS style of, 217–226
    politically incorrect style of, 261–258
    risk taking and, 264–265
    rock star style of, 227–238
    Tao of, 260–263, 268–271
leadership teams, 141–142, 193, 224–225
leadership trends, 217–218
Lexus, 177

limbic system, 24–27, 34–35, 267
LinkedIn, 6, 61, 62. *See also* social media
Little, Mike, 6
loving your work, 87
luck, 77–81

M
Ma, Jack, 69, 100
Maloney, Matt, 125
management teams, 141–142, 193, 224–225
market success, 205–206
marketing, 173–188
    competency in, 179–180
    competition and, 71–72, 75, 138–141, 177–178, 185–188, 283
    competitive analysis in, 194
    competitive edge in, 205–206
    competitive markets and, 138–141
    customer retention in, 182–183
    defining, 174–177, 188
    differentiation in, 139–140, 165–166, 180–182, 185–188
    first to market concept, 178
    innovation and, 178–179
    product as brand in, 57, 184–185
Marketing High Technology (Davidow), 176, 181
Marketing Imagination, The (Levitt), 175
McKenna, Regis, 174–175
meritocracy, 241, 256–258

messaging, 185
Microsoft, 200, 211
Millennials, 10–16, 19, 31
mobile computing, 6–10
money, running out of, 204–205
motivation, 128–130, 283
Mullenweg, Matt, 6, 11
Musk, Elon, 29, 79, 90

N
Nadella, Satya, 280
National Semiconductor, 7
natural selection, 35
networking, 61–62, 148–149. *See also* social networking

O
obsessions, 23, 55, 79, 96
opportunities, 80–81
opportunity cost, 55
OrderHub, 198
organizational culture. *See* company culture
organizations, 78
Organizing Genius (Bennis), 130
over-communication trend, 232–237

P
Page, Larry, 5
Pao, Ellen, 254–255
passion, 113, 127–128
PayPal, 6
PepsiCo, 200
personal accountability, 30, 99, 254, 256–257
personal branding, 55–57, 59
personal productivity, 83–91

personal responsibility, 99, 256–257
pitches, 169–170
pitfalls, 204–213. *See also* failure
platforms, 56
Platt, Lew, 274
politically incorrect leaders, 261–258. *See also* leadership
PortalPlayer, 7
positioning, 181–182
priorities, 85–86, 88–91
problem statements, 137–138
product as brand, 57, 184–185
productivity, 83–91, 266
proving oneself, 67–70

R
Rand, Ayn, 30–31
Ravikant, Naval, 185–186
recruiting and retention, 247–248, 252–256
relationship building, 147–160
    credibility and, 148, 149, 157–159
    with customers, 162–164
    engaging with purpose, 152–157
    introversion and, 159–160
    repairing relationships, 157–159
    in sales, 162–164
    schmoozing, 149–151
    trust and, 148, 149, 152, 153, 158
    value of, 147–149, 151–152
Relationship Marketing (McKenna), 174

reputation, 56–59, 66, 184. *See also* credibility

responsibility, 99, 224–225, 241, 256–257. *See also* accountability

risk, 42–50, 80–81, 122, 199, 264–265

Robbins, Tony, 17

rock star leadership style, 227–238. *See also* leadership

running out of money, 204–205

S

sales, 161–171. *See also* relationship building

    cold calling, 168–170

    committing to big customers, 164–166

    customer needs and, 137–138, 162–164

    defining, 161–162, 171

    genuineness in, 170–171

    selectivity in, 166–167

    you're always selling, 167–168

SAP, 246

schmoozing, 149–151

Schultz, Howard, 70, 125

Seidenberg, Ivan, 69

selectivity in sales, 166–167

self-awareness, 74–75, 248–249

self-censoring, 26

self-image, 237–238

self-improvement, 79

self-promotion, 232–234

Sequoia Capital., 6

service businesses, 200

services as brand, 57

skill development, 49, 109–111

Skinner, B. F., 25–26

smartphones, 7, 9–10

Snapchat, 234. *See also* social media

social behavior, 23–26

social collective. *See* Web 2.0

social conformity, 26–28

social connectivity, 25–28. *See also* Web 2.0

social entrepreneurship, 95

social media, 16, 59–66, 89

social networking, 6, 27–28, 55, 59, 61–62, 65–66, 98. *See also* networking; Web 2.0

social norms, 26

social web, 5–6, 10, 25–32, 287

Son, Masayoshi, 67–69

Sony, 200, 209

Southwest Airlines, 246

Spiegel, Evan, 234

spiral of silence effect, 26–28

Stac, Inc., 50, 52

startups

    adaptability and, 167

    business plans for, 142–144

    competitive barriers for, 185–188

    competitive markets and, 138–141

    decline in, 15–16

    funding, 121–122, 133–145, 207, 255

    growing, 196–201

    management teams in, 141–142

    problem statements and, 137–138

reasons for failure of, 134–136.
See also failure

status quo, 245

stock option backdating, 253

strategic planning, 33, 193–196

strategy and vision, 190–193

stress, 67–72, 75

success, 190, 205–206. *See also*
failure

success attributes, 30, 99, 282

Sun Microsystems, 192, 210

survival instinct, 24–28, 244

SWOT (Strengths, Weaknesses,
Opportunities, Threats)
analysis, 194

T

Tao of leadership, 260–263, 268–
271. *See also* leadership

Tao of Leadership, The (Heider),
236, 260–263, 270

Tao Te Ching (Tzu), 268, 269

teams, 141–142, 193, 224–225

thinking differently, 245–246

thinking vs. feeling, 265–268

time off, 87

time wasters, 89–90. *See also* social
media

Toyota, 177

transparency, 193–194. *See also*
authenticity; trust

trial by fire, 47–50

trust, 148, 149, 152, 153, 158. *See
also* authenticity; transparency

turning points, 78–79, 189–190,
264

Twitter, 6, 27, 59, 61, 62, 195. *See
also* social media

U

Uber, 79, 96–97, 99–100, 138, 198

underdogs, 243–245

unemployment rates, xviii, 16

Unti Vineyards, 58–59

user-generated content, xvii, 5, 16,
59, 94

V

venture capital (VC), 121–122,
137–145, 207, 255

vision, 207–208

vision and strategy, 190–193

visionary leaders, 230–231. *See also*
leadership

W

Web 2.0. *See also* collectivism;
social networking
business and, 19
diversity of thought and, 27
leadership and, 217
mediocrity and, 31
Millennials and, 10–11
personal branding and, 59
rise of, 5–6
social connectivity and, 25–28
social media in, 16
wealth gap and, 31–32

Whitman, Meg, 279–280

wisdom, 47

WordPress, 5–6, 59

work ethic, 86

work-life balance, 88, 90

workplace issues, 251–258

Wozniak, Steve, 125

X

Xerox PARC, 211

Y
Yahoo!, 209–210, 231
You Are Not a Gadget (Lanier), 31
your story, 285–286
YouTube, 6, 59. *See also* social
  media

Z
Zuckerberg, Mark, 6, 11, 90, 128,
  138–139, 218–219, 265